INVENTING INDIA

Inventing India

A History of India in English-Language Fiction

Ralph J. Crane

MACMILLAN

First published 1992 by
THE MACMILLAN PRESS LTD
Houndmills, Basingstoke, Hampshire RG21 2XS
and London
Companies and representatives
throughout the world

ISBN 0–333–56363–8

A catalogue record for this book is available
from the British Library.

Printed in Great Britain by
Antony Rowe Ltd
Chippenham, Wiltshire

10   9   8   7   6   5   4
04   03   02   01   00   99   98   97

For Joy, of course,
and for Jennifer Livett

Contents

List of Plates

Prefatory Note

In the interests of consistency, I have referred to the British community in India as Anglo-Indians throughout this study. Similarly, I have used the term Eurasian to describe the mixed-race community, despite the fact that after the census of 1911 these people were officially recognised as Anglo-Indians.

Many Indian words have no definitive English spelling. As Olivia writes in O. Douglas's *Olivia in India*: 'One trait [Hindustani] has which appeals to me is that one can spell it almost any way one likes'. I have been consistent throughout my own text, but various spellings of words like chapati and Muslim appear in quotations.

Acknowledgements

This book was first conceived as a doctoral thesis at the University of Tasmania. I am indebted to that institution for the provision of the Estelle Taylor Postgraduate Research Award from November 1985 to October 1989. I would also like to express my appreciation to everyone in the English Department at the University of Tasmania, for their encouragement during four very happy years.

* * *

I am grateful to the following for their kind permission to reproduce photographs: the Leicestershire Museums for *The Flight from Lucknow*; Messrs John Dewar and Sons Ltd for *The Monarch of the Glen*; the Verwaltung der Staatlichen Schlösser und Gärten, Berlin, for *L'Embarquement pour L'île de Cythère*; the Tate Gallery, London, for *The Boyhood of Raleigh*. *The Relief of Lucknow* and 'The Courtyard of the Secunderbagh' appear courtesy of the Director, National Army Museum, London. *The Jewel in Her Crown* appears courtesy of Granada Television, Manchester, England.

It is not down on any map; true places never are.

(Herman Melville, *Moby-Dick*)

1
Introductory: Fiction as History

Historicity is part of human certainty – it makes man real.[1]

In *Midnight's Children* (1981), Salman Rushdie's narrator, Saleem Sinai, tells us that in 1947, 'a nation which had never previously existed was about to win its freedom'.[2] Or, to put it another way, India was invented, not for the first time, nor for the last, at the time of Independence. Every novelist who has written about India has re-invented that country. As Veronica Brady explains in a review of Bharati Mukherjee's novel *The Tiger's Daughter* (1987), 'India is a psychic as well as a physical fact, personal even before it is political'.[3] To invent India, it is necessary to imagine the landscape too, because the novelist is inevitably inventing the history of a particular place, as well as a particular period in the history of that place. It is noticeable how many novels begin with detailed descriptions of the topography of India – including four of the novels discussed in this study; J.G. Farrell's *The Siege of Krishnapur* (1973), E.M. Forster's *A Passage to India* (1924), John Masters's *Bhowani Junction* (1954) and Manohar Malgonkar's *The Princes* (1963).

Various fictional means can be employed to re-invent a country; in *The Siege of Krishnapur*, J.G. Farrell:

> based his narrative largely on histories and memoirs of the Siege of Lucknow but transferred the action of his novel to a fictitious settlement, Krishnapur (which means 'city of Krishna'). This allowed Farrell to use history in a very flexible way.[4]

By re-naming Lucknow, J.G. Farrell has immediately *re-invented* that town, but because of the historical events which occur in his novel, it is still recognisable.

By contrast, John Masters *invents* Bhowani and the neighbouring princely state of Kishanpur, which may correspond roughly to Jhansi, but are not recognisable in anything but the most general of senses. R.K. Narayan invents his own fictional world in Malgudi and its environs, which provides the setting for all his novels and stories. None of these places is to be found on any map, but they are, nevertheless, 'true places'.

They are true places, at least in part, because of the strange marriage between history and fiction, and because there is no single truth, no single India, no single Krishnapur. Each work of history, each novel which attempts to interpret the Siege of Lucknow, for example, is likely to be rooted in the same 'facts' or 'truths'. The historian who examines these sources, inevitably, in telling his or her version of the true story, imaginatively reconstructs the events he or she describes. Character, then, may suggest a distinction between the work of the historian and that of the historical novelist, as Manohar Malgonkar recognises in his novel *Distant Drum* (1960):

> But of course, the official histories made no mention of what Ropey had said on that occasion, nor did they say anything about the state of morale of the Satpura men at this particular stage in the battle of the bridge. Official histories merely told you about the way an action was fought; they did not say much about what people said or felt.[5]

Ever since Aristotle, attempts to define the distinction between history and fiction have been at best hazy, and appear only to have confirmed the similarities between the two. In the nineteenth century, literature and history were considered branches of the same tree. Serious writers of historical fiction, like Scott and Bulwer, aimed at historical accuracy to the extent that, 'Bulwer's novels were reviewed as history rather than fiction'.[6] It was a period when novelists and historians influenced each other considerably; Macaulay was indebted to Scott, as Dickens was to Carlyle. Indeed, Carlyle's *History of the French Revolution* and Macaulay's *History of England* rivalled works of fiction in popular appeal. And from 1860 to 1869 the Regius Professor of History at Cambridge University was the novelist Charles Kingsley (whose younger brother, Henry, wrote a novel on the Indian Mutiny entitled *Stretton* [1869]). In the early nineteenth century the historical novel reached the height of its popularity, and most of the major practitioners of the Victorian novel wrote at least one historical novel – Dickens in *A Tale of Two Cities* (1859), George Eliot in *Romola* (1863), for example.

Although in the popular market the historical novel remained as much in demand as ever, by the late 1870s it was dying in intellectual estimation, a near-death from which it is only just recovering. The last decades of the nineteenth century gave birth to Realism and Naturalism, which shared the belief that the lives of the lower and middle classes of the day provided the ideal subjects for serious literature. The advent of Modernism, with its rejection of the values of the past, inflicted yet more wounds to the body of historical fiction.

It was only in the 1960s, and more importantly in the 1970s, that a serious interest in historical fiction was renewed, and new life was breathed into the ailing body by Postmodernism. The use of history in fiction was, effectively, re-discovered, and as Linda Hutcheon shows, postmodern theory has challenged the traditional attempts to explain the separation between literature and history: 'recent critical readings of both history and fiction have focused more on what the two modes of writing share than on how they differ'.[7] Historiographic metafiction, she attests,

> refutes the natural or common-sense methods of distinguishing between historical fact and fiction. It refuses the view that only history has a truth claim, both by questioning the ground of that claim in historiography and by asserting that both history and fiction are discourses, human constructs, signifying systems, and both derive their major claim to truth from that identity.[8]

The change is primarily from a mimetic to a metaphorical representation of reality in the novel. In Postmodernism, history and geography are major vehicles for metaphor, but they, paradoxically, imply reality since they are factual, can be proved to have happened or exist.

India has captured the British imagination in a way that no other part of the Empire ever managed to do. This was due, in part, to the British discovery in India of a civilization as rich in culture and learning as their own. In the nineteenth century India provided the ideal link between, on the one hand, the strong English literary tradition of adventure novels and historical fiction, and, on the other, the problems of Empire and the human spirit. The sheer volume of prose and poetry which uses India as its subject is testimony to this. India also provided the background to much nineteenth-century

British fiction, notably to the novels of William Makepeace Thackeray, and as Patrick Brantlinger points out, even in such 'domestic' novels as Jane Austen's *Sense and Sensibility* (1811), Charlotte Brontë's *Jane Eyre* (1847), and Mrs Gaskell's *Cranford* (1853), India is a place where people return from, or have visited.[9]

India continues to hold a unique place in the British imagination even today, over forty years after Indian/Pakistani Independence. In the first ten years of the Booker Prize, for example, no less than four of the winning novels, J.G. Farrell's *The Siege of Krishnapur*, Ruth Prawer Jhabvala's *Heat and Dust* (1975), Paul Scott's *Staying On* (1977) and Salman Rushdie's *Midnight's Children*, were set in India. Further, India's hold on the British imagination can be seen in the success of films such as *Gandhi, Heat and Dust* and *A Passage to India*, television films such as *Staying On*, and television series such as *The Jewel in the Crown* and *The Far Pavilions*.

The history of British India provided the inspiration and setting for a great many Anglo-Indian novels between the Mutiny in 1857 and Independence in 1947. It is also true that the majority of these novels do not deserve much critical attention on literary merit alone. They have been dealt with quite thoroughly in such studies as Bhupal Singh's *A Survey of Anglo-Indian Fiction*, Allen J. Greenberger's *The British Image of India*, Benita Parry's *Delusions and Discoveries* and Shailendra Dhari Singh's *Novels on the Indian Mutiny*. Of these, Greenberger's study of what he describes in his subtitle as 'the Literature of Imperialism 1880–1960' is particularly useful. Benita Parry's book, subtitled *Studies on India in the British Imagination 1880–1930*, deals with individual novelists rather than with the whole canon of her subject. None of these studies considers the novels which have been written since the revival of the historical novel. David Rubin's recent study, *After the Raj*, which is concerned with *British Novels of India Since 1947*, does look at some of these novels, but his book, like the earlier studies, does not deal with British and Indian novels in tandem, as I intend to do in this study. Since as a general rule British novelists tend to write about the British in India, whilst Indian novelists are interested primarily in Indians, a full picture of the period can only be drawn by looking at both sides of the literary imagination. Rather than discussing novels from various periods, as Greenberger does, or individual novelists, as Parry and Rubin do, I shall look at various historical periods and show how those historical periods have been imagined in the novels of Britain and India.

There is no simple explanation for the hold India has had on the British imagination, nor is there a simple interpretation of the events which surrounded the growth of Empire, and the literary interest in India. In *Victorian People and Ideas*, Richard Altick maintains that: 'When Disraeli bestowed upon the Queen the additional title of Empress of India in 1876, her country was approaching the height of its influence and achievement as an imperial power'.[10] He suggests that after Disraeli the emphasis on Empire waned. Yet, contrary to Altick's beliefs, Jerome Buckley argues that the interest in Empire heightened with Gladstone: 'The tide of jingoism, however, mounted steadily throughout the eighties and nineties till it reached a peak in the "foolish pride and frantic boast" of the Diamond Jubilee celebrations'.[11] This controversy is reflected, too, in attitudes to literature. Some critics, including Buckley, argue that Rudyard Kipling lost faith in Empire (hence the elegaic tone of *Kim* [1901]), whilst others see him as consistently pro-Empire.

India proved to be a popular setting for the adventure novel, which continued to flourish throughout the second half of the nineteenth century. *Kim* uses aspects of the style of these romantic adventure novels, but it also shows India being treated in a more intellectual vein. It is the first important British novel inspired by India, and it attempts to present a genuine picture of Indian life. The next serious British novel to use India as its setting is E.M. Forster's *A Passage to India*. It has had a remarkable effect on the literature of India, both British and Indian. Echoes of that novel can be found in Christine Weston's *Indigo* (1944), and Ruth Prawer Jhabvala's *A New Dominion* (1972) and *Heat and Dust*. Paul Scott admits to the tremendous influence *A Passage to India* had on his fiction.[12] And even Indian writers owe a debt to Forster, as Manohar Malgonkar acknowledges, indirectly, in his novel *A Bend in the Ganges* (1964):

> Was it his youth that made him so shallow, he wondered, or was it part of the Indian character itself? Did he in some way, represent the average Indian, mixed-up, shallow and weak? Like someone out of *A Passage to India*, Aziz, or someone even more confused, quite despicable, in fact, like that boy whose name he had forgotten, Rafi, that was it. Was he like Rafi?[13]

Malgonkar is also aware of Kipling's tremendous influence on the popular image of India, particularly British India. In *Distant Drum*, he writes: 'It was like a thousand other mess nights. At least in the army messes, so little had changed that even Kipling might have felt perfectly at home'.[14]

L.H. Myers is another author whose works have had a profound effect on the ways in which India has figured in the British imagination, and the ways in which serious British novelists have since approached India. His novels, including his great trilogy *The Root and the Flower* (1935), are set in a sixteenth-century India under the reign of Akbar. Consequently, his influence, though considerable, is not as obvious as that of Kipling and Forster, and not germane to the present study, which deals with novels set in a specific period of Indian history which post-dates the arrival of the British.

Many of the novels discussed in this study, like *Kim* and *A Passage to India*, are not historical novels, but do, nevertheless, have a strong sense of history, and have become, with the passing of the years, what could be termed historical source documents. As Max Beloff recognises: 'the role of the novelist in exploring the relationship between the two peoples has always been a crucial one; and novels are an historical source that we are only now beginning to exploit'.[15] *Kim*, *A Passage to India*, and such Indian novels as Kushwant Singh's *Train to Pakistan* (1956) fall into this category. Novels like *Train to Pakistan* and Bhabani Bhattacharya's *So Many Hungers!* (1947), however, are written by those who experienced the events they have recorded. The stance is significantly different in novels like *Kim* and *A Passage to India*, where, although Kipling spent his early childhood in Bombay, and Forster almost certainly fictionalises some of his own experiences in India in his portrait of Fielding in Chandrapore, the lives of the authors are remote from those of the main characters.

This leads to the question of how far in the past an historical novel needs to be set? L.P. Hartley, in an interesting introduction to his novel *The Go-Between* (1953), makes the following general points which are of interest here:

> Someone, perhaps wanting to please me, pointed out that many of the greatest novels had been written about periods of time forty years before the date at which the novelist was writing – and this is roughly true of *War and Peace*, *Vanity Fair* and *Wuthering Heights*. Their authors found it was the point of time – not too near and not too far away – on which their imaginations could most easily focus.[16]

Similarly, in his introduction to *Waverley* (1814), subtitled *Or, 'Tis Sixty Years Since*, Sir Walter Scott suggests that sixty years is an appro-priate period of time to separate historical events from their cele-bration in fiction.[17] Hartley further suggests that 'the reader's imagination can't accept the recent changes as it accepts the different state of affairs that exists in a historical novel'.[18] This is perhaps a major reason why historical novels are rarely set in the recent past.

There is also the possibility that a novelist writing about recent events may be unable or unwilling to prevent strong emotions from distorting his or her presentation of those events. The question of the rate of change of ethos or ideology must be considered, too. It may well be that a writer in 1790, writing about a period circa 1710 would be closer to his or her subject than a writer in 1920, writing about a period circa 1880, although the time gap is actually shorter in the latter case. Thus the question of distancing is not simply a matter of time (forty years or sixty years or a lifetime) or of space (writing about India from Britain), but a matter of objective distancing. The better writers of historical fiction are *emotionally* distanced from their subject. It is, perhaps, remarkable that in *Train to Pakistan*, Kushwant Singh is able to maintain an emotional distance from the terrible events of Partition only nine years after they occurred. Even in writing about events of a century ago this can present problems; writing about the Mutiny, for example, John Masters is not detached emotionally and therefore objectively, whereas J.G. Farrell is. This is evident in Salman Rushdie's novel *Midnight's Children*, too, which is not as strong at the end, when the past is more recent. In the later stages of the novel Rushdie is not as emotionally or objectively detached. This is shown, metaphorically, through the film screen; close up the picture is out of focus, whereas from a distance it is perfectly focused. The same is true of writing about the past.

It is possible to think that an event which happened a hundred years ago is the past, and that it need not trouble us today; it may be interesting, but it is nothing to do with our lives. Yet an author writing with a strong sense of history *will* put the reader there, will make the reader present in 1857 or 1947, and therefore remove the reader's emotional detachment, whilst maintaining his or her own. The writer may make the reader realise that what was happening then may be also happening now, both literally, in that the present history of India is a direct result of historical events, and also in terms of the 'eternal now' of psychological realism, which suggests

that human nature never changes; and this is particularly the intention of Rushdie, and of the South-American magic realists. Thus,
whilst the writer must remain emotionally detached, the reader
must not be allowed to remain so. In the case of the early Mutiny
novels, prevailing ideological myth and emotional involvement prevented the novelists from presenting any true sense of history in
their work. As Frank Kermode has observed:

> The decline of paradigmatic history, and our growing conscious-
> ness of historiography's irreducible element of fiction, are . . .
> contributions to what Wilde called 'the decay of lying.' . . . We
> know that if we want to find out about ourselves, make sense, we
> must avoid the regress into myth which has deceived poet, histo-
> rian, and critic.[19]

The early Mutiny writers, far from writing about the past objectively, became myth-makers in their own right; E.M. Forster, however, and some of the later adventure-story novelists, like John
Masters, made good use of these myths in their novels.

Inevitably, no writer can write of his or her own time in the same
way that the period would be treated by a writer who has the benefit
of hindsight. The historical novelist's role, and this may well be a
predominantly postmodernist view, is not to portray the past as
past, but to include the present in the portrayal of the past. As Marc
Bloch argues, the study of the past as past is the function of the
antiquarian. The historian – and the historical novelist – is concerned
with life and must study the past and present together.[20] Or as Hayden
White rather more graphically suggests:

> anyone who studies the past as an end in itself must appear to be
> either an antiquarian, fleeing from the problems of the present
> into a purely personal past, or a kind of cultural necrophile, that
> is, one who finds in the dead and dying a value he can never find
> in the living.[21]

There is, however, no one set way of using history, but as many
ways as there are authors.

In his novel *Waiting for the Mahatma* (1955), R.K. Narayan does not
make Gandhi his main character; rather his novel is the story of
those whose lives Gandhi influences, and his concerns are with the
whole period. Manohar Malgonkar's novel *The Devil's Wind*, on the
other hand, tends towards being an historical biography of Nana

Saheb, rather than an historical novel of the Mutiny since he is concerned primarily with the character of Nana Saheb himself. In *Aspects of the Novel*, E.M. Forster identifies a danger which novelists like Malgonkar face, when he suggests that if a character in a novel is *exactly* like an historical character (he uses Queen Victoria as his example) then the character *is* that historical figure, and the novel, therefore, becomes a memoir:

> A memoir is history, it is based on evidence. A novel is based on evidence + or – *x*, the unknown quantity being the temperament of the novelist, and the unknown quantity always modifies the effect of the evidence, and sometimes transforms it entirely.[22]

It has been accepted since Scott and Bulwer that facts are essential, and that everything an historical novelist adds or subtracts must be in keeping with historical authenticity. A novelist like Malgonkar, then, must bring out what Forster calls the 'hidden life' of his characters, but in such a way that he produces a character who may not be the Nana Saheb of history, but who *could* be. A novelist cannot leave a gap in the story where there is a gap in the documentary evidence, but must allow his or her imagination to leap in; the historian, on the other hand, must say that there is a gap if there is one. This is particularly relevant in the case of *The Devil's Wind*. An historian or a biographer would have had to admit any gaps in Nana Saheb's story, whereas Malgonkar can use the imagination and freedom of the novelist to fill those gaps, whilst, of course, his account must be in keeping with the documentary evidence he does have.

When historical figures are the central figures in works of fiction, there is a danger that the novel will not present the atmosphere of the age, but a picture of an individual in that age. To avoid this Lukács claims that Scott, 'lets his important figures grow out of the being of the age, he never explains the age from the position of its great representatives'.[23] Ideally, the protagonist of an historical novel should be a fictitious character within whom the wider and often conflicting pressures of the period can be seen to be at work. Fleury in J.G. Farrell's *The Siege of Krishnapur* is such a character, and so, in a very different way, is Saleem Sinai, the narrator of Salman Rushdie's *Midnight's Children*. Saleem is typical of the protagonists of historiographic metafiction, who, Hutcheon argues, 'are the excentrics, the marginalized, the peripheral figures of fictional history.'[24]

As a genre, the historical novel is as loose and baggy as Henry James's monsters of fiction. *A Passage to India*, for example, cannot, by generally accepted criteria, be called an historical novel. Yet the actual historical events of the period are a kind of echo in the novel, and there is more than a little sense of history about it. But Forster was not primarily interested in history, and as Avrom Fleishman suggests, 'what makes a historical novel historical is the active presence of a concept of history as a shaping force.'[25] There must, then, be an intention on the part of the author to write an historical novel. A sense of history is something that is deliberately brought to fiction, and it exists at the time of writing; it is not something that is developed with age like the bouquet of a good wine. It does not come about by laying a realist novel down for a generation or more, but is created by the writer. Anita Desai, for example, is primarily interested in human relationships, not in history. Thus whilst the flames of Partition burn in the distance in *Clear Light of Day* (1981), Desai's interest lies in Bim's relationship with the various members of her family rather than the history of the period. It is writers like Kamala Markandaya, in her novel *The Golden Honeycomb* (1977), who turn back to the days of the Raj, and display a strong sense of history in their work.

After the late-nineteenth-century and early-twentieth-century rejection of historical fiction by the realist, naturalist, and modernist movements, an interest in history was not renewed until the 1960s. Consequently, the majority of novels discussed in this study were written after 1960. The obvious exceptions are *Kim*, *A Passage to India* and *Kanthapura* (1938); but these, I think, can be accounted for by recognising the prophetic voices of the authors, Kipling, Forster and Raja Rao, or perhaps because these writers were prepared to reject the literary fashions of their age. At any rate, the *zeitgeist* in these novels is deliberate, and not an accident of time. The stance of the reader is important in relation to these novels, too. British and Indian readers may well approach novels like *Kim* and *A Passage to India* with different attitudes, and the novels may well mean different things to each.

I am concerned in this study less with works which neatly conform to definitions of the historical novel, than with works which in a more or less perennial way present aspects of India's past – works which manifest a sense of history and in so doing shape, in important ways, our imaginative responses to India.

2

The Great Revolt: 1857

They themselves were fiercely proud of their unswerving loyalty to their race, their religion, and above all to their employers. And yet a similar drive among the Indians was unthinkable to them.[1]

The events which began on 10 May 1857 are known variously as the Indian Mutiny, the Sepoy Mutiny, the Sepoy Rebellion, the Sepoy Revolt and the First War of Independence. That those events should have come to be known by so many names illustrates the vastly different ways in which they have been interpreted, and suggests the general air of confusion, fuelled by emotion, which has always surrounded them. It was not an Indian Mutiny because the revolt was largely restricted to the northern regions of India. It was not simply a mutiny or rebellion by the Bengal sepoys, as many Victorians saw it, because, although it was by no means embraced by the whole population, it was not confined solely to the sepoys either. Nor was it truly envisaged as a war of independence, though it may well have been the seed which gave rise to the independence struggle in later years. It was perhaps a mixture of all these things – the truth lying somewhere between the extremes of contemporary imperialist interpretation and more recent nationalist interpretation.

The Indian Mutiny provided the inspiration for a great many novels in the late nineteenth and early twentieth century. In 1897 the author of "The Indian Mutiny in Fiction', an essay which appeared in *Blackwood's Edinburgh Magazine*, noted that, 'Of all the great events of this century, as they are reflected in fiction, the Indian Mutiny has taken the firmest hold on the popular imagination'.[2] Despite the number of mutiny novels written in the forty years between the Mutiny and the publication of that article (Shailendra Dhari Singh lists twenty-six in her bibliography in *Novels on the Indian Mutiny*[3]), the author maintains 'that *the* novel of the Mutiny is still to be written'.[4] The interest in the Mutiny continued for some years into the twentieth century, and by the time of Independence the Mutiny had been the subject of at least forty-seven novels.[5] Throughout this period, either because of the proximity in time to the events of the Mutiny, or later because of the growing demand for Independence, and because almost all of the writers had spent time in India as civil servants, soldiers or the wives of such men, their views were far from objective, and the majority of their works suffered from a sense of outrage or sentimentality. The result was a number of romantic adventure novels in which the Mutiny was no more than a setting; the same stories could as easily have been set against the backdrop of any conflict in history. They have little sense of history and create no real sense of the country in which they are set; rather these novels use the India already invented by the myths of the British Raj. Thus many of them do draw on the heroes of the Mutiny to lend truth to their tales, but not one of them captures the feeling of the age. As Olivia contends in *Olivia in India* (1912); 'There is room, don't you think, for a really good book on the Mutiny?'[6]

In the two decades prior to Indian Independence no Mutiny novels were published – possibly because no one wanted to add more fuel to the growing fire of Indian nationalism, but also because this period was the high-water mark of Modernism. However, once India had gained her Independence, and Britain at the same stroke had effectively lost her Empire, the Mutiny again attracted the attention of British novelists. Both Greenberger, in his study *The British Image of India*, and Singh discuss John Masters's *Nightrunners of Bengal* (1951) and M.M. Kaye's *Shadow of the Moon* (1957) in their respective studies. In a more specific study of recent Mutiny fiction, Dinshaw M. Burjorjee discusses eight post-Independence Mutiny novels, including *Nightrunners of Bengal, Shadow of the Moon* and J.G. Farrell's *The Siege of Krishnapur*. Of these novelists Farrell stands apart; others, whom Burjorjee describes as 'a succession of inferior writers',[7] perpetuate the myth that British rule was good for India.

Nightrunners of Bengal and *Shadow of the Moon* are two novels which use the hero myth that has been an important part of the British portrayal of the Mutiny. This is not surprising when the backgrounds of the authors are considered. John Masters came from a family whose continuous association with India dates back to 1805. He himself was born in Calcutta and served in the Indian Army until shortly after Independence.[8] M.M. Kaye's ties with India and the Raj are similarly strong. It is perhaps inevitable that they, like the earlier writers, should support the role of the British in novels which are essentially celebrations of the Raj. To condemn British rule would have been to pass a judgement on their own and their families' roles in India. Masters quite unequivocally suggests that the peasants were better off under British rule than they were in the princely states. In his novel Farrell asks why, if this were true, was there not an exodus from the native states to British India? Apathy, the answer he puts in the mouth of a British official, is deliberately unconvincing.

Neither *Nightrunners of Bengal* nor *Shadow of the Moon* differs markedly from earlier Mutiny fiction, and both are, in many respects, true to the typical plot that Singh outlines in her study:

> The hero, who is an officer, meets the young charming lady, just out from England, or who happens to be in India from before, and falls in love or both come to India in the same ship, and strike a liking on board the ship itself. In India the historical situation is already ripe for mutiny, and the lovers are suddenly pitched into the upheaval. . . . The hero takes a lead, he plans, and soon, by his courage, strategy, perseverance and luck, the action begins and the opposing forces are gradually defeated. His rival in love, if any, is discovered to be a villain, and any other complication is resolved by the death or disappearance of the person causing obstruction. In this way the two parallel plots of action are resolved by the hero, who, in most of the cases, gets a V.C., as well as a wife, if not also an estate and a title to lord it over at home in England.[9]

Further, Bhupal Singh, in the introduction to his *Survey of Anglo-Indian Fiction*, makes the following observation about Anglo-Indian novels:

> A common theme of these novels is the unhappiness, misunderstandings, and complexities of married life in India. Of course unhappy married life is not a feature peculiar to Anglo-India. . . . But taking into consideration the comparatively small number of the English in India, it is surprising that year after year novels should be written whose only interest lies in unhappy Anglo-Indian marriages.[10]

Whilst this is not a fair summary of either *Shadow of the Moon* or *Nightrunners of Bengal*, both do have their share of unhappy Anglo-Indian marriages, and are true, in that respect, to the conventions of the past. This summary is, of course, also interesting in relation to such novels as *Heat and Dust, A Passage to India,* J.G. Farrell's *The Hill Station* (1981) and Paul Scott's *Raj Quartet* (1966–1975). However, Burjorjee is right to point out that in *Nightrunners of Bengal* there are 'notable departures from the conventions of the earlier models. Notably, racial prejudice is given its quietus very early in the novel'.[11] It is also worth observing, as Allen J. Greenberger does in *The British Image of India,*[12] that Masters's *Nightrunners of Bengal* is dedicated to 'The Sepoy of India, 1695–1945'.[13] In contrast M.M. Kaye's *Shadow of the Moon* is dedicated to:

> Sir John William Kaye who wrote a history of the Indian Mutiny, Major-General Edward Kaye who commanded a battery at the Siege of Delhi, my grandfather, William Kaye of the Indian Civil Service, my father, Sir Cecil Kaye, my brother, Colonel William Kaye, and to all other men and women of my family and of so many other British families who served, lived in and loved India. And to that lovely land and all her peoples, with admiration, affection and gratitude.[14]

Nightrunners of Bengal was enthusiastically described by one reviewer as 'the best historical novel about the Indian Mutiny.'[15] This was arguably true at the time of writing; however, like the author of the 1897 article some seventy-five years earlier, Singh was moved to write, 'it must be said the best novel on the Indian Mutiny is yet to come'.[16] I would argue that with the publication of J.G. Farrell's *The Siege of Krishnapur* that novel has finally been written.[17]

  The Siege of Krishnapur is an historical novel on a grand scale, based on accurate detail. Indeed Farrell acknowledges the debt he owes to many sources in an afterword to the novel. With so much historical fact behind the novel it is difficult to say that events did not or could not have happened as Farrell describes them. This is not so with the majority of Mutiny novels. In *Nightrunners of Bengal* Masters takes historical events and tales from his army life and moulds them into his story. Thus the famous tale of the Rani of Jhansi, who fought alongside her soldiers and died in the saddle, is the historical truth behind the Rani of Kishanpur, though little resemblance remains in Masters's telling.[18] What he has done, here and throughout, is to allow history in the form of myth or legend to replace the specifically historical element in his story. Like so many of his predecessors, Masters distorts history to write fiction.

To date there has only been a single Mutiny novel written from an Indian viewpoint. Whereas Masters perpetuates many of the myths which have surrounded the British portrayal of the Mutiny in fiction, Manohar Malgonkar, in his novel *The Devil's Wind*, deliberately sets out to destroy those myths, and tell, for the first time, the story of the Mutiny from an Indian viewpoint, or more specifically from Nana Saheb's viewpoint, as the subtitle *Nana Saheb's Story* indicates.

In *Nightrunners of Bengal* John Masters recounts the events of 1857 as they affected the lives of Rodney Savage and the other residents of the British station of Bhowani and the neighbouring princely state of Kishanpur. His carefully constructed story is not concerned solely with the Mutiny itself, but with the events leading up to, and the arguments surrounding the sepoys' rebellion, and in the background there is the debate about the British position in India. It remains, however, primarily the heroic story of Rodney Savage.

Masters makes it clear that there was cause for unrest amongst the sepoy ranks in the early months of 1857 when he describes one of the officers' weekly conferences (p. 107ff.). Rodney's mounting anger prompts him to voice some of the causes of unrest – the loss of field allowances traditionally paid to men in newly-conquered territory, the attempts by Bible-wielding officers to convert the men to Christianity, also non-army matters such as the outlawing of suttee and female infanticide, and Brahmins being made subject to criminal law. As Rodney points out, India is a country of tradition, and it is not easy to change deeply-rooted customs without some consequences. This is highlighted by his treatment of the greased-cartridge affair.

Rodney has already heard one of the sweepers call a Brahmin sepoy a 'licker of cow's fat' (p. 92) – a terrible insult, all the more so because it is a sweeper who is insulting a Brahmin – and now he understands the taunt. Historically, Brahmins, members of the highest caste, had not been subject to the law. The sweepers were Untouchables responsible for sweeping and for emptying latrines. Such was the division between caste Hindus and Untouchables that a caste Hindu could be defiled even by the shadow of an Untouchable falling on him.[19] If the cartridges were greased with a mixture of pig's fat and cow's fat as rumour would have it, both Hindus and Muslims would be defiled. As Philip Woodruff explains:

On the lips of a Hindu cow's fat would be an abomination for which there is no parallel in European ways of thinking; it was not merely disgusting, as excrement would be; it damned him as well; it was as bad as killing a cow or a Brahman. To a Muslim pig's fat was almost as horrible.[20]

It is clear to the modern-day reader that the greased-cartridge affair needed handling with care, but not everyone thought so at the time. Major Anderson's angry response, 'Make 'em all use the cartridges, *and* like 'em, according to regulations. Shoot anyone for mutiny who refuses' (p. 113), was no doubt a typical response, and here it carries more weight than Rodney's plea: 'Can't the musketry wait till after the rains, when this cartridge muddle will be cleared up? It's only ten rounds a man, anyway' (p. 114).

The tension of the early months of 1857 is built up here with the chapati story, which disturbs Rodney, Caroline Langford, and Colonel Bulstrode. Chapatis, circles of unleavened bread, were passed from village to village by the nightwatchmen, probably with the intention of disturbing the lives of the villagers. Masters exploits and exaggerates the story; the chapatis are passed around in twos, one to be broken into five equal parts, the other into ten equal parts, thus carrying the message 10 May, and are followed by pieces of raw goat's flesh, 'with the skin still on them and the hair and outer layers scraped off, so that they're shining white on one side and raw red flesh on the other' (p. 129). The three pieces of varying size carry the message that men, women and children are all to be murdered. The men who distribute these messages, one of whom is found running through the jungle in the dead of night, are Masters's nightrunners of Bengal. Thus Masters has not only fictionalised the chapati story, he has romanticised it too.

Although he comes from, and perpetuates many of the myths of the Raj tradition, Masters does attempt to be sympathetic to both sides, where in the past indignant voices had only bemoaned the treachery and savagery of the Indians. The death, rape, and mutilation caused by the sepoys in the early hours of 10 May (the date of the mutiny in Meerut) is both vividly described and carefully balanced with later, equally gory accounts of British brutality. Rodney, turning a corner in Gondwara during a pause in the sepoy assault:

saw a group of English gunners bending over something green and dirty white. They were kicking it, and he saw it was a sepoy of the 13th. The man knelt in the mud. His coat was a rag, and his bowels hung out of his stomach, trailing on the earth. One gunner held his neck and tried to make him lick the ground; another jerked him back by his hair and rammed axle grease down his throat. (p. 318).

This last action concludes the greased-cartridge affair and is Masters's way of confirming his belief in the truth of the rumour. Similarly, the earlier disarming of the sepoys and the execution of their ringleader are portrayed as both efficient and necessary. The horror of the action though, for Rodney, was not the death of the mutineer, but the faces of the English gunners – 'they had liked doing it. They would behave like animals, and kill every Indian who crossed their path, and burn the land from end to end, and do it joyfully' (p. 302). Here Masters looks ahead to the events that were to follow the Mutiny, just as he had looked back on the events leading up to it. Thus the brutality of the sepoys is preceded by the now accepted fact of British inefficiency and followed by the equally brutal actions of the British soldiers. In this respect Masters is attempting to place the events of his tale in the wider context of Indo-British relations before and after the Mutiny.

Beyond this Masters places those events within the still wider historical context of an Empire he sees as having been built 'by courage and persevering deceit' (p. 19), both of which are evident in the year 1857– the former in the face of the Mutiny, the latter in the events prior to it. A sense of history is further achieved by references to the Crimea, where Caroline worked with Florence Nightingale, and to the murderous society of Thugs, destroyed some twenty-five years earlier, supposedly by Rodney's father, of which Piroo, the carpenter in Rodney's regiment, who later saves Rodney's and Caroline's lives, had been a member. The story of Thugee is told in Masters's second novel, *The Deceivers* (1952), where Rodney's father, William Savage, is responsible for destroying the cult. (In truth William Sleeman was in charge of the operation which brought an end to Thugee.) Piroo's skill with the rummel (the square of black cloth used to strangle victims) adds colour as well as historical detail. However, the presence of the black cloth neatly tucked into Piroo's loincloth destroys, to a considerable degree, the historicity it attempts to achieve. It is quite inconceivable that no one, a mere twenty-five years after Thuggery had been broken, would recognise the rummel, and that Piroo would have worn it so conspicuously if not proudly.

Whilst Masters carefully attempts to outline the historical setting of *Nightrunners of Bengal* he does not neglect the physical setting, and the harshness of the country is made clear, though only at intervals. The threat of rabies which kills Rodney's close friend and fellow-soldier, Julio, and the cholera in the village, which almost kills Caroline, are both described at length, and, indeed, the account of the cholera is one of the great set pieces of the novel; far better in fact than the account of the mutiny in Bhowani.

The British and Indians are compared and contrasted throughout the novel through their appearance, the social events and the drunkenness of both. On the opening page Caroline is seen as 'so cold, so English' (p. 11) in contrast to the warmth of the life that surrounds her. The first news of the trouble in Kishanpur is brought to the club by the Dewan, a 'slight dark Indian' (p. 28), a typical description perhaps, but not so typical is the description, a few lines later, of Colonel Bulstrode, who 'heaved his twenty-stone bulk up-right . . . and waddled away' (p. 28).[21] The sight of the British officers vying for positions appropriate to their rank and importance as they gather to hear the Dewan's news is an interesting parallel to the rigid Hindu caste system. The verbal back-stabbing amongst the ladies of the cantonment is exposed here as being on a level with the gossip of the sweepers, much of which originates in the toilet, literally, and is little better than the intrigues of the Indian courts. Similarly, the apparent debauchery of the Holi celebrations is juxtaposed with the antics at the regimental guest night Rodney has recently left:

> By eleven o'clock he was drinking brandy in the anteroom and flinging himself into the violent games customary on guest nights – wall racing, high-cockalorum, cockfighting. The moon shone on the lawn, the band played, everything was forgotten except the delights of wine, resilient muscles, and fellowship. (p. 120)

And later,

> A knot of revellers broke from the mob in the square and surged yelling down the alley towards him. They carried brass jars full of water dyed red, brass syringes, and bags of red and blue powder. As they ran they splashed and squirted red water over the house doors and over each other, in the rite symbolising the bleeding of women; and they shouted obscenities, because in legend a demoness had once been frightened away from a village

by the villagers' rude words. The leading man had a wooden phallus two feet long strapped round his waist; with one hand he held the vermilion-daubed knob away from his chin, and in the other brandished a small bell. (p. 138)

Whilst the revelry at the guest night is basically the result of drunkenness, the Holi celebrations do have religious significance to the participants. If, throughout the novel, the portraits of India, her customs, and her people are the predictable substance of Mutiny novels over the years, the equivalent portraits of the British, which expose them so clearly, are not. Eighty years earlier, when the first Mutiny novels were being written, the British would never have been shown in such a light.

The attitude of the British towards the Indians at that time is presented by Masters through the rooms metaphor which Caroline uses to describe her impressions of British India. It is penetrating in its accuracy: 'So India is your palace, but you live shut up with yourselves in little rooms like this Bhowani Cantonment, and the next English room is always away at the other end of the palace somewhere?' (p. 25).

Throughout their years of rule the British have carefully kept themselves separate from their Indian counterparts, and the occasional excursions into Indian rooms, the tiger hunts at Kishanpur, the tours by civil administrators and so on, are no more than token gestures, and British and Indians alike know it. Or, as Caroline asks, 'do they not merely visit, instead of live in, the Indian rooms?' (p. 25). The lack of real contact, the inability, or more accurately the refusal, to 'become Indian, gain one set of qualities and lose another' (p. 25) amounts to nothing more than racism, two-sided though it may be. There is tragic irony in Rodney's assertion that 'Indian customs are very different from ours, and we do not want any misunderstandings to spoil things' (p. 25). It is already too late, and the cause is the refusal to 'become Indian'. How can one set of people understand the customs of another, and avoid upsetting a delicately balanced trust unless they make some attempt to enter the Indian rooms? The motif of switching rooms continues in Masters's next two novels, *The Deceivers* and *The Lotus and the Wind* (1953), where Rodney's father, William, and his son, Robin, respectively, spend over half of each novel dressed as natives, and indeed Robin Savage eventually finds it too difficult to return to the life of a British army officer and disappears mysteriously in Peshawar (as we learn later in

Far, Far the Mountain Peak [1957]). Similarly Victoria Jones, the Eurasian heroine of *Bhowani Junction*, dresses in a sari for a time in an attempt to be Indian, only to find that for her the step is too great. In his genuine affection for the sepoys, Rodney is attempting to enter the Indian rooms, and so is Caroline in her effort to learn Hindustani:

> She spoke slowly at the holy man, in Hindustani. . . . She must have studied hard [in Kishanpur], because that Hindustani was surprisingly good. After six years in India, Rodney's wife Joanna knew twenty words, and could use her verbs only in the imperative mood. (p. 12)

Here Masters also points to the fact that the majority of English women thought that when they were able to give orders in the vernacular they had mastered the language as far as it affected them. As Olivia ironically comments in *Olivia in India*, 'You never say "please" and you learn the words in a cross tone – that is, if you want to be really Anglo-Indian'.[22]

This lack of knowledge of local languages also extended into the army, and prior to the Mutiny many officers in native regiments had to speak to their men through interpreters. But it is not only the hero and heroine of *Nightrunners of Bengal* who differ. Surprisingly, perhaps, Masters portrays Colonel Bulstrode (or Curry Bulstrode as he is affectionately called), the Commanding Officer and an important figure in the British hierarchy in India, as another person who genuinely loves Indians. When Rodney and Caroline visit Bulstrode to report the Dewan's nefarious activities they find the Colonel 'wearing sandals, filthy white trousers, and a dress shirt – the latter unbuttoned and not tucked into the trousers' (p. 127). He is quite able to live in the Indian rooms as subsequent comments show:

> 'See that little snake, just moving down there – earth-snake, called *murari sanp*. Lots of superstitions about him; fellahs throw him up in the air to kill him, then bash him with a stone, call it *suraj dekhana* – "show him the sun." The Gonds eat him, farther south; so do I; very tasty dish.' (p. 128)

Here he shows considerable knowledge of the Indians and their beliefs, and none of the abhorrence that many of his compatriots might have shown. In his comment about Holi, 'you ever seen the Holi, miss? Don't. Disgusting business; I like it' (p. 129), he first gives the typical British response and then destroys it with his own.

The failure to understand India, and the insistence on remaining in separate rooms becomes a question of love and humanity, or more correctly, lack of it, which is essentially the theme of *Nightrunners of Bengal*. As Shailendra Dhari Singh holds, 'the conquest of a race requires imaginative grasp of realities, human sympathy, tolerance and constant touch with the people'.[23] The terrible consequences of the loss of humanity are seen in the atrocities of the Mutiny, to which Masters devotes a whole chapter. On an individual level the reader sees the effects that a loss of humanity (or love, or tolerance) has on Rodney. It is shown here as a brief period of insanity, during which he kills his friend Prithvi Chand and one of the villagers of Chalisgon who are sheltering his party at the risk of their own lives; without a restraining hand from Caroline the toll would have been far greater. Here Masters is using Rodney's insanity as a parallel to that of the British in the months following the Mutiny. Humanity is more important than anything else at this time as Caroline urgently expresses when Chalisgon is threatened by cholera: 'At Gondwara, victory is at stake; here it's understanding, love. They're more important. They're more important for England too, in the long run' (p. 257). This view is later echoed at Gondwara by Sir Hector, who has entrusted the final defence of the fort, and thus the lives of everyone inside it, to a troop of loyal Bombay Lancers:

'. . . Perhaps I have done wrong. But indeed' – his voice was metallic – 'if we can trust no one in this whole country, after a hundred years of dominion, we deserve the annihilation our all-wise Father will certainly mete out.' (p. 311)

Rodney, earlier, had had to place his trust in Indians if he was to survive, and on a grander scale so must Sir Hector now, and the whole of British India later. They could never fight the whole of India, and without humanity they can never hope to gain the trust they need to remain there.

The opportunity to develop his theme of love and humanity through Rodney's relationship with Sumitra, the Rani of Kishanpur, says Burjorjee, 'is lessened to a damaging extent by sexual considerations': had he 'avoided the British image of the "lascivious" Rani of Jhansi' his final gesture would have been all the more effective.[24] However, the fact that Rodney does give the Rani his horse and thus the opportunity to escape after the battle of Gondwara remains a sign of humanity, as Caroline's words echoing in his mind remind us – 'nothing's worth the loss of your humanity' (p. 320). It is too late for Rodney and Sumitra to leave their rooms, but at least they are both aware of the need to, which is an important beginning, and Sumitra's sudden request that Rodney should raise her son, and his agreement to do so, offer hope, in a sentimental fashion, for the future. Robin and the young Rajah will not live in separate rooms, but will grow up together, learning each other's ways. This would have been the ideal, and it is perhaps right that Rodney looks towards it at this juncture. However, in view of later historical events it is perhaps a rather optimistic conclusion.

Throughout the relationship between Rodney and the Rani, the latter's ruby ring is used as a symbol of acceptance and rejection of India. The initial gift marks a closer relationship, which is destroyed when Rodney meets Sumitra during the Holi celebrations – when the reader is beginning to see the extent of the mutineers' plot – and is further rejected when it is offered to him by Prithvi Chand. In both cases he somewhat misjudges the situation, and in the second instance he clearly loses his own humanity; in this state he cannot possibly wear the ring. By putting the ruby ring back on his finger, unthinkingly, outside Gondwara, Rodney is symbolically accepting an end to the violence that can only be overcome and forgotten through love. Whilst it is clear what Masters is trying to achieve through the relationship between Rodney and the Rani, it is unnecessarily romantic and far better suited to the romantic adventure tradition than to a serious historical novel.

The Silver Guru story is also unnecessary and somewhat ridiculous, particularly when everything is apparently explained by the man's Irish background: 'They were not North Sea eyes but Irish Channel eyes. An evil cloud lifted from Rodney's mind. Whenever he'd thought of the Guru, the man's treason had soiled him and every Englishman with its filth' (p. 282).

It is possible to interpret Rodney's relief in two ways. Firstly, whilst it was so difficult for Rodney to believe an Englishman capable of treason, it is no longer so difficult when that 'Englishman' is an Irishman. Secondly, and more likely, Masters is drawing an awkward parallel between Ireland and India, suggesting, presumably, that neither the Irish nor the Indians can be guilty of treason as they are actually fighting for the freedom of their own countries. Whichever interpretation the reader chooses to accept, the story remains wholly out of place, and too far removed from the historical Moulvi of

Fyzabad, whose story no doubt provided the inspiration for Masters's Silver Guru, to add to the novel's sense of history. As an attempt to place the Mutiny in India in the wider context of British history it fails miserably.

At times, too, the author's style is particularly awkward. The many ominous and foreboding references, firstly to 10 May 1857 and then to the centennial anniversary of Plassey ('On June 23, 1757, India's native rulers bowed to the English: on June 23, 1857, she would try to make the English bow in their turn' [p. 244]) are overdone and as a result fail to build up any real tension. Indeed, the many early references to 1857 should not be the prime means used to establish the age for the reader; every aspect of the novel should suggest the 1850s, which does not occur in this work. His use of Sumitra, and later Caroline, to ask questions about British India that require long descriptive replies obviously intended for the reader, is especially irritating. If Masters wishes to describe, for example, a sepoy camp, or explain resettlement, he ought to be able to introduce a description less obviously than the Rani's 'Tell me about it' (p. 58) or Caroline's 'What is resettlement?' (p. 157). Such questions are clumsy and fail to bring any historical feeling to the novel. The pages of italics used in Chapter 16, the account of the slaughter at Bhowani, is a further example of the author's technical shortcomings, and the scene which sees the Silver Guru strangled in the middle of rehearsing his death speech borders on melodrama.

Despite these problems of style, in *Nightrunners of Bengal* Masters shows that he is a fine storyteller. However, he is not a fine historical novelist. As an historical novel the greatest deficiency of *Nightrunners of Bengal* is that it fails to capture the specific qualities of its age.

One of the major differences between *Nightrunners of Bengal* and *The Siege of Krishnapur* is that Masters excludes the present from his story, whilst Farrell includes it in a number of ways, making full use of hindsight. He has succeeded in writing a 'Victorian novel' with the awareness of a late-twentieth-century writer. As a result, Farrell's characters are able, as Lukács explained of Scott's characters, to express themselves in a way which is clear to the modern-day reader.[25] No author writing in 1857 could have allowed his characters to express themselves as Farrell's do.

The Siege of Krishnapur is concerned with the people and events central to the siege which gives the book its title, and whilst the action of the novel is restricted to that which directly involves a small group of Britons, he skilfully makes that group representative of the whole of British India, and even of Victorian society in England. His characters are representatives of the age, and despite the fact that the events of the siege are largely based on the historical siege of Lucknow, his characters do not represent particular historical figures in the way that some of Masters's do.

Like *Nightrunners of Bengal, The Siege of Krishnapur* is set in its military age with the aid of references to the Crimean war. We learn early in the novel that the real reason for Fleury's visit to India 'was the need to divert his recently widowed sister, Miriam, whose husband, Captain Lang, had been killed before Sebastopol'.[26] Miriam's association is rather less romantic than Caroline Langford's, and indeed Farrell consistently destroys any romantic notions of the Mutiny. Thus he presents two different pictures of the massacre at Captainganj. Firstly there is Harry's belief 'that because of his sprained wrist he had missed an adventure at Captainganj' (p. 106), and secondly that of his fellow officers who: 'listened quite enviously to Harry talking about the musket shot which had "almost definitely" been fired at himself and Fleury. They wished they had had an adventure too, instead of their involuntary glimpse of the abattoir' (p. 106). By presenting these two views of the massacre Farrell is destroying the popular nineteenth-century idea of young soldiers going abroad in search of adventure and glory. What they actually found was the Crimea and the Mutiny, and there was nothing glorious about either. However, it is worth remembering that although Harry's attitude is eager and naive, the Empire needed such soldiers; without them nothing could have been attempted, let alone achieved. Because of the traditional romantic plot which has been the stock-in-trade of Mutiny fiction, the officers and men of the East India Company Army have been depicted as the heroes of the Mutiny. In *Nightrunners of Bengal* Masters criticised the role of some of the military policy-makers and officers in the events which gave rise to the Mutiny; his criticisms, however, were limited and, true to the tradition in which he is writing, in times of crisis no British officer ever failed in his duty. Farrell, on the other hand, does not pull any punches in his appraisal of the military. His description of General Jackson, the senior officer at Captainganj, is as alarming as it is amusing, coming as it does only days before the massacre:

As one might have expected in an Army where promotion strictly attended seniority, the General was an elderly man, well over seventy. . . . As he advanced stiffly towards the portico both men [the Collector and the Magistrate] noticed with foreboding that instead of a walking stick the General was carrying a cricket bat. Knowing that his memory was no longer quite what it once had been, the General frequently carried some object as an aide-mémoire; thus, if he had come to discuss horses he might carry a riding crop, if the topic was gunnery he might juggle a couple of musket balls in his pocket. (p. 71)

Obviously this startling portrait is of one man only, but it is not long before Farrell widens his criticism to include the majority of senior officers. As the Collector gathers the survivors from Captainganj, Farrell comments that '(for once the senior officers had borne the brunt of the slaughter)' (p. 103) – the parentheses effectively giving this aside the full weight of the author's voice.

The early signs of trouble at Krishnapur are seen in the ominous distribution of chapatis, which in this novel appear in fours in various unexpected places such as inside the Collector's despatch box. Though Farrell's account of the chapati distribution has none of the sinister overtones that Masters developed, it does acknowledge the unease that the chapatis caused amongst at least some of the British. In this novel, however, unrest is carried without the dramatisation that accompanies Masters's telling, and interest in the chapatis soon wanes, leaving the Collector isolated in his concern. That the Collector remains worried by the phenomenon carries considerable weight with the reader, just as Rodney's concern does in *Nightrunners of Bengal*. The use these novelists make of the chapati story again illustrates how history can be used by both the romantic adventure novelist and the serious postmodernist novelist with quite different, but in both cases effective, results.

At no point does Farrell make any attempt to list the various causes of the Mutiny, though he does enunciate a number of them, if at times obliquely. The only one he chooses to highlight directly is the greased cartridges, which is presumed to have been the final spark which ignited the fire:

that's what worried Jack Sepoy! Somehow he got the idea that the grease comes from pork or beef tallow and he didn't like it touching his lips because it's against his religion. (p. 35)

This remarkable understatement illustrates the lack of understanding which existed between the English and the Indians, and in this case between the officers and men of the Indian Army in the months prior to the Mutiny. The tremendous sense of futility and waste which surrounded the whole affair is shown when Farrell describes Lucy busy making cartridges in the final days of the siege: 'Lucy's grease, however, was a mixture of beeswax and rancid butter. A Hindu could have eaten a pound of it with pleasure' (p. 334). In the end the British have to adapt to their circumstances and use a grease which would have been acceptable to the sepoys. The great tragedy is that the trouble over the grease could so easily have been avoided, and the irony is driven home as Lucy weeps bitterly over 'the neat rows of cartridges she had made and which were no longer needed' (p. 341).

During the course of *The Siege of Krishnapur* few Indian characters are developed to any great degree. In one respect this reflects Farrell's own lack of knowledge of Indians compared to Masters's wealth of experience. More importantly, in terms of portraying history through fiction, it reflects the gulf which existed between the British and the Indians at this time. The only Indian that the British have any social contact with is Hari, the Maharajah's son and heir. Our first view of Hari reveals the fruits of his education under a British tutor:

> Near a fireplace of marble inlaid with garnets, lapis lazuli and agate, the Maharajah's son sat on a chair constructed entirely of antlers, eating a boiled egg and reading *Blackwood's Magazine*. Beside the chair a large cushion on the floor still bore the impression of where he had been sitting a moment earlier; he preferred squatting on the floor to the discomfort of chairs but feared that his English visitors might regard this as backward. (p. 79)

This description is an incongruous mixture of East and West; the English furniture contrasts with the Indian cushions, and even the chair, because it is made of antlers, is a mixture of the two cultures. Hari appears out of place in his Indian surroundings, hence the boiled egg and *Blackwood's Magazine*, yet ill at ease in British surroundings, preferring to squat on a cushion rather than sit in a chair. He is, here and throughout the novel, uncomfortably stranded between East and West. Thus his English is full of misused idioms and misquoted Shakespeare, and his interest in daguerreotype, a skill he sees as truly advanced, is pursued in a room which 'was laden with mercury vapour and a variety of other fumes no less toxic, emanating from crystals and solutions of chlorine, bromine, iodine, and potassium cyanide' (p. 91). With this account and particularly the stress on cyanide achieved by its final position, his learning is portrayed as unhealthy for him rather than as a step on the road of progress. The knowledge of phrenology he later acquires, again quite useless to him, perhaps symbolises the imprisonment of his mind by his British education, whilst he is literally a prisoner in the tiger hut during the early part of the siege. Farrell's sense of comedy, particularly his ability to portray the greatest misfortunes in a comic way is reminiscent of Thomas Love Peacock, who satirised phrenology in his delightfully comic novel *Headlong Hall* (1816). Throughout the novel Farrell chooses the most absurd historical examples he can find and juxtaposes them to the greatest comic advantage. Peacock, incidently, was an employee of the East India Company, though he never served in India.

There are, of course, other Indian characters, but none is developed to the extent of Hari. The Maharajah, and Hari's constant companion, the Prime Minister, are almost caricatures of how Indians were seen by the English of the day. But if the Maharajah is overfond of women, Hari has noticed a similar truth beneath the moral Victorian exterior, and immediately offers to show Fleury a collection of lewd paintings. This suggests that British society is no more moral than Indian society, and that British civilization is no better than Indian civilization. Rather, judging by the behaviour of certain representatives of British society, it is infinitely worse.

Farrell uses the 'tea' that Fleury is invited to at Rayne's to show the British at their least admirable. On top of the disgusting treatment of the servants, named after various animals and presumably treated with as much respect, there is the arrival of Lieutenant Cutter who rides his horse into the room waving his sabre and continues to ride around the room until the horse refuses to jump the sofa for a second time and he finally falls to the floor. Through Fleury, the only sober man at this drunken gathering, we are able to view the antics which amuse the others with a detached clarity. Farrell underlines his point with marvellous irony as Fleury, evidently out of place, decides to take his leave: ' "What? Can you be off already?" exclaimed Rayne. "I haven't yet had a chance to talk to you . . . A talk about civilization, that's what I wanted to have!" ' (p. 66). The reader may well recall the report Fleury has been commissioned to write on the advances of civilization in India!

The gulf between the two races is further illustrated by Farrell's comments on language. There is little evidence of the British characters being able to speak any Indian languages, and on the one occasion when the vernacular is used Harry Dunstable has trouble understanding and being understood, his 'grasp of the language being limited to a few simple commands, domestic and military' (p. 48), despite the fact that he was born in the country. In raising this issue Farrell is identifying another of the underlying causes of the Mutiny. The newcomer Fleury has difficulty understanding even his own language when it is spoken by an Indian, and Harry has to interpret for him. The impression is that the British, immediately prior to the Mutiny, simply did not understand Indians.

This distance in understanding is further illustrated by the way Fleury views India through English eyes, as Farrell comically exposes: 'The carriage had slowed down to pass through a densely populated bazaar. Fleury gazed out at a sea of brown faces. . . . A few inches away two men sat cross-legged in a cupboard' (p. 30). And on entering the Krishnapur bazaar 'an incongruous picture came into Fleury's mind of a hundred and fifty people squatting on the floor of his aunt's drawing-room in Torquay' (pp. 47–8). When on occasions he does begin to show some understanding of India, as he does when he warms to Hari's feelings for his religion, it is only short-lived:

> Fleury, however, glanced at [Hari] in dismay: he had forgotten for the moment just what sort of religion it was that Hari enjoyed . . . a mixture of superstition, fairy-tale, idolatry and obscenity, repellent to every decent Englishman in India. (p. 84)

Because Farrell makes such moments of insight brief and infrequent, they carry little genuine conviction or hope. Fleury's is the pre-conceived idea of Hinduism that the English took with them to India, and which prevented any hope of breaking down the barriers between the two races. Farrell's comic irony also exposes the short-comings of the missionary zeal prevalent in India at that time, and now seen as another cause of unrest amongst the sepoy ranks.

If Fleury illustrates the prejudices and limited viewpoints of the 'griffin', or newcomer to India, Harry Dunstable comes out with some astounding comments which reflect the 'stiff-upper-lip' attitude common amongst the military and much of the civilian population in India. His advice to Fleury, 'You have to be careful thrashing a Hindu, George, because they have very weak chests and you can kill them' (p. 77) is all the more disturbing coming from such a young man, and shows the depth of prejudice that prevailed at the time. It is, perhaps, the Collector alone of the Krishnapur residents who displays any true feeling for India and her inhabitants. His thoughts on Mr Willoughby, the magistrate, show his own understanding and also the magistrate's lack of it: 'Even after all these years in India Willoughby doesn't understand the natives. He's too rational for them. He can't see things from their point of view because he has no heart' (p. 98). And it appears that few of the British residents have. The immature Fleury does at times display such a heart, but it is the enthusiasm of his youth that carries him away rather than any deeply felt commitment. India is often seen as a parenthetical pause in the 'real life' of England – as a time and place for a youthful flirtation with ideas. This is certainly true of Fleury, whose meeting with Mr Hopkins at the end of the novel suggests that his idealism was just part of his youth. The Collector, too, has given up in his attempt to gain a genuine understanding of the truth about British rule in India, and Farrell shows the reader, through heavy irony, how far away the Collector still is from any understanding, though he thinks he is making great strides. He muses on:

> the perplexing question of why, after a hundred years of beneficial rule in Bengal, the natives should have taken it into their heads to return to the anarchy of their ancestors. One or two mistakes, however serious, made by the military in their handling of religious matters, were surely no reason for rejecting a superior culture as a whole. (p. 176)

Only at the end does he realise that the 'fiction of happy natives being led forward along the road to civilization could no longer be sustained' (p. 249). Dr McNab alone, perhaps a representative of the post-Raj viewpoint (which Farrell always keeps in sight through the presence of his narrator), was aware of this from the start. Farrell is showing us just how deeply the British believed (as did some Indians like Hari) that it was a superior culture. And indeed, it is the whole idea of Victorian culture that Farrell is exploring in this novel.

From the beginning of the novel through to the end there is a feeling that the British have had and will have little impact on India. The opening description of the village where 'often there is just a well to be worked from dawn till dusk by the same two men and two

bullocks every single day in their lives' (p. 10), manifests the Collector's final impression of India: 'he knew that the same two men and
two bullocks would do this every day until the end of their lives'
(p. 343). The repetition of this description at the end of the novel
expresses the timelessness of India and Indian life (as does the
punkah wallah in *A Passage to India*); the events of the novel, so
monumental in importance to the survivors of the siege and so
central to British rule in India, are no more than a parenthetical
pause in the life of India, with the two men and two bullocks signal-
ling the parenthesis.

The opening paragraphs firmly establish the Indianness and,
therefore, the alienness as far as the British are concerned, of the
setting in a way that is clearly reminiscent of Forster's description of
Chandrapore at the beginning of *A Passage to India*:

> Except for the Marabar Caves – and they are twenty miles off – the
> city of Chandrapore presents nothing extraordinary. Edged rather
> than washed by the river Ganges, it trails for a couple of miles
> along the bank, scarcely distinguishable from the rubbish it de-
> posits so freely. . . . In the bazaars there is no painting and scarcely
> any carving. The very wood seems made of mud, the inhabitants
> of mud moving. So abased, so monotonous is everything that
> meets the eye, that when the Ganges comes down it might be
> expected to wash the excrescence back into the soil. Houses do
> fall, people are drowned and left rotting, but the general outline
> of the town persists, swelling here, shrinking there, like some low
> but indestructible form of life.[27]

Farrell's opening reads thus:

> Anyone who has never before visited Krishnapur, and who ap-
> proaches from the east, is likely to think he has reached the end of
> his journey a few miles sooner than he expected. While still some
> distance from Krishnapur he begins to ascend a shallow ridge.
> From here he will see what appears to be a town in the heat
> distorted distance. He will see the white glitter of walls and roofs
> and a handsome grove of trees, perhaps even the dome of what
> might be a temple. Round about there will be the unending plain
> still, exactly as it has been for many miles back, a dreary ocean of
> bald earth, in the immensity of which an occasional field of sugar
> cane or mustard is utterly lost. . . .

But if you look closely and shield your eyes from the glare you will make out tiny villages here 'and there, difficult to see because they are made of the same mud as the plain they came from; and no doubt they melt back into it again during the rainy season, for there is no lime in these parts, no clay or shale that you can burn into bricks, no substance hard enough to resist the seasons over the years. (p. 9)

At first the mud huts appear anything but permanent, blending as they do into the background. In contrast a sense of permanency is established in the description of the Residency where 'the walls, which were built of enormous numbers of the pink, wafer-like bricks of British India, were so very thick' (p. 13). Yet despite this impression of permanence and solidity the Residency is strangely at odds with the landscape, so much so that 'it was hard to believe that one was in India at all, except for the punkahs' (p. 17). In other words, it doesn't belong in the way that the simple mud huts do. The pink, wafer-like bricks are out of place, and the fragile adjectives 'pink' and 'wafer-like' undermine the impression of words like 'enormous' and 'thick'. Although they are washed away every year, it is the mud huts that appear the more permanent, and in an Indian sense they are. The once splendid British bungalows, now that Krishnapur had declined in importance, 'were left shuttered and empty' (p. 10). Even in the midst of the still-inhabited compound there is evidence of this decay, as the reader sees when Fleury accepts Rayne's invitation to tea and is led by a bearer 'past an old, deserted bungalow with holes in its thatched roof and a sagging verandah' and, worse when one considers the symbolic importance of the flag in British India, 'beside it, on a little mound, lay the worm-pocked skeleton of a flag-pole' (p. 60). Yet the very fact that such buildings as the Residency and the cantonment bungalows were built is proof of the colonial confidence existing at that time.

In India, as elsewhere in the Empire, the British simply established their own society and culture, imposing their buildings on the landscape and shipping the furniture and possessions to fill them as if it was their right and the natural course for a superior race. The signs of decay symbolically show that the British hold was only transitory after all, and in turn the events of the siege forcibly confirm this, again using the images of mud and bricks: 'For the Collector knew that he had to have earth as a cushion against the enemy cannons; brickwork or masonry splinters or cracks, wood is useless; only earth is capable of gulping down cannon balls without distress' (p. 270). This also reinforces the idea that mud rather than bricks is suited to India. It may appear contradictory, therefore, that the Collector's mud ramparts should be repeatedly washed away by the rains. This is not so as they, like the mud huts, can always be rebuilt; the problem here is time – the besieged victims' lack of it as opposed to the timelessness of the Indian peasants' life. Also, the rains, by washing away the defences, repeatedly expose the bizarre collection of possessions which clearly do not belong there, and in so doing mock the confidence that brought them.

However, the possessions which formerly cluttered the Residency are not merely useless, as Farrell, showing himself a master of the grotesque, makes clear:

A sepoy here was trying to remove a silver fork from one of his lungs, another had received a piece of lightning-conductor in his kidneys. A sepoy with a green turban had had his spine shattered by 'The Spirit of Science'; others had been struck down by tea-spoons, by fish-knives, by marbles; an unfortunate *subadar* had been plucked from this world by the silver sugar-tongs embedded in his brain. A heart-breaking wail now rose from those who had not been killed outright. (pp. 318–19)

As Frances B. Singh points out, 'in the last defense of the compound, the very implements of civilization, progress and science become missiles of pain, horror and death'.[28] Yet the symbol works both ways; those very same implements of civilization, progress, and science also become the missiles which protect the innocent. It is also true to say that these implements were useless in India until they were adapted to a particular situation. The huge busts of Plato and Socrates, formidable representatives of western civilization, are good examples of this. The banqueting hall 'was an unhappy mixture of Greek and gothic . . . but perhaps the most surprising pieces of ornament were outside, the four giant marble busts of Greek philosophers which gazed out over the plain from each corner of the roof' (pp. 109–10). The busts are clearly out of place (one is tempted to question the very need to transport Greek philosophers to India) and are quite useless until adapted, as they are during the siege. Harry, in charge of the cannon:

had had an excellent notion for protecting the gunners, which was to prise off two of the giant marble busts that crowned the roof and have them dragged into position on each side of the cannon . . . now the giant heads of Plato and Socrates, each with an expression of penetrating wisdom carved on his white features surveyed the river and the melon beds beyond. (p. 149)

The same incongruity is true of the British themselves. Farrell points to the celibate condition of so many Anglo-Indian marriages at this time, and to the social activities which are at odds with the climate and situation. Thus the meetings in Calcutta drawing rooms, the balls, references to the Bengal Club Cup and the picnic are all illustrations of the deliberate attempt to re-create British society in India:

The ladies were discreetly watching from an upstairs window the following morning when a rather grimy *gharry* stopped in front of the Dunstaples' house in Alipore. Even Louise was watching, though she denied being in the least interested in the sort of creature that might emerge. If she happened to be standing at the window it was simply because Fanny was standing there too and she was trying to comb Fanny's hair. (p. 25)

Take away the Indian names and scenes like this could have been taken from a Jane Austen novel.

Yet despite all efforts to establish British society in India, and there are moments when it is possible to imagine that social events like the ball 'were taking place not in India but in some temperate land far away' (p. 45), the truth cannot be escaped for long, because in the Indian climate: 'no amount of rice powder could dull the glint of [the ladies'] features, no amount of padding could prevent damp stains from spreading at their armpits' (p. 41). This detail shows the depth of historical observation to be found in Farrell's novel, as well as showing the historical imagination at work. Few historians writing about the Mutiny would take time to describe the nineteenth-century forerunner of anti-perspirant. Such carefully selected detail is a vital part of the technique of good historical fiction. But paradoxically, this verisimilitude involves a fact which would never have been mentioned by Jane Austen or any nineteenth-century writer. It is chosen both as an 'ordinary' example of everyday life, for verisimilitude of atmosphere, and as an 'extraordinary' example intended to shock the reader. At this point, we are conscious of the twentieth-century omniscient narrator at work.

Four of the senses – sight, sound, touch and taste – were to a large degree cut from India off simply by the circumstances of cantonment life. For many women there was very little need to leave the cantonments, and for the men whose work threw them into close contact with Indians, once home in their bungalows or at the club, the sights and sounds of India could be shut out and easily forgotten. Obviously touch was even easier to circumvent. Taste, too, could be avoided, but more often the food eaten by the British was a mixture of English cookery and Indian spices: '. . . the fried fish in batter that glowed like barley sugar, the curried fowl seasoned with lime juice, coriander, cumin and garlic, the tender roast kid and mint sauce' (p. 53). And on the following morning 'the *khansamah* was buttering some toast for Fleury's breakfast with the greasy wing of a fowl' (p. 60). The important point is that despite the Indian additions, the food is essentially English. Smell could not be ignored; whilst it may be possible to cut oneself off from the smells of the bazaar, the sense of smell is always at work in India, where 'one sweet suffocating perfume [gives] way to another' (p. 61). Even the smell of roses, so evocative of the English garden, changes in the Indian environment and becomes a distinct reminder of India, as Fleury unhappily discovers:

> he could smell the heavy scent of the roses . . . the smell disturbed him; like the smell of incense it was more powerful than an Englishman is accustomed to. At that moment, tired and dispirited, he would have given a great deal to smell the fresh breeze off the Sussex downs. (p. 50)

Not only are the smells of India often different, but familiar smells are stronger, too strong for the English nose. The smell of the roses, far from being agreeable is rather an assault on the sense. What Fleury longs for is the ability to shut out the smell of India.

If for the most part the British are able to avoid any serious arousal of their senses, this is not the case during the siege itself when they are forced to live in very close proximity with one another. The billiard room, now housing the women, is in many respects a parallel to the Indian bazaar, and before entering the room the Collector 'had to pause a moment to compose himself for the inevitable assault on his senses' (p. 170). In the following pages each of the five senses is attacked, and at each juncture the Collector compares present with past, which both suggests the changes the British are experiencing and the gulf which normally exists between British and Indian life.

The first sense to be assaulted is sound:

> The noise in this room was deafening, especially if you compared it, as the Collector did, with how it used to be in the days when it had been reserved for billiards. Ah, then it had been like some gentle rustic scene . . . the green meadows of the tables, the brown leather of the chairs, and the gentlemen peacefully browsing amongst them. Then there had been no other sound but the occasional click of billiard balls or the scrape of someone chalking his cue. (p. 170)

As the Collector looks back on the past glory of the billiard room his thoughts evoke the British countryside with an emphasis on peace and tranquillity, and also the male-dominated contemporary British society. Past billiards become, comically, a pastoral idyll, inhabited by bovine males. 'But now, alas, the ears were rowelled by high-pitched voices raised in dispute or emphasis; the competition here was extreme for anyone with anything to say: it included a number of crying children, illicit parrots and mynah birds' (p. 170). The gentle sounds of the English countryside give way to the sound of parrots and mynah birds, whilst the noise of arguing women and crying children replaces the click of balls and the chalking of cues. The description is one that might well have described the noise, and the life, of an Indian bazaar.

> It was now the turn of his eyes to take offence. This room, so light, so airy, so nobly proportioned, had been utterly transformed by the invasion of the ladies. A narrow aisle led down the middle of the room . . . the two pretty Misses O'Hanlon . . . were sitting cross-legged on their bedding in chemises and petticoats. . . . On each side of the aisle charpoys or mattresses or both together had been set down higgledy-piggledy, in some cases partitioned off from their neighbours by sheets suspended from strings that ran from the wall to the chandeliers, or from one string to another. (pp. 170-1)

The charpoys and mattresses arranged in haphazard fashion bear little resemblance to the luxury of a separate room to sleep in. (Though for the Kashmiri villagers in Rumer Godden's *Kingfishers Catch Fire*

[1953] even a separate bed is something to be wondered at: '"A bed each!" said the village, marvelling. "A bed even for the children!"'[29]) The picture of women sitting around in their chemises and petticoats recalls Fleury's first view of the bazaar, 'crowded with people dressed in white muslin' (p. 47) and his musings on where they could all possibly live. The answer is, in surroundings as public as those that the British women are now forced to endure.

The smells of the bazaars have also found their way into this room which was once so thoroughly set apart from Indian life:

> Near the door there was a powerful smell of urine from unemptied chamber-pots which thankfully soon gave away to a feminine smell of lavender and rose water . . . a scent which mingled with the smell of perspiration to irritate his senses. (p. 171)

In Indian streets, particularly the narrow streets of the bazaar, the smells of urine, excrement, and waste are ever present; now they have found their way into the inner sanctuaries of British India.

The Collector's senses of touch and taste are also played upon before he completes his inspection:

> So far his sense of touch had been exercised only in imagination but at this moment a round shot struck the outside wall in an adjoining room a few yards away. The sudden noise caused two of these young bodies to cling to him for a moment . . . and he could not restrain his large hands from comforting them. (p. 174)

In one respect this passage conjures up the typical idea of an oriental harem, whilst in another it points to the sexual exploitation that was rife in Victorian England.

> His mission accomplished, he turned to leave. But his sense of taste, which had so far escaped the assault on the other four, was now confronted with a hastily brewed cup of tea in a child's christening mug (for lack of china) and a rock bun. (p. 175)

The past is again evoked by the lack of a china cup, and the tea, presented in this unusual vessel is another reminder of the bazaar, this time of the tea shop.

This visit to the former billiard room both shows the effects of the siege and compares British and Indian life. British life is shown to have little effect on the senses, whilst in comparison Indian life has a very great effect, suggesting a greater sense of life itself. Or, conversely, the British are, until removed from the environment of their choosing, unaware of their senses, suggesting the repressions of Victorian society. The billiard room further resembles Indian life in that 'the ladies in the billiard room had divided themselves into groups according to the ranks of husbands or fathers' (p. 172), which, like the British officers gathering to hear the Dewan's news in Masters's *Nightrunners of Bengal*, clearly parallels the Hindu caste system, so often criticised by the British, yet little different, in many respects, from the social divisions adhered to by the British residents in India. Even the British attitude of standing together in adversity does not overcome these divisions. Masters makes a similar point in *Nightrunners of Bengal*; at the hot-weather children's party, Joanna Savage is obviously unhappy about having to play croquet with Mrs Hatch, the wife of a non-commissioned officer, and even the Hatch children are seen playing apart from the rest. As the Hindus have their Untouchables so too the British have their outcastes (*sic*), seen here in the figure of Lucy Hughes, the fallen woman. (Though exactly how far she has fallen is never explained. I suspect that like Sarah Woodruff in John Fowles's *The French Lieutenant's Woman* [1969], gossip has been unkind to her). The manner in which Lucy is treated by her compatriots is a further reminder of the position of women in Victorian society, and again sets the novel in its social age:

> Lucy Hughes provided a problem which the Collector was unable to solve. She was ostracized even by the members of the lowest group, in fact, by everyone except Louise. The *charpoy* on which she had spread her bedding had been pushed to the very end of the room, beneath the oven blast of the open window. It was the only bed that had any space around it, for even Louise's bed, which was next to hers, stood at a small, but eloquent distance. (p. 173)

This is Farrell's ironic comment on British condemnation of untouchability.

The physical and mental deterioration of the British during the siege is mirrored by the fortunes of the dogs in and around the compound:

they included mongrels and terriers of many shapes and sizes but
also dogs of purer breed . . . setters and spaniels, among them
Chloë, and even one or two lap-dogs. What a sad spectacle they
made! The faithful creatures were daily sinking into a more desperate state. While jackals and pariah dogs grew fat, they grew
thin; their soft and luxurious upbringing had not fitted them for
this harsh reality. (p. 193)

This passage could as easily be describing the fortunes of the British
survivors as their dogs. As the siege continues it becomes necessary
for both men and dogs alike to adapt to their circumstances or
perish. Thus it is quite right that the British should eat a captured
horse and that the Collector should relish a tasty beetle. It is not
right, though, that the scavenging should fall to the depths it reaches
at the auction, where the survivors are, metaphorically, preying on
one another; it is surely no coincidence that straight after the auction
we see Chloë, the dog Fleury had intended to give to Louise, sink to
a similar level:

> Fleury turned away, sickened, for Chloë had wasted no time in
> bounding forward to eat away the sepoy's face. He told Ram to
> kill her as well and hurried away to take refuge in the banqueting
> hall and try to erase from his mind the scene he had just wit-
> nessed. (p. 297)

Whilst it is clearly necessary to adapt to their plight it is essential that
the besieged men and women keep their humanity and obey at least
some rules. Chloë is to all intents and purposes British, and in eating
the sepoy's face she has degenerated into 'cannibalism', which can
never be acceptable to civilized society. Fleury does not wish to
descend to this level, and thus Chloë is justly shot for failing to abide
by British standards.

But the Victorian public was protected from the knowledge of
much of this, and it is the relief troops, rather than the survivors of
the siege, that the Victorian reader would have seen as 'realistic'. In
other words, it is the relief troops, not the survivors, who fit the
myths of the India invented for and by the Victorian public, as
Farrell exposes here. Indeed the nineteenth-century reader would
have shared Lieutenant Stapleton's opinion of the survivors as an
'extraordinary collection of scarecrows' (p. 339). In R.M. Ballantyne's

The Coral Island (which, coincidently, was published in 1857, the year of the Mutiny) the shipwrecked boys rise to the occasion and behave in the way British boys would have been expected to behave. Or, to put it another way, in a manner that the Victorians (or the relief troops) would have believed likely. In William Golding's *Lord of the Flies* (1954), however, the naval officer who discovers the children 'inspected the little scarecrow in front of him. The kid needed a bath, a hair-cut, a nose-wipe and a good deal of ointment'.[30] The truth of this is paralleled in Farrell's description of the Krishnapur survivors. In both Golding's and Farrell's books twentieth-century pragmatism takes the place of nineteenth-century idealism and romanticism.

Farrell closes his penultimate chapter with the General musing on how the relief should be shown to the world:

> Even when allowances were made, the 'heroes of Krishnapur', as he did not doubt they would soon be called, were a pretty rum lot. And he would have to pose for hours, holding a sword and perched on a trestle or wooden horse while some artist-wallah depicted 'The Relief of Krishnapur'! He must remember to insist on being in the foreground, however; then it would not be so bad. With luck this wretched selection of 'heroes' would be given the soft pedal . . . an indistinct crowd of corpses and a few grateful faces, cannons and prancing horses would be best. (p. 342)

This is what the Victorian public expected, and as Thomas Jones Barker's *The Relief of Lucknow* (Plate 1) shows, it is indeed how the relief was recorded by artists of the day as well as by novelists. The truth of the photograph, which shows the courtyard of the Secunderbagh after the Relief of Lucknow (Plate 2), stands in marked contrast. Farrell, writing with twentieth-century licence, has demythologised the 1850s. He has successfully recreated the feelings of that time whilst stripping it of romanticism and adding truths not found in the literature of the day. In his genteel, polite way he has deconstructed the myths of the Raj.

An example of Farrell's attention to detail can be seen in the reactions of Fleury and Harry as they scrape the swarm of cockchafers from Lucy's naked body:

> The only significant difference between Lucy and a statue was that Lucy had pubic hair; this caused them a bit of a surprise at

first. It was not something that had ever occurred to them as possible, likely, or even, desirable. (p. 256)

This detail is not strange to us as we know that women have pubic hair, but it gains its impact because we recognise that it *is* strange to Fleury and Harry. Thus Farrell is viewing the disjunction between our society and society at the time of the Mutiny, and this is characteristic of the way Farrell uses history, creating a gap between the two ages to create what could be called 'context shock'. Perhaps Farrell's idea for this scene came from Mary Lutyens, who suggests that a similar discovery by John Ruskin about his wife Effie was the cause behind his failure to consummate their marriage.[31] However, although this description is accurate as a Victorian response it may not be accurate in its Indian setting. Fashions in the Colonies tended to be some years behind those of England (witness the interest in Fleury's coat), and British society in India at the time of the Mutiny would probably have had more in common with the freer Regency period than with the Victorian austerity of contemporaneous society in England. But Farrell is not worried by this and simply uses artistic licence to ignore what might be seen as a minor anachronism, and he has been able to describe the incident as a writer of the time could never have done. It is not an anachronism, however, when it is used with deliberate point, as in many novels of the 1970s.

Debates on the religious and medical controversies of the time rage throughout Farrell's novel. The religious climate of the time is principally illustrated by the ongoing argument between the Reverend Hampton and Fleury. The former had, in his college days, experienced 'the seething religious atmosphere of Oxford' (p. 56) though he wisely concentrated on rowing. In other words he did not get caught up in the Tractarianism of the Oxford Movement, and now, as the siege continues he takes up the dogmatic standpoint of the Evangelicals, insisting on the literal truth of the Bible. Fleury's at times lively interjections, on the contrary, put forward the liberal views of the broad Church. It is because of Fleury's liberal thinking that Reverend Hampton hounds him throughout the siege, and makes such wily comments as 'I hear, Mr Fleury, that in Germany there is much discussion of the origin of the Bible . . .' (p. 220), in an attempt to draw out and in some way defeat the arguments of the younger man. Fleury's assertion that the question of whether the Bible is literally true or not does not matter places him in agreement with Coleridge and the German critic Strauss, author of *Das Leben Jesu* (first published in 1835, and translated into English in 1846 by Mary Ann Evans, the young George Eliot), who both argued that the importance of the Bible lay in its moral teaching rather than whether or not it was accurate as fact. The unsuitability of Reverend Hampton's evangelical fervour is emphasised by the theme of the sermon he preaches to the all but empty church: 'Go ye into all the world, and preach the gospel to every creature' (p. 123). With heavy irony Farrell has the Revd Hampton outline another of the underlying causes of the sepoy unrest as he continues his sermon:

> He had heard, he declared, that there were those in the British community who blamed their present perilous situation on the missionary activity of the Church. They blamed a colonel of a regiment at Barrackpur who had been preaching Christianity in the bazaar. They blamed Mr Tucker, the Judge at Fatehpur, for the piety which had made him have the Ten Commandments translated into the vernacular and chiselled on stones to be placed by the roadside . . . (p. 123)

And from what we see of the Revd Hampton we can only agree with them. The Padre is also at odds with the Catholic Chaplain Father O'Hara, a dispute which Farrell centres on the graveyard:

> A small portion of the graveyard had been reluctantly allotted to Father O'Hara by the Padre for his Romish rites in the event of any of the half dozen members of his Church succumbing during the present difficulties. But when Father O'Hara had asked for a bigger plot, the Padre had been furious; Father O'Hara already had enough room for six people, so he must be secretly hoping to convert some of the Padre's own flock to his Popish idolatry. (p. 112)

Thus within the walls of Krishnapur Farrell exposes not only the religious activity that directly affected the residents of British India, but also the wider problems of the time.

His references to the German theologians, whose enquiries were based on 'the Testimony of the Rocks' also opens the way to Darwinism – the publication of *On the Origin of Species* was only two years away at the time – and that Fleury puts forward a number of quasi-Darwinian theories during the course of the novel is not surprising: 'Could it not be, he wondered vaguely, trembling on the brink of an idea that would have made him famous, that somehow or other fish designed their own eyes?' (p. 168). In the years leading up to 1859 thoughts along Darwinian lines were being developed, and Farrell uses this as an important factor in establishing the climate of the age. Tennyson's *In Memoriam* (1850) is, of course, a classic example of 'Darwinism' pre-Darwin.

In a literary sense Farrell sets his novel in its age through references to Tennyson, the poet who more than any other epitomises the 1850s. He uses Tennyson to suggest how the Victorian men saw themselves, or at least the ideal, as 'great, broad-shouldered, genial Englishmen' (p. 40), whilst on two occasions the Collector uses the line 'the soft and milky rabble of womankind' (p. 30 and p. 171) – from 'The Princess' – as his eyes fall on a group of women. We might also note that Tennyson wrote a poem entitled 'The Defence of Lucknow'. In that poem he displays many of the attitudes which were apparent in early Mutiny fiction, and glorifies the defence in the same manner as the artist in the painting referred to earlier. The symbolic importance of the flag which Farrell ironically draws our attention to in *The Siege of Krishnapur* is celebrated with vigour in this poem:

> Banner of England, not for a season, O banner of Britain, hast thou
> Floated in conquering battle or flapt to the battle-cry!
> Never with mightier glory than when we had rear'd thee on high
> Flying at top of the roofs in the ghastly siege of Lucknow –
> Shot thro' the staff or the halyard, but ever we raised thee anew,
> And ever upon the topmost roof our banner of England blew.[32]

(To a similar end John Fowles uses a number of extracts from Tennyson as chapter headings in *The French Lieutenant's Woman*.)

The medical differences of the time are shown through the arguments between the civil surgeon, Dr Dunstaple, and the regimental surgeon, Dr McNab. In particular Farrell focuses attention on the wide difference of opinion that surrounded the treatment of cholera. Dr Dunstaple's belief that the disease is carried 'in impure or damp air' (p. 279) and Dr McNab's belief that cholera is caught by drinking infected water, together with the respective treatment each advises (amply illustrated by Farrell), reflect in considerable detail the battle which was being fought within the medical world in the nineteenth century. Dr Dunstaple's treatment of 'calomel, opium and poultices, together with brandy as a stimulant' (p. 184) is similar to the treatment used to cure Caroline Langford in *Nightrunners of Bengal*. Though romantically presented, Masters's treatment is in keeping with the time, and neither Rodney, nor Caroline, despite her experiences in the Crimea, could be expected to be conversant with the latest medical beliefs expounded by Dr McNab in Farrell's novel.

The authorial voice, introduced by such words as 'nowadays', further places the author in the role of historian. The reference to the present (1970s) state of the tombs both reminds the reader of the distance in time, and suggests a definite, tangible link with the past – assuring its validity. A later authorial appearance asks the reader to: 'Picture a map of India as big as a tennis court with two or three hedgehogs crawling over it' (p. 102). Again this interruption makes the reader aware of the role of the author, but in a way which also invites the reader to remember that the author is inventing the country he is describing. Another writer would have been unlikely to use the same image; this is Farrell's India. Of course, on a different level this image of a tennis court also suggests the way the British saw or treated India in the middle of the nineteenth century, and Farrell appears to be suggesting that the British are as out of place in India as hedgehogs on a tennis court. On occasions, though, Farrell refuses to accept that he does know what is happening: 'What would have happened if Dr Dunstaple had replied to Dr McNab's challenge is hard to say' (p. 294). At times like this Farrell is consciously taking the stance of the historian, and pretending to be reporting rather than inventing; yet implicitly, throughout the novel, he makes it clear that he *is* in control. In the closing sentences of the novel Farrell again appears reluctant to say that he knows what the Collector is thinking:

Perhaps he was thinking again of those two men and two bullocks drawing water from the well every day of their lives. Perhaps, by the very end of his life, in 1880, he had come to believe that a people, a nation, does not create itself according to its own best ideas, but is shaped by other forces of which it has little knowledge. (p. 345)

Finally, by examining the effect of India on the senses of the British, both before and during the siege, Farrell shows how India affected the inner lives of the Victorians who found themselves in that country. He is thus using the historical moment of the siege to look behind the Victorian masks and show the characters stripped of historical, cultural, and social trappings and forced to look at their raw selves, as many postmodernist writers do, such as Saul Bellow with Henderson in *Henderson the Rain King* (1959), or Patrick White with Mrs Roxburgh in *A Fringe of Leaves* (1976).

* * *

Manohar Malgonkar's intention in *The Devil's Wind* is to invent an *Indian* India of the years 1857–58. To achieve this he writes 'Nana's story as . . . he might have written it himself' (p. x). To this end the treatment of Nana Saheb is one-sided. As Malgonkar explains in an Author's Note (and as Nana Saheb himself discovers during the course of the novel), Nana Saheb 'replaced Napoleon Bonaparte as the hate object of a nation' (p. ix), which Malgonkar believes was due to an unjust interpretation of the facts, fuelled by the strong emotions which gripped Britain at that time, and by the deliberately censored picture the people of Britain received. Thus, for example, the horrors of Satichaura Ghat and the Bibighar were amply dwelt upon by British writers, whilst little mention was made of the atrocities perpetrated by such men as Neill and Renaud, or the murder of the Princes by Hodson, other than in a context which portrayed the British as heroes. But as Nana Saheb insists during the course of his narrative: 'What the British did to Lucknow cannot be balanced against a hundred Satichauras, cannot be washed away by banning all mention of it from history books' (p. 234).

Malgonkar concludes his Author's Note with an appeal to the authoritativeness of his work: 'It is fiction; but it takes no liberties with verifiable facts or even with probabilities' (p. x). This is a remarkable claim, though perhaps understandable in its naivety; historical fiction does take liberties with verifiable facts, and certainly with probabilities, and it is impossible to believe that Malgonkar has been able to produce a work of fiction that does neither. Yet there appears to be nothing in this novel which is actually contradicted by the history books, though, of course, there are a number of events which are not actually confirmed by historians. In fact, there is historical accuracy in virtually every detail of this novel. For example, Christopher Hibbert describes an incident which occurred in Kanpur (or Cawnpore) shortly before Wheeler's entrenchment was besieged:

There *had* been an unpleasant incident when a cashiered subaltern drunkenly fired an ill-aimed shot at a patrol of the 2nd Cavalry who had challenged him as he staggered out of his bungalow in the dark; but at the young man's trial it had been held that his state of intoxication excused his conduct and that his fire-arm had gone off by mistake. The sepoys of the 2nd Cavalry 'muttered angrily that possibly their own muskets might go off by mistake before very long'; and one of them complained to W.J. Shepherd that 'if we natives had fired upon a European we should have been hanged'.[33]

In *The Devil's Wind* Malgonkar recounts the incident which Nana Saheb believes started the storm in Kanpur:

Tantya's voice sounded unnaturally calm, and his eyes flashed with excitement. 'His name is Cox,' he told me. 'Last night he got drunk and sat in the middle of the road in front of his bungalow and fired at the nightly patrol of the 2nd Cavalry going on its rounds – he fired several rounds, swearing obscenely all the while, yelling that they were dung worms and pig's spawn.' . . .

And it was exactly what Tantya had predicted and what Tika Singh had hoped it would be. The court assembled on June 4 and went through a mock trial. The verdict was 'not guilty.' Cox, the court held, was stupefied with drink and therefore not responsible for his actions, and his firearm had been 'discharged by accident.'

'Our firearms too will have to be discharged by accident,' the sepoys wailed.

'If a sepoy had fired at a patrol of redcoats, he would have been hanged.' (pp. 145–6)

The details each provides are almost identical – only the telling differs, and even that only differs in the way Malgonkar allows his characters to comment on the events, allows them, that is, to voice their subjective feelings. His portrayal of the objective facts must to some extent be affected by subjective feeling, and he admits as much when he suggests he is attempting to redress the balance of the portrayal of Nana Saheb in history and fiction. This novel is, of course, fiction because Malgonkar is attempting to explore the emotions of his character Nana Saheb. An historian would not attempt this and would necessarily have to maintain a distance that only a third-person narrative can achieve. Malgonkar, on the other hand, as a writer of fiction is able to allow his imagination to take over where there is a gap in the historical accounts. Like the historian he selects his material, but he uses the novelist's imagination to interpret that documented evidence. This imagination is most clearly at work in Part III, 'Gone Away', because what actually happened to Nana Saheb, and to Eliza Wheeler, who did survive the massacre at the Satichaura Ghat, has always been uncertain. However, although this section of the novel is the most 'romantic' or fanciful, much of it is still based on documented evidence, as Hibbert shows:

> At the Satichaura Ghat in Cawnpore, the women and children who had survived the massacre, about 125 of them, were pulled out of the river and collected together on the sand by some of the Nana's men . . .
>
> One of those retained by their captors was General Wheeler's youngest daughter, a girl of eighteen, whose supposed fate was enacted in theatres and described in magazines and books all over the world. She had, it was said, killed her captor, a young trooper named Ali Khan, as well as his entire family, then thrown herself down a well. In fact, so it appears, she had agreed to become a Muslim and to marry him. Many years later a Roman Catholic priest in Cawnpore came upon an old lady in the bazaar who told him on her deathbed that she was Miss Wheeler. She said she had married the sepoy who had saved her from the massacre, that he had been good to her and that she did not want to get in touch with the British authorities.[34]

Malgonkar's claim to historical accuracy raises the far-reaching question of the boundaries of the novel in other directions. The term 'documentary novel' springs to mind, but I doubt the term can be applied to a work that looks back over one hundred years into the past.

Like Masters, Malgonkar treats many, if not all, of the causes of the Mutiny. Obviously, because this is Nana Saheb's story, considerable emphasis is placed on Dalhousie's Doctrine of Lapse, the cause which affected Nana Saheb and other Indian rulers most directly:

> The Doctrine of Lapse was an instrument of confiscation so crude that it might have been devised by a child, so tyrannical as to resemble an act of God. If a ruler died without a son, Dalhousie simply 'annexed' his domain. (p. 46)

Indeed Malgonkar suggests that it is the annexation of Oudh which makes a revolt inevitable:

> The seizure of Oudh brought us face to face with the reality of the Company's rule. It made us lift our eyes from our little fish-pond world and look around. And suddenly, like some complex mathematical equation that only in its final step yields a simple, uncomplicated answer, the solution emerged in one word: revolt. (p. 57)

Malgonkar also suggests that the impetus for revolt was backed by Zeenat Mahal, a Mogul Queen who wanted her son named heir to the Mogul Emperor (in reality a powerless figurehead), Bahadur Shah, whom the British had allowed to continue to live in the Red Fort in Delhi. In her cause she was aided by Ahmadulla Shah, the Moulvi of Fyzabad, commonly known as the Mad Mullah, and in turn they were supported by another Queen, Hazrat Mahal, Queen of Oudh:

> So we had these two queens backing the revolt, Zeenat of Delhi and Hazrat of Oudh, and both were guided by the Mullah. In the event, the Queen of Delhi never left the Red Fort; the other, Hazrat, took an active part in the fighting. (p. 106)

Masters, though obliquely, borrowed much from these historical figures to contribute to the melting-pot characters of the Rani of Kishanpur and the Silver Guru in his novel. Malgonkar, conversely, always attempts to be faithful to the historical figures he represents in his fiction. In his history of the Mutiny, Christopher Hibbert quotes Charles Ball's description of the Mad Mullah:

> an inspired prophet or fakir . . . a tall, lean, muscular man, with thin jaw, long thin lips, high aquiline nose; deep-set, large dark eyes, beetle brows, long beard, and coarse black hair, falling in masses over his shoulders.[35]

Malgonkar's description of the Mullah is fairly similar: 'Immensely tall, with limbs that are all bone and no flesh, face like a falcon, eyes hooded as though the light hurt them, beard the colour of fire' (p. 74). In other words, Malgonkar's Moulvi of Fyzabad may not be the Moulvi of Fyzabad of history, but he could be. And the same is true of almost every character in this novel.

The chapati distribution that Masters embellishes so vividly in *Nightrunners of Bengal* is treated far more objectively by Malgonkar. We learn only two things about their movement. Firstly 'they are to be passed by hand, from village to village. Each village that receives one has to bake four more and take them to four villages, and so on' (p. 74). Secondly, their message, which Masters makes so specific, remains obscure and confused in *The Devil's Wind*. But as the Mad Mullah is quoted as saying: 'The essence of a rumour is its ambiguity' (p. 74).

In this novel too, the grease that was smeared on the cartridges for the new Enfield rifles is seen to be the straw which apparently broke the camel's back. Rumours that this grease was made from pig and cow fat were widespread, and the truth of the rumours is supported here by the sympathetic Wheeler who describes the cartridges as 'Obnoxious! Disgusting! Smothered in rancid fat. . . . It's all mixed – and it's all filthy!' (p. 101). Masters uses the sympathetic Bulstrode for the same purpose in *Nightrunners of Bengal*. The taunts aimed at high-caste Hindu sepoys in *Nightrunners of Bengal* are also seen again in *The Devil's Wind*, as is the cruelty meted out to those objecting to the cartridges:

> So, on May 9, under a livid sun, and when the heat was like a fire lit under the earth so that you could not have stood on the parade ground with unshod feet, the whole of the Meerut garrison, British and Indian, was lined up to witness the spectacle of soldiers being 'broken.' The offenders were stripped of their equipment and uniforms and made to stand in their breechclouts while the blacksmiths called up from the city riveted fetters on their wrists and legs. (p. 113)

Perhaps the most obvious method Malgonkar uses to stress the historicity rather than the fictionality of his novel is that, unlike other historical novelists, he changes neither the names of historical figures, nor the names of places. His India is one which can be traced on a map, and the characters that populate his India are, with a few exceptions, ones who can be found on the pages of a history text. Thus whilst Masters's fictional Bhowani may geographically be close to the real Jhansi, and the events that occur there close to those which took place in Meerut, it is neither Jhansi nor Meerut. Similarly the town of Krishnapur in Farrell's *The Siege of Krishnapur* is clearly based on Lucknow, but disguised by fictionality. Malgonkar's fiction wears no such disguises; his Meerut *is* Meerut, his Lucknow *is* Lucknow and his Kanpur *is* Kanpur, though of course each is a reinvented one. The use of fictional names allows an author to borrow characteristics from a variety of historical figures and add to those others of his or her own imagining to form a character for his or her fiction. Because he uses real names, Malgonkar cannot legitimately do this, and consequently the opportunities open to him as a writer of fiction are restricted.

Historicity is further achieved by having Nana Saheb return, years after the Mutiny, to Kanpur where he sees the monuments erected by the British in the Bibighar and on the site of Wheeler's entrenchment. As Nana Saheb reads the inscriptions on the monuments Malgonkar is able to show how British history has recorded those events:

SACRED TO THE PERPETUAL MEMORY
OF A GREAT COMPANY OF CHRISTIAN PEOPLE
CHIEFLY WOMEN AND CHILDREN
WHO, NEAR THIS SPOT
WERE CRUELLY MURDERED BY THE FOLLOWERS
OF THE REBEL DHONDU PANT OF BITHOOR
AND CAST, THE DYING WITH THE DEAD
INTO THE WELL BELOW
ON THE 15TH DAY OF JULY 1857

(p. 286)

and,

IN A WELL UNDER THIS CROSS WERE LAID
BY THE HANDS OF THEIR FELLOWS IN SUFFERING
THE BODIES OF MEN, WOMEN, AND CHILDREN
WHO DIED HARD IN THEIR HEROIC DEFENCE
OF WHEELER'S ENTRENCHMENT
WHEN BELEAGUERED BY THE REBEL NANA

(p. 289)

Nana Saheb did not, of course, live to see the memorial raised to him after Independence which reads:

KNOWING THE DANGERS
HE EMBRACED A REVOLT
HIS SACRIFICE SHALL LIGHT OUR PATH
LIKE AN ETERNAL FLAME

(p. ix)

Having him compose his own memorials that could stand on the sites of Daryanganj and Bithoor allows Malgonkar, and effectively Nana Saheb, to bridge the almost one-hundred-year gap and include at least the spirit of the post-Independence Indian memorial in his novel in an attempt to show the unsuitability of the British compositions, and to balance the limited perspective they embraced. Nana Saheb's years in the Terai jungles of Nepal are also a kind of hiatus, a period of lost time. His decision to return to Kanpur, and to see the evidence of the battle shows him effectively returning from the wilderness to confront history. In this respect, *The Devil's Wind* has much in common with the literature of late Modernism. At moments such as this Malgonkar is at his best as an historical novelist, notably moments where he does breathe subjective feeling into his work – moments where he is most obviously a writer of fiction not of history.

Malgonkar also quotes history in the form of an extract from Queen Victoria's proclamation which states her desire to show mercy towards India by 'pardoning the offences of those who had been misled' (p. 253). But as Malgonkar shows it, this mercy appears to be of the kind shown by the court of Venice towards Shylock. It was an offer of mercy that would not extend to such figures as Nana Saheb, nor did it save the many who were hung from trees by groups of Britons scourging the Indian countryside in the months after the Mutiny. This is shown by the extract quoted from Queen Hazrat Mahal's proclamation in reply to the British monarch's: 'It is the unvarying custom of the British never to condone a fault, be it great or small. No one has ever seen, not even in a dream, that the English forgave an offence' (p. 253).

Malgonkar's choice of the intimate and seemingly trustworthy first-person narrative is a further attempt to exclude the presence of an author other than Nana Saheb from the pages of his work, and one which is no doubt intended to lend credence to his claim to be telling Nana Saheb's story.

That the Mutiny, synonymous in this novel with 'The Devil's Wind [which] would rise and unshackle Mother India' (p. 104), broke in Meerut on the morning of Sunday 10 May 1857 is a fact well documented here and in other Mutiny fiction. Although Masters saw fit to set the outbreak in his fictional Bhowani during the night hours, no doubt to add to the *'Boy's Own'* atmosphere he creates at times, his brutal description of the horrors is one with which Malgonkar fundamentally agrees. As Malgonkar concludes, 'Meerut was not so much a declaration of war as a plunge into barbarity' (p. 116). And although he is deliberately attempting to destroy the myths which have so long surrounded the British view of the Mutiny, the Mutiny that Malgonkar invents for his readers shares considerable common ground with that which Masters invents. Thus in *Nightrunners of Bengal* the sepoy violence is carefully balanced by examples of British barbarity, and in *The Devil's Wind* Malgonkar writes this of the slaughter at the Bibighar: 'But, of course, even granting that the details have been exaggerated, the fact remains that every single woman and child in the place was killed' (p. 206). So, although he is showing the Indian side of the medal, he is aware, as is Masters, that it is a two-sided medal that he is describing. Or, to return to *The Merchant of Venice*, Malgonkar might well be asking the question asked by Shylock in that play:

> . . . If a Christian wrong a Jew, what should his sufferance be by Christian example? Why, revenge! The villainy you teach me I will execute, and it shall go hard but I will better the instruction.[36]

Whilst Malgonkar might show Nana Saheb willing to admit the facts and the shame they bring, he does so in the light of British savagery:

> Then our men saw something else: a village being sacked with military thoroughness and its women dishonoured. Fattepur, by being in the vicinity of the place where our troops had offered battle, had had its fate sealed. They saw it being cordoned off and set on fire. Those who tried to escape, even women and children, were thrown back into the fire or shot while escaping. (p. 202)

Thus the horror of the massacre at the Bibighar is recounted only after the atrocities perpetrated by Neill and Renaud have been described.

Similarly, the humanity which was evident in *Nightrunners of Bengal* is also seen in *The Devil's Wind*. On the one side the humanity of Nana Saheb is emphasised at various and frequent stages of the novel, and on the other side British humanity is seen in Michael Palmer, once a house-guest at Bithoor, who does not expose the fleeing Nana Saheb, though this could be seen as the repayment of an old debt as Nana Saheb is aware: 'Was he, I wondered, repaying his debt to me?' (p. 247). Indeed, Nana Saheb spoke of the money he lost to Palmer as an 'investment', and if he thinks that Palmer would have exposed him were it not for the debt, then perhaps this is not a clear example of humanity. But Nana Saheb also knows that, 'In letting me go he was as good as throwing away a lakh of rupees' (p. 248). It is important to show that not all Indians and not all the British became monsters during the Mutiny.

In much the same way as Farrell illustrates the physical and mental deterioration of the British in *The Siege of Krishnapur*, so Malgonkar illustrates the deterioration of the besieged in what became known as Wheeler's Entrenchment:

> I saw a pie-dog, tail tightly curled and ears torn by many fights, stomach bloated with carrion and body hairless from a mange brought on by a surfeit of rotted meat, straying close to the wall of the Entrenchment where the blackening bones of the dead bull still lay beside the vulture-cleaned skeleton of the white soldier. For a time I watched the dog as it listlessly tore away at the cartilage around the bull's knee and then, when it turned and began to gnaw the skull of the soldier, idly, without thinking about it, raised my rifle and brought its bead against the dog's chest. For a few seconds I waited, holding my breath, knowing that I was being watched, before squeezing the trigger. The dog fell and as it rolled over, its legs stiffened. (p. 154)

Nana Saheb's actions show that he wishes to keep his humanity, and that despite the course events are taking, he wishes both sides to obey some of the rules of civilized society. The gnawing of the soldier's skull by the pie-dog parallels the eating of the sepoy's face by Chloë in *The Siege of Krishnapur*. Fleury prevents Chloë, a British dog, from eating the face of a sepoy, whilst Nana Saheb prevents the pie-dog, an Indian dog, from gnawing the skull of a soldier who is presumably British. Neither Fleury nor Nana Saheb can accept this degeneration to 'cannibalism'.

Where Malgonkar does differ from Masters and other Raj novelists is in his view of the sepoys. The sepoy of the East India Company Army (known affectionately as Jack Sepoy and John Company respectively) has frequently been referred to in such endearing terms as 'the salt of the earth' by British novelists, biographers, and historians, and much has been made of the special relationship between the native sepoy and his British officer. That, however, is the British viewpoint. Malgonkar sees the relationship in an entirely different light:

> The sepoys were self-professed mercenaries; for a pittance, they served an alien master's army. They would just as readily have served other foreigners such as the Chinese or Africans. Soldiering to them was no more than a means of earning a livelihood. They worked only for 'bread and salt,' as they were wont to explain; and in exchange for a specific quantity of bread and salt, they gave back a specific quantity of loyalty. And that was the entire basis of their allegiance. (pp. 97–8)

Whether this is a true picture or not is perhaps not as important as seeing that by describing them in this way Malgonkar has re-invented the sepoy.

Like Masters and Farrell, Malgonkar sets his story in its age through references to the Crimean war. In *Nightrunners of Bengal* the presence of the Crimea is brought to India by Caroline Langford and in *The Siege of Krishnapur* by Miriam Lang; in *The Devil's Wind* it is brought, more significantly, by Azim, Nana Saheb's secretary, who visited the Crimea on his return from England where he had been appealing, on Nana Saheb's behalf, against Dalhousie's actions in Bithoor. Because news of the Crimea is brought by an Indian who had been an admirer of the British, in this novel it serves to show that the British can be defeated in war and is seen as an encouragement to those Indians plotting revolt.

Cholera, like the Crimea, is only mentioned briefly, but even the brief mention helps to set the novel in its age, in a medical sense, when Nana Saheb, reporting the death of his first wife, tells us 'that many doctors are now convinced that cholera spreads through water' (p. 25), something Masters never considers, though the cholera Rodney and Caroline face is important in the action of his novel. Masters's treatment pushes historicity into the background in favour of fictionality, when in fact the two should enhance each other. In *The Devil's Wind*, the lack of historical *manners* means that the novel lacks a sense of time. Emily Wheeler, for example, seems unlike a young lady of the 1850s. It is, undoubtedly, on one level a very accurate account of the Mutiny, but it fails to transcend that particular occasion; it is *only* about the Mutiny. Unlike J.G. Farrell's *The Siege of Krishnapur*, there is nothing universal about *The Devil's Wind*; it tells us nothing about the present or about how people would be likely to behave again. Our perception of the novel, or perhaps more particularly the postmodernist historical novel, depends on its achieving greater universality than *Nightrunners of Bengal* or *The Devil's Wind* do. It is perhaps for this reason that *The Siege of Krishnapur* appears now to stand out as the best novel of the Mutiny to have yet been written.

3

The Period of the Great Game

'Show me the cuts.' Kim bent over the Mahratta's neck, his heart nearly choking him; for this was the Great Game with a vengeance.[1]

Hagan . . . half-turned and raised an arm to indicate his companions who had meanwhile dismounted a few yards away and were making a great game of banging the dust from each other's clothes.[2]

Between 1858 and the end of the nineteenth century the Raj was at its height politically, but problems of Empire were growing at the same time. In 1858 the rule of India passed from the hands of the East India Company to those of the British government, but as early as 1813 Lord Grenville had stated: 'The British government is *de facto* sovereign in India'. This view was reinforced by the Acts of 1813, 1833 and 1853, each of which asserted the sovereignty of the Crown and defined the limits of the Company's influence. The 1858 Act was simply the final step.[3] Then in 1877, though she had never visited the country, Queen Victoria was proclaimed Empress of India. The Second Afghan War was quickly won. In 1885 the Indian National Congress was formed, but the demand for Independence did not begin to gather real momentum until the early years of the twentieth century. Prior to that, the collapse of the secure and confident Raj could not be seriously considered.

It is not surprising, therefore, that this period has not attracted Indian novelists, and that almost all the British novels set in this period are in the romantic adventure tradition. Despite this, the period is worth considering for two major reasons. Firstly, it is important historically. Secondly, the importance of Rudyard Kipling's *Kim* on the British imagination and its influence (like that of Forster's *A Passage to India*) on later fiction set in India, like M.M. Kaye's *The Far Pavilions*, cannot be overlooked. There are other British novels, like John Masters's *The Lotus and the Wind*, which could be discussed in this chapter, but again this is a novel which, like *The Far Pavilions*, owes much to *Kim*. It was only in the 1980s, with the publication of J.G. Farrell's, sadly, unfinished novel *The Hill Station*, that this period was treated in a way which transcends the romantic adventure tradition with which it has so long and almost exclusively been associated.

The popular image of the period, then, is one of adventure; it is the period of 'the Great Game', and Rudyard Kipling's *magnum opus*, *Kim*, is the novel which epitomises this image. *Kim* is far more than a picaresque adventure story; it tells us a great deal about India in the late nineteenth century. And, of course, by 1901 many British people had had some contact with India, and the Indian influence on England was, perhaps, at its height. Words like kedgeree, jodphurs, polo and bungalow had all found their way into everyday English, and a large number of cottages in the English countryside had names like Sikkim or Mussoorie. *Kim* is both a successor to the adventure novels that followed the Mutiny, and a predecessor to works like *A Passage to India* which used the East–West encounter as a symbol of universal collisions of the human spirit. It is also one of the few novels written by an Englishman that succeeds in creating an India of Indians. Typical of the adventure novels set in this period is M.M. Kaye's *The Far Pavilions*, which, like *Kim*, reinforces the image of adventure along the North-West Frontier. A novel of an entirely different nature set in this period, distant in space from the frontier and the Great Game which seems to be constantly played out there, is J.G. Farrell's *The Hill Station*. Yet Farrell *uses* the style of the adventure novel, which shows the influence of *Kim* and the strong link between this period of Indian history and the adventure story tradition:

> Teddy Potter, meanwhile, was explaining to the ladies and especially to Emily that the road to Simla was positively infested with hostile tribesmen, with thugs and dacoits of every shape and description who were, moreover, particularly interested in making away with fair young English damsels . . . yes, it was jolly lucky that he and Woodleigh and Arkwright, under the 'awe-inspiring command' of the 'universally dreaded' Captain Hagan, should be on hand 'in the nick of time' to prevent Miss Anderson being carried off to become the unwilling bride of a hook-nosed Pathan chieftain with a dagger in his belt. Why, most likely the rascal was already watching them from behind those very trees!
> (p. 44)

And, a few lines later:

> 'But why are you fighting them with your bare hands?'
> 'Because our guns have missed fire, of course, as they always
> do according to *Blackwood's*.' (p. 45)

These *'Boy's Own'* style excerpts clearly parody the style of the
romantic adventure tradition in general and the type of stories which
appeared in *Blackwood's* in particular. And parody, which is an
important aspect of postmodernist fiction, also shows that the popular image of the period is a distorted one. Indeed, even the popular
view of this period as that of the Great Game, is parodied in *The Hill
Station*, which is full of people playing games – croquet, charades
and even arm-wrestling.

In the final paragraphs of *The Siege of Krishnapur* Farrell describes
a meeting, 'one day, in the late seventies' (p. 344), between the now
portly figures of the Collector, and Fleury. During the course of this
brief meeting Fleury gives the Collector news of some of the survivors of Krishnapur:

> His own sister, Miriam, the Collector probably did not know, had
> subsequently married Dr McNab and they, too, had remained in
> India.
> 'Ah yes, McNab,' said the Collector thoughtfully. 'He was the
> best of us all. The only one who knew what he was doing.' He
> smiled, thinking of the invisible cholera cloud, and after a moment
> he added: 'I was fond of your sister. I don't suppose I shall see her
> again.' (pp. 344–5)

There is a touch of playful irony here. The Collector may not see
Miriam again, but the reader of *The Hill Station* will, and I suspect
Farrell was aware of this when he wrote those words.

The Collector's description of McNab as 'the best of us all' confirms
our opinion of the Civil Surgeon, and establishes him as a figure we
can trust. This is important because, whilst the Collector had, in
effect, been our guide to the mid-Victorian period, it is McNab who
takes us with him to the late-Victorian period, some two decades
later, and acts as our guide to that age.

McNab's role as our guide is established from the outset with the
journey from the heat of the plains up to the cooler climate of Simla,
the summer capital of British India. This journey has a number of
purposes; it takes us up to Simla, the perfect microcosm for Farrell's

intentions, and it takes us back in time from the present to the past of the 1870s. By taking us back with an awareness of the present in our minds, Farrell will be able to compare past and present, and make full use of hindsight. This parallel sense of past and present is achieved in the opening sentence of the novel: 'Nowadays the railway goes all the way up to Simla, but before the turn of the century it stopped at Kalka' (p. 3). These words take us immediately from the present to a nineteenth-century past, which is made specific in the opening line of the second chapter: 'One day in March 1871' (p. 7). (There is an inconsistency late in the novel when Farrell refers to McNab as 'a physician who had exercised his profession throughout the third quarter of the nineteenth century and a little beyond' [p. 98], but *The Hill Station* is an unfinished novel and the editor has allowed minor inconsistencies to stand.)

As the McNabs travel towards Simla with Emily, their niece, Farrell, through the journey he describes, by train, landau and tonga, begins to create the atmosphere of the period, and during the course of the train journey a number of important character are introduced, including the Reverend Kingston, central to Farrell's discussion of religious debates of the time, and Mrs Forester, the protagonist of the sub-plot, who join the McNabs in their carriage. Less important characters are in the surrounding carriages or on the station platforms. These chance introductions prepare the way for the two stories Farrell develops in this novel, the major one being the exploration of the still-raging religious debate of the time, which his meeting with the Revd Kingston draws McNab into, and the other being predominantly social, involving Mrs Forester and which we follow through Emily, that reflects the society of the late-Victorian period. Farrell also uses the introduction of these characters to help establish the age; as Emily talks to Mrs Forester on the train she refers to 'her voyage out by way of the wonderful new Suez Canal' (p. 17), which was completed only two years earlier in 1869, and would still have been something of a novelty.

The journey to Simla effectively removes the events of the novel from the India of Indians. Simla was the summer capital of the Raj, and Farrell's major players are all British. The Indianness of India is never established in this novel, not even to the extent that it is in *The Siege of Krishnapur*. Farrell's focus is on British India, and the small group of characters which populates his Simla is representative of late-Victorian England. Through those characters, in their deliberately isolated setting, he is able to explore the whole spectrum of late-Victorian society.

The social structure of the British in India at this time remained, in many respects, similar to the Hindu caste system, and Farrell makes this clear when McNab refers to 'the rigid caste system among the British in Simla' (p. 36). McNab is surprised, therefore, that Mrs Forester should ask Emily to travel from Kalka up to Simla in her landau. Through the plot surrounding Mrs Forester there are frequent examples of this caste system at work, and the consequences suffered by those who have, in Victorian terms, fallen, and have thus, in Hindu terms, lost caste. This is evident when Mrs Forester is snubbed as she and Emily parade along the mall in their *jampans*, or Indian sedan-chairs:

> It was a snub. Not just a snub either, but a snub administered to Mrs Forester . . . [Mrs Forester] raised a hand and with a pretty smile and in her most ingratiating voice she called: 'Good afternoon, Mrs Cloreworthy!' The lady in question took a brief look at Mrs Forester . . . and turned her face resolutely and quite deliberately to look in another direction. (pp. 83–4)

The fact that she turns 'to look in another direction where, as ill-luck would have it, one tattered mongrel had just mounted another and was pumping vigorously, unaware that ladies were in the vicinity' (p. 84) suggests the sexual misdemeanours of Mrs Forester, and lends comic absurdity to the snub. It also suggests that Mrs Forester's behaviour is not unusual in Victorian Simla or in Victorian England. Further, it is one example of people being forced to see things they do not wish to see. It is Mrs Forester who on a number of occasions forces Emily to see what she would rather not have seen:

> Once she had touched Emily's hand and pointed, smiling. Emily had looked, shielding her eyes, and would rather not have seen what she did see, an eagle with a baby rabbit in its talons rising as if without effort from a ridge at a little distance. (p. 37).

And not long after, an embarrassed Emily finds herself, in the company of Mrs Forester, spying on the Revd Kingston and his bearer kneeling before a chapati:

> At Emily's side Mrs Forester was shaking with suppressed hilarity at this curious sight. Emily herself felt ashamed to be

watching it. And because it seemed as if they might go on like that
for ever, the clergyman in an ecstasy of prayer, the bearer writh-
ing and dribbling with anticipation, she detached herself from
Mrs Forester's hand and retreated softly back down the path they
had come. (p. 39)

This seeing and also not-seeing, the desire to see only what one
wishes, is, as these two examples show, both a social and a religious
problem.

Through the newly-arrived Emily, Farrell is able to make it clear
that the British caste system is not exclusive to India but reflects the
social divisions which existed in England at the time:

Emily, brought up a Miss Anderson of Saltwater House, could not
help but feel that when she was with the McNabs she suffered
a slight but perceptible loss of rank. She felt that people saw her
as Miss McNab instead of Miss Anderson. She saw her uncle
and aunt as being a kind, cautious, respectable, but limited couple. They lacked that little touch of aristocratic *ampleur* in their
attitude to life, it seemed to Emily. If you were a person of 'a good
family' as Emily was, you benefited by a little extra freedom
from the self-imposed constraints and prejudices of the *petite
bourgeoisie*. (p. 80)

The exposing of what John Spurling calls 'Emily's blinkered view of
class'[4] opens the way for Farrell to extend the sense of history in his
novel by introducing an important figure of the age, Karl Marx:

It would be harsh to blame Emily for not having re-invented the
class-stratified view of the world she had inherited from her
parents along more egalitarian lines. (In any case, as Emily, light
as a feather, went bobbing away on the strong brown shoulders of
her *jampanis*, a few thousand miles away in London a familiar
bearded leonine figure sucking a pencil turned a little in his seat
in the British Museum to see the hands of the clock at the northern
quarter of the Reading Room, and thought, 'Soon it will be closing
time.') (pp. 80–1)

The first volume of *Das Kapital* (written in the British Museum
Reading Room) had been published in 1867, four years before the
events of *The Hill Station* took place. This is a good example of how

the historical novel can make connections that would be impossible for anyone to see at the time. And as Ronald Binns observes, Marx 'did indeed spell "closing time" for Emily's world of privileged supremacy'.[5] It is curious that Farrell writes 'a familiar bearded leonine figure'; surely the implication is 'now-familiar', that is, familiar to the reader.

Farrell uses Emily's ignorance of British India to draw the reader's attention to the 'parade of fashionable people' (p. 82) strolling through Simla:

> Just for a moment it struck her as a little incongruous that here, buried deep in the mountains miles from anywhere, people should be strutting and giving themselves airs as if they were spending the summer in Marienbad or Deauville. Did they not realise, wondered Emily, that if someone caught them in a butterfly net and pinned them in a collector's case beside the real thing, that's to say, a *really* fashionable person caught last year in Deauville, not to mention Marienbad or Vichy, they would look like country bumpkins! (p. 82)

In certain respects Farrell fulfills the role of lepidopterist, and through Emily's observations he illustrates that the fashions of British India are slightly out of step with those of Europe. But whilst they may be out of step, they dance to the same music:

> Emily was not by nature a detached observer interested in the comparative strength of frenzies of fashion in this or that place. If she saw people being fashionable she wanted to join in, learn the rules and, if possible, be more so. That is why, after her first reaction of surprise and disdain, she wasted no further time before turning a critical and calculating eye over the faces and *toilettes* of the passing throng, paying particular attention to the dresses of the ladies. (p. 82)

Thus whilst the fashions, *per se*, may be behind those of Britain, the behaviour of the British in India is no different from the British in England. Farrell also adds to the historicity of his story with the naming of the fashionable resorts of the period, Deauville, Marienbad and Vichy, and the Champs-Elysées.

Through the plot which deals with the Mrs Forester and her circle Farrell dispels a number of popular notions about Victorian prudery, and reveals, to an extent, a truer picture of Victorian sexual ethics. Farrell here reflects the scholarly interest in the Victorian period, which had been awakened in the 1960s and 1970s. It appears that Mrs Forester, who is shunned because she has 'fallen', is shunned not because of her affairs, but because they have been rather too blatant. The crime is not so much in the act as in the discovery of the act. Below their masks, the Victorians were not the moral creatures they have often been thought. They projected their own view of themselves; *we* see a different view. Farrell comically exposes this as Emily is being helped out of her *jampan* 'by trembling blue-veined hands' (p. 85) at Mrs Forester's gate:

> she felt what in any other circumstances she would have inter-
> preted as an attempt to pinch her bottom through the stuff of her
> riding-coat. However, since there was no one within range but the
> two white-haired old gentlemen who had been helping her, one
> of whom bore a striking resemblance to her Grandfather Anderson,
> she assumed she must have been mistaken. (p. 85)

However, the real exposé of Victorian sexual mores comes soon after as a group of inebriated visitors arrive at Mrs Forester's bungalow, in a scene which is reminiscent of Rayne's tea party in *The Siege of Krishnapur*. Such parties are always wonderful scenes in Farrell's novels, and in this instance the role of detached and shocked ob-server played by Fleury in the earlier novel is performed by Emily. As she looks on from the position of an outsider we see the morals of the British to be far short of popular notions of Victorian morality: 'Mrs Bright by this time was sitting half on the arm of the sofa and half on his lap as if she were a harlot and not a respectable mother of three. And this was how Emily later remembered her upsetting introduction to Simla society' (p. 93). It is a portrait that the reader, too, remembers.

Farrell, like many postmodernist writers, introduces into his text direct comparisons between past and present. This can be seen, for example, when he describes Emily's *jampanis* (the Indians who carry *jampans*):

> Not only were they not well turned out, they were not even well
> assorted as to size, one being bigger than average and another
> smaller. The result was that however they arranged themselves
> Emily found herself listing slightly. It is not at all easy to create the

right impression if you are not quite on an even keel; she felt as someone would with a flat tyre in a motor parade today. (p. 83)

Similarly, he uses the present to explain the social standing of a doctor in the 1870s: 'it was simply that he was a *doctor*. A hundred years ago the social position of a doctor was better than, say, that of a grocer, but by no means what it is today' (p. 80). Such comparisons show that Farrell is always willing to set historicity aside for a moment. Jolts like this are not inartistic, however; rather, Farrell is making the reader uncomfortable, and asking him or her to apply all this to now, insisting, therefore, that it is not all over.

There seems to be some difference of opinion about the direction that *The Hill Station* would have taken had Farrell been able to complete it. In his appreciation which accompanies the novel, John Spurling suggests 'that religion was to have been the main burden of *The Hill Station*'.[6] In his review of the novel for *The Sunday Times* Paul Theroux argues that ritual, social as well as religious, would have been the central concern of the novel.[7] Ronald Binns, in his study of the author, acknowledges that the plot centres on a doctrinal row about ritualism, but suggests that: 'the real thrust of *The Hill Station* would seemingly have been less concerned with either religious ritual or social satire than with a development of Farrell's interest in the theme of sickness',[8] which has been a feature of many twentieth-century British novels.[9] Indeed Farrell does begin to open up the medical debate which surrounded tuberculosis. He does this by again looking at this subject from the distance of the present: 'At that time it was widely believed in the medical profession . . .' (p. 115), and then going on to outline the varied beliefs about 'phthisis or pulmonary consumption, as tuberculosis used to be called' (p. 115), current in Europe at that time. In the following chapter the threat of a rabies epidemic is comically introduced when a shopkeeper attempts to sell McNab first a muzzle and then a pair of ankle-protectors.

The doctrinal battle between the high and low churches is treated in some detail in the nineteen chapters we have. The religious debate opens as soon as the Revd Kingston seats himself on the train, and McNab is able to glimpse the title of the book he is reading: 'It was Keble's *The Christian Year*. The title stirred some faint memory from years ago but he became drowsy and fell asleep before he could seize it' (p. 8). (Readers of *The Siege of Krishnapur* will know that the faint memory stirred is the religious argument that raged within the walls of that besieged town.) It is not surprising that the Revd Kingston should be reading this particular book, as sales of *The Christian Year* were phenomenal. Soon after, Mr Lowrie, owner of Lowrie's Hotels in Simla and Kalka, and an intractable gossip, tells McNab:

> that there have been certain . . . ah . . . difficulties at Saint Saviour's in the past few weeks. The parishioners have been upset by certain rituals of what one would have to call . . . ah . . . a Puseyite cast, quite unknown to our Protestant traditions. Kingston is thought to be . . . ah . . . going 'over the Tiber' . . . Do I make myself clear? (p. 35)

The mention so early in the novel of Keble and Pusey, two of the founders of the Oxford Movement, and reference to certain rituals, takes us to the heart of the doctrinal disputes of the time. The Oxford Movement was also known as 'Tractarianism' and 'Puseyism', the latter, Altick explains, was common in Victorian fiction, and it was 'customarily used with disrespectful or even worse intention'.[10] And this is certainly true of the way Lowrie uses the word.

The importance of the doctrinal debate Farrell takes up in this novel is seen when the author refers to the time as one 'when religious tracts, verses and exhortations were flowing from Indian presses almost as freely as they were from those in England' (p. 63). Here he links the events he describes in Simla to those occurring in England at the time, and there surely must have been a sense of irony in Farrell's decision to set his exploration of the doctrinal debates of the Church of England in Simla where the British are cut off from India and wrapped up in their own religious controversy, and apparently oblivious to the whole spectrum of Indian religions.

The form that ritualism was taking at this time is amply described when the Bishop outlines the complaints made about Saint Saviour's. These complaints include lighted candles on the altar table, choirboys dressed in surplices and singing the psalms and responses, processions with a crucifix, kissing the prayer book, using wafer bread and making the sign of the cross.

The church service that the McNabs attend at Saint Saviour's is further evidence both of the ritualism of the time and the opposition to it. Spurling informs us that:

> to judge from the notes there was to be a second and even more disgraceful church service in which peashooters were used from the gallery, prayer-books thrown, windows smashed, dogs

released and a pitched battle fought with the choir (supported presumably by the gallant officers) at the chancel gates.[11]

And if this seems too fanciful for the imagination, Spurling goes on to explain that:

> Most of this actually happened at St George's-in-the-East, Stepney, in 1859. Farrell simply shipped it to Simla together with Bo'sun Smith (a real person), elements of Bishop Tait, Bishop of London and later Archbishop of Canterbury during the heyday of anti-Ritualism, and much curious material from Michael Reynold's biography (*Martyr of Ritualism*) of the Rev. A. H. Mackonochie, Vicar of St Alban's Holborn.[12]

The presence of Bo'sun Smith, Dr Bateman and, to a lesser degree, Mr Lowrie, brings the presence of the evangelicals to *The Hill Station*, and thus both sides of the religious controversy of England are brought to India and debated in Farrell's Simla.

In the lecture he delivers at Lowrie's Hotel, Bo'sun Smith takes his listeners, and the reader, back to 6 July 1838 when 'that great Bishop of Calcutta, Bishop Wilson . . . conceived that the greatest dangers threatening the Church arose from the publication of *The Tracts for the Times* and the ritualistic movement which it spawned' (p. 103). Here Farrell brings to the forefront the major players in the ritualism controversy. The ritualistic movement he refers to is, of course, the Oxford Movement, and *The Tracts for the Times* were the series of ninety position papers published by the leaders of the group between 1833 and 1841. Indeed Bo'sun Smith goes on to refer to Newman and his dramatic decision to join the Church of Rome in October 1845. By naming Newman, Farrell has named, during the course of the novel, the three leaders of the Oxford Movement; Keble, Pusey and Newman.

There are a number of wonderful caricatures of Evangelicals in Victorian fiction, amongst them Robert Brocklehurst in Charlotte Brontë's *Jane Eyre* (1847). Altick suggests that 'Brocklehurst was drawn from life. His original was William Carus Wilson, a nationally known Low Churchman'.[13] Other contemporary novels, like Anthony Trollope's *Barchester Towers* (1857) also caricature the clergy. Farrell, in keeping with this tradition uses the real Bishop Wilson of Calcutta to add to the feeling of the age that he has established in the novel.

Whereas *The Hill Station* looks at the British in India, and is concerned, ultimately, with the present as much as the past, *Kim* is concerned with the India of Indians, at a particular time in history.

The picaresque qualities of *Kim* have frequently been discussed,[14] and Kim is indeed a picaresque hero; he is also our guide in much the same way as McNab is our guide in *The Hill Station*. And it is significant that he is a guide who is on intimate terms with India, yet who is above all else a sahib:

> Though he was burned black as any native; though he spoke the vernacular by preference, and his mother-tongue in a clipped uncertain sing-song; though he consorted on terms of perfect equality with the small boys of the bazar; Kim was white.   (p. 1)

Thus Kim can perform his task as our guide to the Indian India, whilst at the same time being in a position to enter the world of British India. This enables Kipling to establish a picture of a particular segment of British India, as well as allowing him to contrast the two worlds, Indian India and British India. If Kim had not been British, Kipling could never have done this, just as Farrell cannot have McNab guide us through Indian India. Kim's position as 'Little Friend of all the World' (p. 4) enables Kipling to present a selected picture of parts of northern and north-western India in the late nineteenth century. And because, through Kim, Kipling offers what is essentially a child's view of the world, he is able to present an unbiased picture, and, more importantly, to avoid the controversies of religion and so on, which are such an important part of Farrell's novel.

The Indianness of India is established from the beginning of the novel as Kim plays with his friends and later begs food for the Lama in the Lahore bazaar. But it is on the Grand Trunk Road that we see the real variety of Indian life:

> . . . the Great Road which is the backbone of all Hind. For the most part it is shaded, as here, with four lines of trees; the middle road – all hard – takes the quick traffic. In the days before rail-carriages the Sahibs travelled up and down here in hundreds. Now there are only country-carts and such-like. Left and right is the rougher road for the heavy carts – grain and cotton and timber, fodder, lime and hides. . . . All castes and kinds of men move here. Look! Brahmins and chumars, bankers and tinkers, barbers and bunnias, pilgrims and potters – all the world going and coming. (pp. 80–1)

This variety of Indian life, which the Ressaldar sums up as 'a river of life as nowhere else exists in the world' (p. 81) is vividly captured by Kipling as Kim and the Lama journey along the road, and Kim delights in 'new people and new sights at every stride' (p. 86). Kipling's description of the Grand Trunk Road (pp. 86ff.) is one of the great set pieces of the novel, and probably the best description of Indian life to have been written by an English novelist. And the exchange between the old lady, whom Kim and the Lama travel the Road with, and the Englishman, a District Superintendent of Police, allows Kipling to point to one of the problems of British India at this time. The Englishman, it transpires from the brief exchange, was born and bred in India, and thus the old lady comments: 'These be the sort to oversee justice. They know the land and the customs of the land. The others, all new from Europe, suckled by white women and learning our tongues from books, are worse than the pestilence' (p. 107). Despite the lessons of the Mutiny, India was still being ruled by people who did not understand her customs. Yet in another sense the task of ruling must have been harder for men like this than for men who came out to India simply to govern and felt no pull of conflicting loyalties.

Apart from describing the variety of Indian people on the Grand Trunk Road, Kipling describes the animal life and the physical landscape, albeit of a small geographical area of the country. The impression is there, however, that if one continued to journey along the full fifteen hundred miles of the Road one would indeed see the whole of India pass by.

Similarly we are shown another slice of Indian life when Kim and the Lama travel by train. These train journeys have the same function as the train journey in *The Hill Station*. In *The Hill Station*, however, the view is the limited view of the British in India; in *Kim* the view is of Indian life in all its rich variety.

The India that Kipling creates for the reader is frequently a timeless India. This sense of timelessness is achieved through the descriptive elements of the story. The description of the Grand Trunk Road establishes an image of India, but it does not establish a particular time period. Many of the descriptive passages, whether it is the opening description of the gun, Zam-Zammah, which still stands in front of the Lahore Museum in what is now Pakistan, or the description of the journey in what is obviously a third-class railway carriage, apply equally to the late-twentieth century as they do to the

late-nineteenth century. As Angus Wilson comments of the Grand
Trunk Road:

> When you make the journey down the empty highway today,
> passing an occasional government carrier van, it seems that it can
> hardly have changed since the last decades of British rule, even
> back to the days of Kipling and Kim, save that its noisy, human
> busyness has been replaced by emptiness.[15]

This sense of timelessness is found in Kipling's description of the
religious spirit of India, which, of course, is centred on Kim's wan-
derings with Teshoo Lama. Indeed Kipling captures the religious
spirit of India when he writes: 'All India is full of holy men stammer-
ing gospels in strange tongues; shaken and consumed in the fires of
their own zeal; dreamers, babblers, and visionaries: as it has been
from the beginning and will continue to the end' (pp. 45–6). And the
fact that the Indians are, for the most part, tolerant of these holy men,
whatever their religion, stands in marked contrast to the doctrinal
divisions eating away at the Church of England in *The Hill Station*.
The lack of tolerance of the British in matters of religion can also be
seen in Kipling's novel when Kim first finds his Red Bull on a green
field, and comes face to face with the Reverend Bennett and Father
Victor. Even Bennett is aware that: 'Between himself and the Roman
Catholic Chaplain of the Irish contingent lay . . . an unbridgeable
gulf' (p. 120). And as to the Lama: 'Bennett looked at him with the
triple-ringed uninterest of the creed that lumps nine-tenths of the
world under the title of "heathen"' (p. 124). This is in marked contrast to the Lama's tolerance of the two British churches: 'Dignified
and unsuspicious, he strode into the little tent, saluted the Churches
as a Churchman, and sat down by the open charcoal brazier' (p. 124).
Kipling has not transferred the high and low church debate of late-
Victorian England to his India, but that is because his India is primarily the India of Indians, and the British who enter the story are not
the British who would have been involved in the debates that interest Farrell. Teshoo Lama highlights the difference between the bick-
ering of religion and the strength of faith. Kipling, through the
character of Teshoo Lama, shows that the path to enlightenment, or
to God, can be achieved beyond the confines of the Christian Church.

The education systems of India in the late Victorian period are
also illustrated in *Kim*. There is the traditional Hindu education
system, as Bhaskara Rao explains: 'This was the famed "Guru-Kula-
Ashrama" type of learning by living with the teacher and his family.

The spirit of this system is carried out, in part, by the Lama and Kim'.[16] The other educational options available to Kim, as a sahib, are outlined by Father Victor: 'The Regiment would pay for you all the time you are at the Military Orphanage; or you might go on the Punjab Masonic Orphanage's list . . . but the best schooling a boy can get in India is, of course, at St. Xavier's in Partibus at Lucknow' (p. 133). The brief period Kim spends with the Regiment at Umballa is enough for Kipling to give a very negative impression of a barrack school. And despite his assertion that the reader 'would scarcely be interested in Kim's experiences as a St Xavier's boy among two or three hundred precocious youths, most of whom had never seen the sea' (p. 175), Kipling gives a vivid picture of life in an Indian public school for the sons of sahibs and half-sahibs run on western line. A western-educated Indian is seen in the form of Huree Babu, a graduate of Calcutta University, which was founded in 1857. The first of these systems evokes the timeless quality of India, but the long-established St Xavier's, where 'generation followed sallow-hued generation' (pp. 175–6), and Calcutta University suggest a more particular period – the late nineteenth century.

Wilson is right to assert, in his introduction to the Macmillan centenary edition of the novel, that 'Kim's India is also the India of the late Victorian times'.[17] Against the backdrop of a timeless sub-continent Kipling does establish his novel in its age. We have already seen this in his treatment of education and religion. He also achieves this through establishing the political climate of the time, which is brought into focus through Kim's involvement with the Great Game. More importantly, Kipling establishes the age, and brings a definite sense of history to *Kim* through a series of specific historical signposts which are scattered throughout the novel.

The political theme, as Bhaskara Rao rightly suggests, is not paramount in *Kim*, though his suggestion that it is paramount in *A Passage to India* is one which I would agree with less readily.[18] However, although less central to the novel than the Lama's Search, it is Kim's involvement in the Great Game, the Anglo-Indian and Russian espionage and counter-espionage activities on India's northern borders, that firmly establishes the novel in the late-Victorian period. The expectation of war with Afghanistan was constant throughout the late 1880s; the message that Kim carries for Mahbub Ali and the movements of the Mavericks reflect this. War with Russia also threatened during this period, and Kipling exploits this in his Great Game, to set *Kim* in a definite political age.

A number of specific historical references further establish this age. Huree Babu refers to Herbert Spencer on at least four occasions in the novel. The clearest reference is to Spencer's concept of 'Social Darwinism', as expressed in his *Principles of Psychology* (1870): 'I am good enough Herbert Spencerian, I trust, to meet little thing like death, which is all in my fate, you know' (p. 319). And Huree, when 'he thanked all the Gods of Hindustan, and Herbert Spencer' (p. 342), misapplies Spencer as clearly as Spencer misapplied Darwin. Kipling, it appears is making fun of both his Bengali character and Spencer.

The figure of the old Ressaldar, a loyal veteran of the Mutiny, is included to add a sense of history to the novel. He brings with him the memory of the Mutiny, and the fact that he 'told tales of the Mutiny and young captains thirty years in their graves' (p. 71) and now has three sons, 'grey-bearded officers on their own account' (p. 66), supports a late 1880s setting.

The most specific historical reference in the whole novel also comes from the old Ressaldar who remembers 'when the Kaisar-i-Hind had accomplished fifty years of her reign, and all the land rejoiced' (p. 75). The Kaisar-i-Hind is, of course, Queen Victoria, and she celebrated her golden jubilee in 1887. The action of the novel, then, definitely takes place post-1887. Critics who have suggested that Kim was born in 1865 (the same year as Kipling) and that he met the Lama in 1878 could not have read the novel thoroughly.[19] They have missed Kipling's clearest historical signpost.

Another point of historical interest in the novel is elucidated by Angus Wilson:

> Lurgan was drawn from the mysterious Armenian Jew, A. M. Jacob, who arrived in Simla in 1871. He dealt in precious stones, and had friends in high places, and was only ruined in 1891 after a long-drawn-out legal case with the Nizam of Hyderabad concerning the sale of a fabulous diamond.[20]

Kipling has transformed the historical figure of Jacob, to create the fictional character of Lurgan.

On a more personal note, *Kim* reflects the age through recalling Kipling's own childhood. Kipling, we know, thought and spoke in Hindustani as a young child, as did many young English children brought up by native *ayahs*. We are particularly aware of this when Kim, who thinks in the vernacular, has to translate his thoughts into

English when he speaks to Bennett and Father Victor. Perhaps Kim is the figure that Kipling would have liked to have been, and through whom he can act out the influences of his own childhood.

Kipling has often been criticised for his imperialism, and perhaps such criticism is fair when applied to some of his stories. The measure of Kipling's success in *Kim*, however, can be judged by Bhaskara Rao's conclusion to his chapter '*Kim* and the Indian Synthesis', in his balanced study of Kipling, a study that is not afraid to praise as well as to criticise: 'If I were asked to name one novel written by an Englishman which genuinely interprets the India of every-day life, the India of the common people, I would unhesitatingly give that honor to Kipling's *Kim*'.[21]

Kim may well have the qualities of a picaresque novel, it may well have the qualities of a boy's adventure story; but it is also a novel about India, and a novel set firmly in a particular time.

Writing about *Kim*, Edward W. Said remarked that 'although it can be read with enjoyment by adolescents it can also be read with respect and fascination both by the general reader and the critic alike'.[22] A novel such as M.M. Kaye's *The Far Pavilions*, which belongs to what can loosely be referred to as the romantic adventure tradition of the novel, or, in more deprecating terms, as 'popular fiction', may not appeal to adolescents in the way that *Kim* does, and it may not be read by critics with as much respect as *Kim* is, but it should not be dismissed simply because it has such appeal for the general reader.

The important question that needs to be asked when looking at popular novels is why *are* they so popular? A novel like *The Far Pavilions* is popular because it has a rollicking good story that keeps the reader's attention. Bhupal Singh has observed that 'much of what has been written since the publication of his Indian stories, and especially *Kim* (1901), has directly and indirectly been influenced by Kipling'.[23] This is certainly true of *The Far Pavilions*; it would even be true to say that Kaye has borrowed her story from Kipling. In Kaye's novel Ash, like Kim, is orphaned early in life and brought up as an Indian. Whereas Kim finds the Mavericks, his father's old regiment, Ash reports to the Guides, his Uncle's regiment. The proof of Kim's identity is carried in his amulet, the proof of Ash's identity in the small packet of letters and papers wrapped in oiled-silk. Kim is sent to St Xavier's for his education, Ash is sent to England. In the holidays Kim visits Lurgan Sahib or spends time on the road with Mahbub Ali, Ash visits Anderson Sahib. Both Kim and Ash have the

gift of being able to pass for natives in India. Neither Kim nor Ash is
able, or indeed allowed to forget that he is a sahib. This leads to trials
of identity for both – Kim's haunting question 'Who is Kim – Kim –
Kim?' (p. 265) and Ash's 'Who was he? Ashton . . .? Ashok . . .?
Akbar . . .? Which?'[24] This trial of identity, however, comes to nothing in *Kim,* as Edmund Wilson points out in his famous essay 'The
Kipling that Nobody Reads':

> Now what the reader tends to expect is that Kim will come
> eventually to realize that he is delivering into bondage to the
> British invaders those whom he has always considered his own
> people, and that a struggle between allegiances will result.[25]

The struggle which never eventuates in *Kim* does take place in *The Far
Pavilions.* It is possible, of course, that Kipling could not allow such
divided loyalties to play any greater role in his novel, whereas Kaye,
writing in a very different political climate, did not feel restricted in
the same way. Both Kim and Ash undertake a journey, Kim on the
Grand Trunk Road, Ash to Bithoor. Both are involved in the Great
Game.

The second reason for the popularity of a novel like *The Far
Pavilions* is that it has some interesting and appealing characters. On
the English side there is Wally Hamilton, and on the Indian side a
host of colourful characters including Koda Dad Khan (who has a
namesake in Kipling's story 'The Head of the District'), his sons and,
of course, Ashok. Thirdly, there is the exotic appeal of the East. India
has long fascinated the British imagination, and Kaye very successfully responds to this with her colourful Indian characters and
the wealth of background detail she supplies about the country.
Fourthly, it contains the conflicts of love and war, which appear to
have universal appeal. Here the love story is made more dramatic by
the conflicts of East and West, and the wars that occupy the Guides
on the North-West Frontier and in Afghanistan are made more gripping by the inclusion of the Great Game in which Ash is the
protagonist.

In other words, *The Far Pavilions* has, quite deliberately, all the
ingredients of a best-seller. It also, again quite deliberately, aims to
be an historical novel of sorts. The novel can roughly be divided into
three sections. By far the largest is the middle section, the love story
which takes up almost half of this massive novel. This section includes
the journey to Bithoor, during which time the romance between Ash

and Juli, the Indian princess who was his childhood friend, flourishes, and Ash's dramatic rescue of Juli from Bithoor. This section is full of colourful details but it contains little of any historical interest. The other two sections, however, the first which covers the 1850s and 1860s, and the final section which is set in the late 1870s, do contain much historical detail. Yet most of this really amounts to no more than padding; it is interesting and appeals to the general reader, but does not succeed when approached critically. This is because such detail simply satisfies the reader's curiosity, whereas a novelist like Farrell analyses and reflects on his historical detail.

Kaye (and the same is true of Masters in *The Lotus and the Wind*) attempts to use many of the techniques of the historical novelist which are so successfully used by Farrell and Kipling, but one of the differences between her use of the techniques, and I suppose a generic difference between popular, romantic historical fiction and fiction which is successful in an historical sense, is that Kaye is clumsy in her attempts at historicity. Look, for example, at the following passage:

Ash had returned to India in the late summer of 1871.

It was a year that had not been without interest to many millions of people. France had seen the capitulation of Paris, heard Prince William of Prussia proclaimed Emperor of Germany at Versailles, and once again declared herself a Republic. In England, Parliament had finally legalized trade unions, and an end had been put to the long-established and iniquitous system by which commissions in the British Army could be purchased by the highest bidder, irrespective of merit. But none of these events had been of any interest to Ashton Hilary Akbar, compared to the fact that he was returning at last to the land of his birth after seven long years in exile. (p. 125)

The date in this passage only confirms that the action of the novel took place at a particular time, and the regular dating throughout the novel only establishes the chronology of the action; it does not create the feeling of the period. Kaye does attempt to provide an historical backdrop to the action by reference to contemporaneous events in Britain and Europe, and the year 1871 may well be of interest to the general reader, but I would suggest that the events Kaye refers to here do nothing to enhance the story or to convey the period with any vividness. Such details have greater effect if they form an integral part of the web of the novel; the details in this passage, which reads like a short history lesson, amount to no more than stuffing for the curious mind.

Indeed, the fact that Kaye's historical references do not blend in and are not an essential part of the whole is perhaps the single most important difference between historical fiction that appeals to the general reader and historical fiction that achieves literary distinction. In *The Hill Station* and *Kim* historicity, in different ways, pervades each work and is an integral part of the writing; in *The Far Pavilions* the historical references stand apart. *The Far Pavilions* does achieve a limited sense of history, but it does not capture the spirit of the time as *The Hill Station* and *Kim* do.

4
Bridges

Would she like a Bridge Party? He explained to her what that was – not the game, but a party to bridge the gulf between East and West; the expression was his own invention, and amused all who heard it.[1]

Despite such events as the massacre at Amritsar in 1919, the 1920s still saw an outwardly confident and settled British Raj. This is the India of E. M. Forster's *A Passage to India*, probably the best-known of all Anglo-Indian novels, and the period too, of one of the two narrative strands in Ruth Prawer Jhabvala's *Heat and Dust*. Both *A Passage to India* and the earlier of the two stories in *Heat and Dust* are set firmly in the Civil Stations of British India with occasional excursions into the exotic world of Indian India, whether it be the bazaar Fielding visits or the Nawab's palace where Olivia spends more and more of her time. And whilst they both deal with the cross-cultural conflicts of the time, *A Passage to India*, in the context of this discussion, has much to tell us about English society of the period, too. Raja Rao's *Kanthapura*, set almost a decade later, portrays a wholly different India, not because of the time-lapse but because it presents an Indian India where the British, not the Indians, are the outsiders. Raja Rao, along with such writers as Mulk Raj Anand and R.K. Narayan, was at the very forefront of the emergence of Indian writing in English, which, although Rao could hardly have known it at the time, would, fifty years later, be at the cutting edge of world literature written in English. *Kanthapura*, set in an Indian village, is dominated by the Independence Movement and the influence of Gandhi, who, despite his tremendous impact on Indian politics, is never referred to directly in *A Passage to India* and only once in *Heat and Dust*.

There are, however, some important similarities which link these novels. Like *A Passage to India* and *Heat and Dust*, *Kanthapura* is concerned with the relationships and the gaps which exist between East and West, but concentrates on the conflicts these cause within Indian society in the early 1930s. The objectives of Gandhi's early *Satyagrahas* were to break down the economic, caste and religious differences that existed within the Indian community. The Nationalist

75

Movement's agenda was to build genuine bridges between the Indian communities, rather than to dismantle the bridges that existed between East and West.

The historical signposts which so clearly mark such novels as *The Siege of Krishnapur* are not readily found in Forster's work, because he did not care at all about historical accuracy. Forster was interested in India primarily as a rich and suggestive context, or even symbol, for human relationships. Like *The Siege of Krishnapur*, the novel begins by creating a sense of timelessness rather than a particular sense of time. Unlike Farrell, however, Forster maintains a certain sense of timelessness throughout his novel. That is, he is deliberately invoking cosmic time rather than historical time. I have already referred to the opening paragraph of Book One of *A Passage to India* in my discussion of *The Siege of Krishnapur*; the same sense of timelessness is achieved in the opening paragraphs of the second book, and indeed almost throughout the third book. The sense is that whatever events occur, the backdrop of India, which represents the whole geological indifference of the planet itself towards man, remains unchanged; in a political context the British still rule India.

Yet *A Passage to India is* about a particular time: British India in the early 1920s. Prior to its publication Forster made two trips to India, the first in 1912–13, the second in 1921–22, and I think it is safe to conclude that some of the early chapters are set in pre-World-War-One India. In those chapters the Club members are performing *Cousin Kate* (a comedy by H. H. Davies, first produced in 1903, and revived in 1911), and it is implied that this is a play or musical that has recently been on the London stage since Mrs Moore has seen it there. When the memsahibs consider *Quality Street* (by J. M. Barrie, the first London production was in 1902) and *The Yeomen of the Guard* (written in 1888 by Gilbert and Sullivan) the suggestion is that they are trying to keep fairly well up to date with the English stage. This would be consistent with Oliver Stallybrass's discussion of the manuscripts of *A Passage to India* in which there is evidence to suggest that a number of chapters (including Chapters 1–7) were written before World War One.[2] Forster, because he was not interested in history, appears not to have been worried about re-setting these chapters definitely in the 1920s, despite the fact that the bulk of the novel is clearly set in that period. And here I disagree with such critics as Paul Scott who writes: '1913 – which I think has to be agreed as the year Adela popped over to India'.[3] Santha Rama Rau, on the other hand, sets the scene as follows in her dramatic adaptation of Forster's novel: 'The action of the play takes place in the small provincial town of Chandrapore, in Eastern India, near Bengal. The time is April of a year in the early twenties.'⁴

It is possible that Forster did not attempt to combine these two periods for a number of reasons. Whether they were aware of it or not, like the British in England, the British in India were artificially, even deliberately, preserving a way of life that belonged to pre-World-War-One Britain; thus in their acting, 'they had tried to reproduce their own attitude to life upon the stage, and to dress up as the middle-class English people they actually were' (p. 60). And that attitude, Forster has already told us, 'was the public-school attitude, flourishing more vigorously than it can yet hope to do in England' (p. 60). Perhaps more importantly, his purpose was not to write an historical novel, and this is further evidenced by the absence of any direct references to important political figures of the time. Gandhi is noticeable by his absence, yet Aziz's question to Fielding: 'how is England justified in holding India?' (p. 124) surely reflects the questions being asked at this time by such figures as Gandhi. And in a novel which for the most part avoids politics, it is a noticeably political question. The National Movement must also be at the back of Ronny's mind when he tells his mother and Adela that 'the educated Indians will be no good to us if there's a row' (p. 59).

The clearest reference point in this novel, however, is Queen Victoria's funeral (1901); Hamidullah remembers fondly his days in England, particularly those he spent with the Bannisters and their young son, Hugh: 'I took him up to the funeral of Queen Victoria, and held him in my arms above the crowd' (p. 35). The boy cannot have been very old if he was held up in this manner, yet now he is 'a leather merchant at Cawnpore' (p. 35) and must certainly be in his twenties. In a later reference to his days in England, Hamidullah recalls 'how happy he had been there, twenty years ago!' (p. 120), clearly suggesting that the present is 1921.

Various references are made to cars; Dr Panna Lal is afraid of motors when he is out with his horse (p. 75), which suggests that quite a few are about; at different times various members of the English community arrive or depart in cars, and the Nawab Bahadur first had a car nine years earlier (p. 113). It is extremely unlikely that Indians would have been driving much before 1912. The nine years may be a reference to the period that separated Forster's own visits to India and this would clearly establish the year as 1921 and Fielding's later visit in 1923, the year of Olivia's story in Jhabvala's *Heat and Dust*. The references to the Asirgarh motor-omnibus (p. 294) and freezer ships carrying mangoes to England (p. 90) also point to the post-war years.

Forster claimed that *A Passage to India* was not a political novel,[5] but it was seen as political by many early readers, and it certainly has political content. Similarly, whilst many readers approach it with an interest in Anglo-Indian history, and indeed time has lent it a sense of history (not in a literary sense, but as an historical document), *A Passage to India* is not an historical novel by any definition. Frank Kermode was obviously aware of this when he suggested that Forster: 'wrote a book that was very successful with a public uninterested in secrets, willing to read it as a study of the British in India and approve or condemn it for its accuracy or its partiality'.[6] The major political events of the time, which may not be specifically voiced, are nevertheless mentioned. The novel is certainly set post-World-War-One or why does Aziz, in the closing scene, refer to 'the *next* European war' (my italics) (p. 315)? And if there is any doubt that this refers to the Second World War, Forster makes the following comment in his Prefatory Note to the Everyman edition: 'There was a Second World War (foreseen by Aziz on p. 315)'.[7] No novel set in India in the early 1920s can justifiably fail to mention the Amritsar massacre if it is to have any historical credibility, and Forster alludes to this event on at least four occasions, as Oliver Stallybrass details in his notes to the Penguin edition of the novel. The first reference occurs when the Club takes on its besieged attitude after the Marabar incident. This immediately recalls the Mutiny and the besieged Residency of Lucknow, but Stallybrass suggests that Forster was also referring to the events that took place at Amritsar in April 1919, 'starting on the 10th with the arrest of two Indian doctors who were supporting Gandhi's civil-disobedience campaign, and the consequent rioting in which five Europeans were killed and an Englishwoman seriously injured' (note to p. 188). The Collector's desire to 'flog every native that he saw' (p. 190) refers, as Stallybrass again explains, to the fact that the assault on the Englishwoman at Amritsar 'was avenged in part by the flogging, in several cases into unconsciousness, of six Indians allegedly "implicated in the assault"' (note to p. 190). Further, the fact that 'the dread of having to call in the troops was vivid to [the Collector]' (p. 190), along with the Major's 'Call in the troops and clear the bazaars' (p. 194), must surely be further references to the Amritsar massacre where on 13 April 1919 General Reginald Dyer opened fire on an unarmed crowd estimated at between 5000 and 20 000 in the Jallianwalah Bagh. He fired 1650 rounds of ammunition, killing 379 people and injuring over 1000 more, and stopped firing only when there was no ammunition left (379 is the official death toll, but some Indian sources put the total dead between 500 and 1000). The suggestion that women and children 'should be packed off at once in a special train' (p. 191) refers to the special trains which had been used to evacuate women and children from Amritsar and Lahore (note to p. 191). The final allusion of interest occurs immediately before the trial when Mrs Turton exclaims: '[Indians] ought to crawl from here to the caves on their hands and knees whenever an Englishwoman's in sight' (p. 220). Six days after the massacre, Dyer issued an order that all Indians using the street where Miss Marcia Sherwood, a doctor from the Zenana Missionary Society, had been attacked by a group of Indians on 10 April, must crawl on all fours. These allusions to the disturbances and ensuing slaughter at Amritsar are of course veiled, but they do capture the mood of the period. Importantly, Stallybrass tells us that: 'an even clearer allusion to the Amritsar Massacre occurs in a rejected draft for part of this chapter [Chapter 20]' (note to p. 194).

There can be no doubt that *A Passage to India* is set in the early 1920s. The historical evidence I have discussed above does not establish the period so much as confirm it. Whilst these references need searching out to confirm the age, the reader knows instinctively that Forster is writing about the 1920s – because his work embodies the intellectual questions and disquiets of the twenties, he projects the feelings of that age.

Forster engages with his period on two distinct levels, yet blends them perfectly because the splits in India are an ideal vehicle for Forster's treatment of such modernist concerns as the scientist and artist, the conflict between youth and age, and the conflict between male and female. Like J.G. Farrell he successfully captures the feelings and tensions of British India, whilst at the same time evoking the mood of contemporary England, in Forster's case the 1920s. Thus Philip Gardner is quite wrong when he suggests that: '*A Passage to India*, published in 1924, is a novel only of the British in India, not in England, whose life after the First World War Forster never described in fiction'.[8]

Gardner's suggestion wholly ignores the fact that for Forster India is a symbol as well as a real place. Conversely, Ramlal Agarwal is rather unjust when he suggests that Forster's *A Passage to India* does not provide 'an accurate picture of Indian life and character because it does not deal with Indians in their families or in their own social groups'.[9] This is true to an extent, but it must be remembered that Forster does offer more of an Indian view than most British novelists had done. We certainly do not get the picture that we might expect from a novelist writing today, with the value of hindsight, but we do not get such a picture of the British either. Forster, during his own visits to India, was not a government official and therefore not in the same position as Fielding is in the novel; rather his position was more like that of Miss Derek, who works for a Maharani and is much disapproved of by the British Civil Station. Forster, then, was in something of a no-man's-land between British India and the India of Indians, in much the same position as Harry in *Heat and Dust*. What *A Passage to India* does offer is a remarkable picture from the Indian point of view *for the time*. For example, Forster opens the narrative of his novel in Chapter 2 with Aziz and his friends rather than with the British community. This is very significant as Forster always uses the opening paragraphs of his novels to introduce his most sympathetic characters. Chapter 2, which includes the gathering of Aziz and his friends at Hamidullah's house, Aziz's subsequent calling away by the Civil Surgeon, his humiliation at the hands of the two memsahibs who take his tonga, and finally his meeting with Mrs Moore in the Mosque, is deliberately organised to give a positive impression of the Indians, and in particular their tolerance of the British. When the British are introduced, on the other hand, no such tolerance of Indians is in evidence; we hear comments like that of the ex-nurse, Mrs Callendar, who says 'the kindest thing one can do to a native is to let him die' (p. 48), which are a great shock to the reader.

Forster is interested in the relationship between the two cultures, British and Indian, a theme which Christine Weston also treats very successfully in her novel *Indigo* (1944). This aspect of *A Passage to India* can be seen from the outset, and examined by looking at the three parties that take place; the ironically named Bridge Party, Fielding's tea party and the ill-fated picnic and expedition to the Marabar caves. Each of these parties is an exploration of the gulf that separated the British and Indian communities in India.

The initial description of Chandrapore, where the divisions between the Indian, Eurasian and British parts of the city and Civil Station are outlined, firmly establishes the gulf between the cultures. Indeed the gaps between the two cultures are kept in mind throughout the novel by the liberal use of such words as 'split', 'crack' and 'fissure'. Thus the Indian earth itself highlights the gulf which separates the two races. As Forster concludes in the opening paragraphs, the Civil Station had nothing in common with the Indian city 'except the overarching sky' (p. 32), which joins them in spite of themselves.

Following this description which establishes the division in the reader's mind, Forster introduces Aziz and his friends, Hamidullah and Mahmoud Ali, who 'were discussing as to whether or not it is possible [for an Indian] to be friends with an Englishman' (p. 33). This question, and the obverse, whether it is possible for an Englishman to be friends with an Indian, are central to the novel. It is also part of Forster's larger question, treated in all his novels, about whether it is possible for any two people to maintain a close relationship, summed up in that famous phrase from *Howards End* (1910), 'only connect'. This meeting between Aziz and Mrs Moore in the early part of the Mosque section is the most optimistic answer Forster gives to this question in *A Passage to India*. Their friendship, even more than the one between Aziz and Fielding, continues to offer hope throughout the novel. The fact that the discussion at Hamidullah's house is brought to an untimely end by the summons from Major Callendar, the Civil Surgeon, and the loss of Aziz's tonga to the two memsahibs, offers an early, negative answer. The summons also reminds the reader that Aziz is Callendar's assistant, despite the fact the Aziz is the better doctor. The master–servant relationship between British and Indians is confirmed.

From the English viewpoint this question of friendship between the British and the Indians is raised in the figures of Mrs Moore and the naive Adela Quested, who, like Olivia in O. Douglas's *Olivia in India*, desires to meet Indians and see the 'real India'. It is the wish of Adela and Mrs Moore to meet Indians that the Collector chooses to humour when he decides to organise a Bridge Party. The party emphasises the gulf, and as Indians and English gather in their own very separate groups, little attempt is made to cross the divide. Indeed, when Adela and Mrs Moore do wander over to the Indian group it is not without Mrs Turton's stern advice: 'You're superior to them, anyway. Don't forget that. You're superior to everyone in India except one or two of the ranis, and they're on an equality' (p. 61). Adela and Mrs Moore are preparing to cross a cultural bridge and visit the Indian side; Mrs Turton is warning them, if they must visit the Indian side, to remain anchored to the British one. This piece of advice illustrates the common attitude of the British towards the Indians. On a community level, where such attitudes will always be rife, the possibility of friendship between the races does not exist; British society in India will not allow or tolerate it. This is a strong condemnation of the British in India, and of everyone who would welcome a return to Edwardian values in Britain, particularly if it is considered in the light of G. E. Moore's *Principia Ethica* (1903) (which had so much influence on Forster and the Bloomsbury group), where he argued that human relationships are the basis of ethics and morality. By the twenties many artists and intellectuals considered the whole idea of Empire morally indefensible.

The only person who does make a genuine attempt to bridge the cultural gulf is Fielding, the Principal of Government College:

Athletic and cheerful, he romped about, making numerous mistakes which the parents of his pupils tried to cover up, for he was popular among them. When the moment for refreshments came, he did not move back to the English side, but burned his mouth with gram. He talked to anyone and he ate anything. (p. 65)

It is because he discovers that the two new ladies had tried to establish communication with the Indians that he invites them to tea, along with Godbole and Aziz. There is a far greater chance of the gulf being bridged at Fielding's informal party than there was at the formal gathering at the Club. This is evident from the ease with which Fielding and Aziz establish their friendship, and the atmosphere of bonhomie that exists between the two of them continues with the arrival of the other guests. It is only when 'into this Ronny dropped' (p. 92) that the presence of the official community and the attitudes that inevitably accompany it are once more brought to bear on the party. The rift begins to widen once more as Heaslop rudely ignores Aziz and Godbole; he has nothing to say to them because they do not come under his jurisdiction and therefore he has no obvious master–servant relationship with them, and cannot conceive of any other relationship with an Indian being possible. His arrival is a reminder that though formalities may occasionally be dropped by individuals, the community will not tolerate such behaviour, and thus Fielding's party, despite its promise, is brought to an unsatisfactory conclusion for all concerned.

The promise of a friendship between Fielding and Aziz is further developed by the former's visit to Aziz's sick-bed – which culminates in Aziz showing his English friend the photograph of his dead wife. On an individual level the two can meet successfully as friends whether at Fielding's before the arrival of the other guests, or at Aziz's after the other visitors have departed. As a humanist Forster is saying that yes, Englishmen and Indians can be friends, and not only on British soil as Hamidullah has earlier suggested, but also on Indian soil – hence the two meetings between Fielding and Aziz. The first meeting takes place at Government College, on British soil, but it is significant that Government College is housed in an Indian building, and thus, symbolically, Fielding lives in an Indian house. The second meeting is in Aziz's room on the edge of the bazaar, on Indian soil. Consequently, Part One, 'Mosque', concludes with the possibility of friendship: 'they were friends, brothers. That part was settled, their compact had been subscribed by the photograph, they trusted one another, affection had triumphed for once in a way' (p. 133).

Yet we must remember some important points about their friendship. Fielding, like Forster, is not and never has been, nor ever will be truly a member of the Anglo-Indian community: 'Still, the men tolerated him for the sake of his good heart and strong body; it was their wives who decided that he was not a sahib really' (p. 80). Further, it is only because Adela Quested and Mrs Moore are not typical memsahibs that the party at Government College begins so well. As Mrs Turton acidly pointed out before the Bridge Party: 'Fielding wasn't pukka, and had better marry Miss Quested, for she wasn't pukka' (p. 49). Mrs Moore, we know, has already met Aziz on a spiritual level that transcends all divisions of race and community.

However, whilst it is possible to see the 'Mosque' section in an optimistic light, the gap between the two cultures is evident even at this stage of the novel. The Bridge Party had not been a success, and Ronny's arrival at Fielding's had quickly destroyed the atmosphere of that party. When, consequently, Adela and Ronny become engaged (this occurs between the tea party at Fielding's and Fielding's visit to Aziz's), Adela immediately adopts the attitudes that are expected of a memsahib: 'now that Adela had promised to be his wife she was sure to understand' (p. 110). From this point on she ceases to speak up for Indians in general and Aziz in particular; that is left to Mrs Moore who here and throughout the novel remains loyal to Aziz: 'I like Aziz, Aziz is my real friend' (p. 111). The gap between East and West, then, prevails when one views the opening section purely in an Anglo-Indian context; in a more general 1920s context the gap is concealed, temporarily, as polite society succeeds in bridging it on a human level.

Other gaps treated by Forster can be viewed in a similar way, and those gaps apply to English society every bit as much as they do to Anglo-Indian society. The first of these gaps is that between young and old, and this is most obviously bridged by Adela Quested and Mrs Moore, who initially share a common attitude towards the country they are visiting. This bridge, however, begins to crumble when another bridge, that between male and female, between Adela and Ronny Heaslop, is established. Adela's decision to marry Ronny not only effectively severs her relationship with the 'real India', it also damages her relationship with Mrs Moore. The fact that this unsuccessful heterosexual relationship erodes two other relationships (the relationship between Adela and Mrs Moore, and the relationship between Adela and Aziz) may be due, at least in part, to Forster's own homosexuality.

Forster also uses the religion of India, as well as the geography of the country, to structure the novel. In the 'Mosque' section, he uses Islam to suggest that successful bridges can be achieved. Islam provides an apparent sense of social order and stability, which in the 'Cave' section is shown to be fragile and at the mercy of external, cosmic or anti-humanist forces. What could be termed maya (illusion), or evil, splits apart all the connections that have been made, proving that social connections are fragile, and that some deeper, spiritual connection is essential. It is the 'Temple' section which shows that Hinduism precisely recognises this. The Hindu festival is used by Forster as a symbol, for what the British call the 'muddle' of India, but which may also be seen as the fecund, harmonious disorder of creation.

Thus the trip to the Marabar caves is fated to end in disaster from the outset. How wrong Aziz's words, 'this picnic is nothing to do with English or Indians; it is an expedition of friends' (p. 170), prove to be. Whilst Fielding has never been fully accepted as a member of the Anglo-Indian community, Adela Quested, since becoming engaged to Ronny Heaslop, has been adopted by the Anglo-Indians, and thus the expedition *is* to do with English and Indians.

Just how strong those community feelings are is shown after the return to Chandrapore and Aziz's arrest. At the station Turton is quick to call Fielding off as Aziz is taken away. As Turton explains to Fielding, 'I called you to preserve you from the odium that would

1. Thomas Jones Barker (1815–82) *The Relief of Lucknow.*

2. The Courtyard of the Secunderbagh after the Relief of Lucknow.

3. Abraham Solomon (1824–62) *The Flight from Lucknow.*

4. The painting of *The Jewel in Her Crown* prepared for Granada Television's dramatisation of Paul Scott's *Raj Quartet*.

5. Sir Edwin Landseer
    (1803–73) *The
    Monarch of the Glen*.

6. Jean Antoine Watteau (1684–1721) *L'Embarquement pour L'île de Cythère.*

7. John Everett Millais (1829–96) *The Boyhood of Raleigh.*

attach to you if you were seen accompanying him to the Police Station' (pp. 172–3). And indeed, because he will not actively join the English camp, Fielding does become a target for the odium of his countrymen.

Fielding desires to treat the case on an individual level, but in India that is impossible, and although he wants to tread a middle road between the two communities he cannot do so – neither side will allow it, and thus he is forced to take sides: 'He regretted taking sides. To slink through India unlabelled was his aim. Henceforward he would be called "anti-British", "seditious" – terms that bored him, and diminished his utility' (p. 183). (The word 'slink' suggests that this is a cowardly attitude.) Turton and McBryde had tried to keep him on the English side, but in the end Fielding is forced to choose the Indian side, and this is not taken kindly by the Club: 'I only heard a rumour that a certain member here present has been seeing the prisoner this afternoon. You can't run with the hare and hunt with the hounds, at least not in this country' (p. 194).

This sums up the prevalent attitudes perfectly. Individual friendships cannot transgress community lines, and the image, in this case of the British as the hounds, pursuing the defenceless hare, is extremely apt. When Fielding decides not to join the English pack, by remaining seated when Heaslop enters the Club, he has equally made a decision to join the Indian side as far as his countrymen are concerned. Similarly, Adela's withdrawal of the charges in court severs her ties with the English side, who reject her as readily as they had previously adopted her.

When Adela withdraws her charges in court, the male–female bridge and the youth–age bridge are effectively destroyed, and what remains, both in the Adela Quested–Mrs Moore and the Adele Quested–Ronny Heaslop relationships, is no more than the fabric that polite society can draw over the holes. Ironically, the one relationship that does last throughout the novel is that between Aziz and Mrs Moore, which is a spiritual coming together of young and old, male and female, and perhaps more significantly, of East and West. Yet in some respects no East–West gap is bridged in this relationship because Mrs Moore is, in spirit, an Oriental, as Aziz observes at their first meeting:

'You understand me, you know what I feel. Oh, if others resembled you!'

> Rather surprised, she replied: 'I don't think I understand
> people very well. I only know whether I like or dislike them.'
> 'Then you are an Oriental.' (p. 45)

Perhaps Forster is suggesting that it is necessary to absorb some of
the other culture if the gap is ever going to be bridged, or if any
relationship is ever to be successful; Mrs Moore absorbs Indian
spirituality, whilst Aziz adopts Western medicine. Mrs Moore dies
before she reaches England and is buried at sea in the Indian Ocean.
Adela Quested and Fielding can each return to England on their own
terms, but not Mrs Moore.

The final relationship that Forster discusses in *A Passage to India* is
that between the artist and the scientist, which is again an important
concern of the 1920s. Aziz, who is both a surgeon and a poet, embodies
in himself this uneasy relationship. Like so many of the other relationships, this too appears to be successful in Part One; it is only in
the final section, 'Temple', that the gaps are emphasised, as the poet
takes precedence over the surgeon:

> He had to drop inoculation and such Western whims, but even at
> Chandrapore his profession had been a game, centring round the
> operating table, and here in the backwoods he let his instruments
> rust, ran his little hospital at half-steam, and caused no undue
> alarm. (p. 289)

Here it is science that is equated with the West, and art with the East
or with the heart. The conclusion to the novel, then, ' "No, not yet,"
and the sky said, "No, not there" ' (p. 316), suggests, on one level,
that the time is not right for Indians and Englishmen to be friends –
not whilst the British are in India as a ruling power. As long as the
British are in India as the rulers they are maintaining a master–
servant relationship with the Indians, and true friendship is thus
impossible. Similarly the time, the 1920s, is not yet right for genuine
and lasting bridges to be built between young and old, male and
female, and artist and scientist in English society. But in both cases,
some progress towards these relationships has been made. In that
respect it is an optimistic novel.

Like *A Passage to India*, Ruth Prawer Jhabvala's *Heat and Dust* is not
an historical novel, yet like *A Passage to India* it does have a strong
sense of history. This is a result, initially, of the juxtaposition of
Olivia's story and the unnamed narrator's story, the juxtaposition of

an identifiable past, 1923, and an identifiable present. Both past and present time are established in the opening page of the novel. The year 1923 is indicated, and the present is evidently two generations or about fifty years later. (In the Merchant-Ivory-Jhabvala film of the novel the present is 1982).

In this discussion it is Olivia's story, which draws the narrator of the later story to India, that I am concerned with. As the narrator tells the reader at the outset: 'this is not my story, it is Olivia's as far as I can follow it'.[10] Although this need not be taken entirely at face value, there is a deliberate attempt to direct the reader towards the earlier story, towards the past. This allows two relationships between English women and Indian men, both of which result in pregnancy, at two distinct times in history, to be explored. It also exhibits Jhabvala's postmodernist interest in the effect of text on life, in this case of Olivia's letters on the unnamed narrator of the later story.

Jhabvala has never written about British India before, nor have any of her previous novels been set in the past, but it is a past not completely alien to her. It is the past of her screenplay *Autobiography of a Princess* which was released two years before *Heat and Dust*, and the past of Forster's *A Passage to India*, which she had read.[11] Indeed, there are grounds for suggesting that *A New Dominion* (1972) is in many ways a latter-day *A Passage to India*, and in *Heat and Dust* Jhabvala again tells a story similar to Forster's *A Passage to India*, but from a different perspective, and she tells it twice – at a time contemporary to Adela Quested's encounter, and then again fifty years later.[12] Adela, Olivia and the unnamed narrator are all questers trying to find the real India, but Jhabvala's characters are less naive in their attempts. And to take the idea of inter-textuality further, it is surely no coincidence that Jhabvala's major characters in the 1923 story are named Olivia and Douglas. *Olivia in India* by O. Douglas (Anna Buchan, the sister of John Buchan) consists of a series of letters penned by Olivia whilst in India, and in *Heat and Dust* it is the letters of Jhabvala's Olivia which later lead the unnamed narrator to India, where she herself keeps a journal.

The parallel stories do much to achieve a sense of history; the presence of the narrator's story creates a definite sense of the past, just as the presence of Olivia's story creates a definite sense of the present. Further, there are noticeable historical references in the novel, as for instance, when Olivia is talking to Douglas about the future that a child of theirs could expect in India:

'Supposing things change – I mean, what with Mr Gandhi and these people' – but she trailed off, seeing Douglas smile behind her in the mirror. *He* had no doubts at all, he said 'They'll need us a while longer,' with easy amused assurance. (p. 89)

The reference to Gandhi, combined with Douglas's air of confidence and the fact that Independence is still a question rather than an inevitability to Olivia ('supposing' rather than 'when') and probably not even that to Douglas, does help to establish a particular time. There are other references too, which place the story firmly in pre-Independence India: 'In those days Khatm still had a large proportion of Muslim inhabitants (this changed in '47 when they were either killed or emigrated to Pakistan)' (p. 68).

A sense of past is also created by telling the reader in the opening line, though not in any great detail, the conclusion to the story: 'Shortly after Olivia went away with the Nawab . . .' (p. 1). Such an opening is not uncommon (Paul Scott opens his novel *Staying On* in a similar manner), but it does create a sense of the interdependency of past and present. This technique has been successfully used in film also. The film version of *Heat and Dust* opens with Douglas finding that Olivia has left the hospital after Dr Saunders has discovered the twig used in her crude abortion. Similarly, Richard Attenborough's film *Gandhi* begins with the assassination of the Mahatma, before moving back in time to the early part of the century, and the period Gandhi spent in South Africa. This means that in an historical novel, while the reader often brings with him or her a general knowledge of the pattern of events, it is the details of how those events unfold that provide interest. This is distinct from those novels like *The Siege of Krishnapur* in which the author deliberately uses the disjunction between 'true' historical events and fictional events. Forster, of course, could not frame his novel in this way because he was not writing with the benefit of hindsight.

Newly-married and newly-arrived in India, Olivia has, as far as outward appearances suggest, the makings of a typical memsahib. Douglas never doubts this, and the opinion of the English community is voiced by the Burra-Memsahib, Beth Crawford, whose words Douglas passes on to Olivia in an early attempt to reassure her of her position in India:

She said she was sure that someone as sensitive and intelligent as you are – you see she does appreciate you, darling – that you would surely be . . . all right here. That you – well this is what *she* said – that you'd come to feel about India the way we all do. (p. 26)

Olivia, however, is far from reassured by this. She does not like the rest of the English community, and, like Adela in *A Passage to India*, she does not want to become another memsahib, which would separate her from India. It is not only because she does not want to be separated from Douglas that she refuses to go to Simla; she does not want to spend four months with the other English ladies:

> 'You should have gone to Simla.'
> 'And do what? Take walks with Mrs Crawford? Go to the same old boring old dinner parties – oh oh' she said, burying her face in despair, 'one more of those and I'll lie down and die.' (pp. 116–17)

This, of course, is spoken in the privacy of her own bedroom – she never publicly expresses her desire to see the 'real India' as Adela Quested does in her naive fashion, with words that echo around the billiard room. And later we see the same feelings when Olivia thinks the Nawab 'lumps' her in with the rest of the English community:

> 'All are the same,' the Nawab said suddenly and decisively.
> Olivia had a shock – did he mean her too? Was she included? She looked at his face and was frightened by the feelings she saw so plainly expressed there: and it seemed to her that she could not bear to be included in these feelings, that she would do anything *not* to be. (p. 122)

Her life in Satipur offers little diversion from the boredom of Anglo-Indian routine, strictly regulated by the hierarchy of the British community. In her early portrait of Olivia, Jhabvala paints a typical picture of Anglo-Indian life for a woman, in a world that revolved around the duties of the men. Even Hindustani (a mixture of Hindi and Urdu used by the British) is a male domain:

> 'Why? Mrs. Crawford speaks Hindustani; and Mrs. Minnies.'
> 'Yes but not with men. And they don't deliver deadly insults. It's a man's game, strictly.'
> 'What isn't?' Olivia said. (pp. 38–9)

For women, life in India in the 1920s was full of routine and endless hours of boredom, and this is a point Jhabvala makes very clearly; in many ways life for a memsahib was little freer than that of the purdah ladies, as John Masters also observes. And even in Kamala Markandaya's novel *The Coffer Dams* (1969), which is set in post-Independence India, Helen Clinton, whose husband is in charge of the construction of the coffer dams, finds herself faced with the same long hours of boredom with which Olivia is faced. At home Olivia is frequently seen engaged in the same activity, or inactivity, within the confines of her bungalow. As Charles Allen explains, once her husband had gone out in the morning an English memsahib was left alone with Indian servants she could not communicate with and Indian customs she did not understand. He concludes that: 'She had precious little alternative but to turn to other memsahibs and adopt their standards'.[13] Each day sees Olivia lying in bed long after Douglas has left for work, and when she is up she is invariably seen at the piano. The fact that we see her in this way over and over again evokes the sense of routine and boredom Olivia feels: 'And you don't think I *like* sitting around here all day, day after day, staring at the wall and waiting for Douglas to come home, do you?' (p. 130). This is why, initially, she finds the palace so attractive. Khatm is essentially a contrast to her life in Satipur. It offers a whole new world – not the 'real India' perhaps, but it is certainly one India, and one which is very real to her. The contrast between the two is emphasised by the heat and dust which separates Satipur from Khatm. In Khatm Olivia finds a variety of activities to entertain her; and not least, in time, the Nawab himself. The variety of Khatm is a marked contrast to the boredom of Satipur, just as she comes to see the Nawab as entertaining and Douglas as somewhat stuffy. In the final analysis the contrast is between the India of the Indians, as Olivia sees it, and the India of the British. But the Nawab too is bored by his routine and sees his days with Olivia as a pleasant diversion (see p. 149).[14]

The question of East and West is thus raised through these simple contrasts. Olivia, who hears the British complaints about the Nawab's involvement with the dacoits, and also hears the Nawab's complaints about the British who intend to investigate him, finds herself uncomfortably between the two, rather like Fielding in *A Passage to India*. The problem she faces reaches its height after she has told the Nawab about her pregnancy. He is delighted by the news, and never for a moment doubts that the baby is his. His words, ' "Really you will

do this for me?" . . . "You are not afraid? Oh how brave you are!"'
(p. 152) are later echoed by Douglas: '"You're not afraid?" . . .
"You'll really do this for me? How brave you are"' (pp. 154–5).
Douglas is referring only to the problem of childbirth in the Indian
climate, and Olivia can be forgiven for assuming that the Nawab has
the same concerns in mind. However, when Harry tells her that 'he
said when this baby was born, Douglas and all were going to have
the shock of their lives' (p. 161), the Nawab's words take on a
different meaning. It is at this point that Olivia realises she has been
standing on a bridge which will no longer support her. The only
decision left is which side she will jump down on; once made it will
be an irreversible leap. In *A Passage to India* Fielding is able to choose
the Indian side and then return to the English side later, and it is for
this reason that Aziz cannot forgive him. This may have been possible for a man, but not for a woman in Olivia's circumstances. And it
could be argued that Mrs Moore stepped over to the Indian side
without keeping one foot on the English shore, and she too never
returns to England. In *The Devil's Wind* when an Englishwoman comes
out to India to marry an Indian, the Indian is blamed for the scandal,
and the same would probably have been true in Olivia's case had she
not become pregnant, had an abortion, and fled. Her leap was far
greater than the timid step taken by Malgonkar's character or
Fielding's bold stride. The abortion, which she has to prevent the
Nawab having his revenge on Douglas and other British residents of
Satipur is, ironically, also the decisive step to the Indian side. It is
also the step, figuratively, which Adela Quested chose never to
make – whilst her withdrawal of the charges is a step away from
Anglo-India, her next step takes her home to England. Olivia's is a
decision quite unusual for the 1920s, and one which looks forward to
the young questing figures of post-Independence India, which
Jhabvala has written about so often and so well; the narrator of the
later story in this novel is an ideal example.

In *Heat and Dust*, as in *A Passage to India*, the Mutiny is recalled in
times of trouble. Jhabvala does this by likening Olivia's flight to
Khatm to Mrs. Secombe in flight from the Mutineers:

> Harry never knew how she came but presumed it was by what he
> called some native mode of transport. She was also in native dress
> – a servant's coarse sari – so that she reminded him of a print he
> had seen called *Mrs. Secombe in Flight from the Mutineers*. Mrs.
> Secombe was also in native dress and in a state of great agitation,

with her hair awry and smears of dirt on her face: naturally, since
she was flying for her life from the mutineers at Sikrora to the
safety of the British Residency at Lucknow. (p. 172)

Ironically, the flight has been inverted, and Olivia flees *to* the Indian
side, rather than *from* it. Abraham Solomon's *The Flight from Lucknow*
(Plate 3), does not match Jhabvala's description of *Mrs. Secombe in
Flight from the Mutineers* exactly, but it is close, and it does show the
style of painting Harry had in mind. It is significant that Olivia's
final, decisive flight is to Khatm; in *Indigo*, Christine Weston writes:
'The simple white-limed surface bore Hanif's name and his age, and
under these a single word: *Khatm*, which is the Moslem *Finis*'.[15]

The great colonial vision that had been evident in earlier periods
of the history of British India, so apparent in the characters in *The
Siege of Krishnapur*, is still there in the characters in *A Passage to India*
and *Heat and Dust*, but it is not as marked. The reader feels that it is
a confidence deliberately invoked rather than heartfelt. In later periods, as the demand for Independence grew, it would be seen to fade
altogether and, of course, it has vanished completely by the time of
the narrator's visit to India. The only traces are to be found in the
buildings: Olivia's house which is now a number of offices, or the
tombstone of Italian marble, now noseless and chipped, originally
erected for the Saunders's baby, and which still bears testament to
a long-gone confidence.

The radically different form of Raja Rao's *Kanthapura* owes as much
to the oral tradition of India as it does to the literary tradition of
England. As Salman Rushdie comments in an article on his own
novels *Midnight's Children* and *Shame* (1983), 'it is really impossible
to overstress the fact that the oral narrative is the most important
literary form in India'.[16] The shape of the oral narrative is, as Rushdie
goes on to explain, not linear:

> An oral narrative does not go from the beginning to the middle to
> the end of the story. It goes in great swoops, it goes in spirals or
> in loops, it every so often reiterates something that happened
> earlier to remind you, and then takes you off again, sometimes
> summarizes itself, it frequently digresses off into something that
> the story-teller appears just to have thought of, then it comes back
> to the main thrust of the narrative. Sometimes it steps sideways
> and tells you about another, related story which is like the story
> that he's been telling you, and then it goes back to the main story.

Sometimes there are Chinese boxes where there is a story inside a story inside a story inside a story, then they all come back, you see. So it's a very bizarre and pyrotechnical shape. And it has the appearance of being random and chaotic, it has the appearance that what is happening is anything the story-teller happens to be thinking, he just proceeds in that contingent way. It seemed to me in fact that it was very far from being random or chaotic, and that the oral narrative had developed this shape over a very long period, not because story-tellers were lacking in organization, but because this shape conformed very exactly to the shape in which people liked to listen, that in fact the first and the only rule of the story-teller is to hold his audience: if you don't hold them, they will get up and walk away. So everything that the story-teller does is designed to keep the people listening most intensely.[17]

The following single sentence from *Kanthapura* is an example of the style Rushdie describes:

Kartik has come to Kanthapura, sisters – Kartik has come with the glow of lights and the unpressed footsteps of the wandering gods; white lights from clay-trays and red lights from copper-stands, and diamond lights that glow from the bowers of entrance-leaves; lights that glow from banana-trunks and mango twigs, yellow light behind white leaves, and green light behind yellow leaves, and white light behind green leaves; and night curls through the shadowed streets, and hissing over bellied boulders and hurrying through dallying drains, night curls through the Brahmin Street and the Pariah Street and the Potters' Street and the Weavers' Street and flapping through the mango grove, hangs clawed for one moment to the giant pipal, and then shooting across the broken fields, dies quietly into the river – and gods walk by lighted streets, blue gods and quiet gods and bright-eyed gods, and even as they walk in transparent flesh the dust gently sinks back to the earth, and many a child in Kanthapura sits late into the night to see the crown of this god and that god, and how many a god has chariots with steeds white as foam and queens so bright that the eyes shut themselves in fear lest they be blinded.[18]

Kanthapura takes the form of an oral narrative, a *Harikatha* (or a story of God). But the *Harikatha* told by the *Harikatha*-man in the novel is about the birth of Gandhi, and Rao's novel too is a *Harikatha*, a

Harikatha which tells the story of Gandhism as it affects the village of Kanthapura. Ediriwira Sarachchandra suggests, however, that:

> *Kanthapura* can be styled a prose poem, a *gadya kavya* as it would be called in the language of Sanskrit literary criticism. . . .
>
> Although Raja Rao himself says, along with several of his critics, that he follows the old Indian tradition of story-telling, his technique is not as simple as this description might suggest. It is only superficially that the technique appears to be that of the medieval story-teller.[19]

Nevertheless, the oral tradition does provide the framework of the story: 'Our village – I don't think you have ever heard about it – Kanthapura is its name, and it is in the province of Kara' (p. 1). And in the closing chapter the narrator reminds the reader of her presence: 'This Dasara will make it a year and two months since all this happened and yet things here are as in Kanthapura' (p. 248). This use of the oral tradition establishes the Indianness of the novel, but more than that, it sets the events firmly in the recent past and in so doing asserts the fact that the narrator is telling a history of her village. Indeed this idea of Kanthapura being one of many Indias rather than India being a whole, is evident in the novel. This occurs in Heather Wood's *Third-Class-Ticket* (1980), too, where the Bengali villagers who travel around India have great difficulty coming to terms with the concept of being Indian, and India being one country.

Because this is the history of Kanthapura, the political events which pervade the novel are not seen in a national context, but only in a local one, in so far as they affect the lives of the villagers, and the wider political events of the time are not regularly referred to; yet in many ways Kanthapura is a microcosm of India, as C.D. Narasimhaiah asserts, and what happens in Kanthapura reflects what was happening on a larger scale throughout the whole of India at this time.[20]

The age is established partly through references to cars, planes and the growing global influence of the USSR.[21] But the most obvious way that Rao captures his age is through political references, to those 'who fight with the Congress – Kamaladevi and Sarojini Naidu and Annie Besant' (p. 145). These references, however, do not clearly establish the period, as Annie Besant's major period of influence in the Congress spanned the years 1914–18, before a new leader emerged in the figure of Mohandas K. Gandhi, who had returned from South Africa in 1915. It was he who took over the leadership of Annie Besant's Home Rule League after she resigned in 1920. At the same time he also controlled the Gujarat Congress Committee. By the end of 1920 he had gained control of the whole of the Congress movement. Sarojini Naidu, a follower of Gandhi, was an important figure in the Uttar Pradesh political scene in the 1920s. Kamaladevi was Nehru's wife. For all these figures to be known in a village like Kanthapura points to the end of the 1920s rather than the beginning.

It is through references to Gandhi and the Independence Movement, and such practices as the boycott of foreign cloth, begun in 1920–21, that the age is most obviously signposted. The most significant of these historical signposts is the reference to Gandhi's salt march to Dandi beach:

Do you know, brothers and sisters, the Mahatma has left Sabarmati on a long pilgrimage, the last pilgrimage of his life, he says, with but eighty-two of his followers, who all wear khadi and do not drink, and never tell a lie, and they go with the Mahatma to the Dandi beach to manufacture salt. (p. 164)

Gandhi began his salt march on 12 March 1930 and arrived at Dandi beach twenty-five days later on 6 April. This clearly suggests that the events of the novel took place during the months preceding and following this march.

In *A Passage to India* any reference to the Nationalist Movement was carefully veiled, partly because Forster did not want the book to be read as a political novel or simply as a novel about the British in India. Rao, on the other hand, when publishing *Kanthapura* fourteen years later, did want his book to be read as a political novel. Thus he openly writes a novel that is concerned with the influence of Gandhi, and the inhabitants of Kanthapura can freely call themselves Gandhi-men. There are, of course, consequences; the political content of Jayaramachar's *Haikatha* about Gandhi and *Swaraj* leads to his arrest:

But hardly had he finished the *Harikatha* and was just about to light the camphor to the god, than the Sankur Police Jamadar is there. Moorthy goes to him and they talk between themselves, and then they talk to Jayaramachar, and Jayaramachar looks just as though he were going to spit out, and we never saw him again. (p. 17)

Ediriwira Sarachchandra is right to suggest that: 'It is into the pattern of religious rituals that the political movement is woven, as if the rituals formed the vessel into which the political fervour was poured'.[22] Moorthy must take on the role of religious leader before he can be a political leader, but the ironical knot means that in order to become a political leader, he must turn his back on important religious rituals, and, for example, accept food from the hands of Untouchables. It is apt, therefore, that this deliberately political novel should take the form of a *Harikatha*.

The division between the Indians and their rulers is made clear from the outset of the novel: 'There, on the blue waters, they say, our carted cardamoms and coffee get into the ships the Red-men bring, and, so they say, they go across the seven oceans into the countries where our rulers live' (p. 1). The distance between the two cultures, between the rulers and the ruled, is implied by reference to geographical distance – 'across the seven oceans' rather than simply 'across the water'. The suggestion is that the gulf is an enormous one which will always be difficult to bridge. Notice also that Rao's Indians refer to the British as the 'Red-men' rather than the 'White-men', which recalls Hamidullah's reference to Heaslop as the 'red-faced boy' in *A Passage to India*. This is a good example of the British being seen the way others see them, rather than the way they see themselves, or would like to be seen.

The gulf between East and West is emphasised by the division between Kanthapura village and the neighbouring Skeffington Coffee Estate, a separation made clear by the fence and gates which keep the Estate workers in and the villagers out. In many respects the Coffee Estate has similarities with British imperialism. It is a reminder of the fact that Britain's hold on India began with the trading of the Honourable East India Company. The Sahib that the coolies meet is portrayed as a benevolent father-figure who gives peppermints to a crying child. This illusion does not last long, however, and the white sahibs are soon seen in the role of oppressors – the old Skeffington Estate owner beating the coolies and allowing the corruption of his Indian maistris (overseers), and the new owner sexually abusing the young women:

> He is not a bad man, the new Sahib. He does not beat like his old uncle, nor does he refuse to advance money; but he will have this woman and that woman, this daughter and that wife, and every day a new one and never the same two within a week. (p. 76)

The accuracy of this picture is supported by Geoffrey Moorehouse's description of coolies being recruited for the tea plantations:

> Coolies were recruited by the hundred in every tea district on the promise of wages that were not paid in full, they were despatched from the recruiting towns to the gardens in unsanitary conditions which produced many deaths, and they were liable to flogging for petty offences or merely for failing to work hard enough.[23]

In *A Passage to India* the division between East and West is highlighted in the court-room scene, and in Rao's novel too, the court system serves to emphasise the gaps. Evidence of this is seen in the Skeffington Coffee Estate when the Sahib shoots and kills a Brahmin who refuses to give him his daughter. Nothing comes of the ensuing case because 'the Red-Man's Court forgave him' (p. 77). The courts are the Red-man's as the following exchange illustrates:

> 'Moorthy! The Red-man's judges, they are not your uncle's grandsons,' and Moorthy simply said, 'If Truth is one, all men are one before It,' and Ranganna said, 'Judges are not for Truth, but for Law, and the English are not for the brown skin but for the white, and the Government is not with the people but with the police.' (p. 119)

Moorthy, echoing Gandhi's sentiments, says that this must change, and that Truth will change it. His impending imprisonment recalls how many went to prison in 1921, the probable year, coincidentally, of Aziz's trial in *A Passage to India*.

During the Marabar incident the Mutiny is recalled by the members of the Club; in *Kanthapura* the Mutiny is also recalled, but with very different sentiments. The story of Lakshmi Bai, Rani of Jhansi, is used to strengthen the resolve of the women of Kanthapura. The events of the Mutiny are not as important here as the causes:

> suddenly the army rose against the Red-man, for the Red-man wanted the Hindus to eat cow's flesh and the Mohomedan to eat pig's flesh, and the army rose and fought against the Red-man. (p. 144)

Here Rao, through Rangamma, dwells on the causes of the Mutiny. The Indians remember the Mutiny as a revolt against injustice, and this is equated to the struggle of the Gandhi movement, though eighty years after the Mutiny the methods of struggle are different. The point of the story is that the same strength of resolve is required for this fight.

The account of the Mutiny given by Rangamma to the other village women is an interesting parallel to the account the narrator gives of the way the coolies are recruited for the Skeffington Coffee Estate:

> Once upon a time when the English were still not masters of the country, there were many, many kings, and one king could not bear the other. So the English went to this king and said, 'We shall help you to rule your people. We shall only collect taxes for you and you shall live in your palace and be a king,' and they went to another and said, 'Why, you have enemies in the south and the east and the north, and you have to defend yourself against them, and we have a strong army, and we have much power and powder and we can defend you,' and the Raja said, 'Well, that is a fine thing!' and he gave them titles and land and money. And so the English would go from one Maharaja to the other and one day they would be the kings of India. (pp. 143–4)

and,

> the maistri that had gone to their village, and to the village next to their village, and to the village next to that . . . he came and offered a four-anna bit for a man and a two-anna bit for a woman. (p. 62)

But in *Kanthapura*, as in *A Passage to India* and *Heat and Dust*, the East–West encounter is not clear cut. In *A Passage to India* Fielding is prepared to stand up in the Club and speak out on Aziz's behalf, and here there is an Indian prepared to stand up at the Congress rally and support the British: 'if the white men shall leave us tomorrow it will not be Rama-rajya we shall have, but the rule of the ten-headed Ravana. What did we have, pray, before the British came – disorder, corruption, and egoism' (p 122). Just as not all British were anti-Indian, so not all Indians were anti-British, and this highlights one split in the Indian community, though the real split is caused by money and caste.

This split, anti-British and pro-British, or those who support Gandhi and those who do not, is only one of the divisions within the Indian community. The major division, now as in the past, remains along caste lines. This can be seen clearly by the geographical division of Kanthapura into quarters: 'Till now I've spoken only of the Brahmin quarter. Our village had a Pariah quarter too, a Potters' quarter, a Weavers' quarter, and a Sudra quarter' (p. 7). These divisions *within* the Indian community are as strong as those which geographically separate the British and Indian communities in Chandrapore.

However, whilst a person like Fielding, and to a lesser extent Olivia Rivers, may try to bridge the gaps between East and West, the Gandhi men in Rao's novel, and perhaps Forster's Aziz and Jhabvala's Nawab, ultimately wish to widen the gaps. The bridges the Gandhi men want to build are bridges that draw the various Indian communities together.

5

Swaraj

I thought that the whole bloody affair of us in India had reached flash point. It was bound to because it was based on a violation.[1]

Whereas the Mutiny has been the subject of many novels by British authors, and of only one Indian novel, Independence has been treated by many Indian novelists, and noticeably fewer British writers.

In R.K. Narayan's *Waiting for the Mahatma* the often complicated merging of history and fiction is suggested by the subtitle, *A Novel of Gandhi*. In this novel, as in Raja Rao's *Kanthapura*, and indeed in all the Indian novels of Independence, the British are in the background, whereas in the Anglo-Indian novels dealing with the period, the British remain in the foreground. The Indian novels are concerned with the struggle for Independence and the opening of a new era of Indian history; the British novels are concerned with the closing down of an era of British history. This is clearly the case with Paul Scott's *Raj Quartet* (*The Jewel in the Crown* [1966], *The Day of the Scorpion* [1968], *The Towers of Silence* [1971] and *A Division of the Spoils* [1975]. British and Indian novels alike show that the shadow of the Second World War cannot be separated from the Independence years.

I have argued that all novelists who write about India do, inevitably, in their presentation of that country, invent their own India. Narayan goes one step further, he invents his own, fictional, town of Malgudi, and sets all his novels within its boundaries. Malgudi is thus a microcosm of India in which Narayan can play out, on a confined stage, the political events of the continent. As A.V. Krishna Rao has suggested, 'R.K. Narayan invents Malgudi to provide a symbolic setting for the interplay of character and incident'.[2] In *Waiting for the Mahatma* Narayan departs from the usual style of his Malgudi stories to write a novel which has a strong sense of history, about a very specific time; for rather than leave Malgudi behind, he encompasses the history of the period within the limits of his fictional world.

Kanthapura was concerned with the Gandhi movement in the early 1930s, the time of the Second Non-Cooperation Movement; *Waiting for the Mahatma* looks at the final period of the campaign from 1942 through to Independence, and concludes with the death of the Mahatma in 1948.

Although *Waiting for the Mahatma* deals with a major period of Indian history, Narayan's story is primarily that of Sriram, and his love for Bharati (aptly named: 'Bharat is India, and Bharati is the daughter of India'[3]), who is a follower of the Mahatma. The waiting of the title is their five-year wait for the Mahatma to approve their marriage. Through the naive Sriram, and his involvement with the National Movement (not through conviction, but because he is attracted to Bharati), the various political movements of the time are displayed before the reader.

Whilst the fictional story at the heart of *Waiting for the Mahatma* revolves around Sriram, the historical elements of the novel revolve around Gandhi's role in the National Movement. Thus there is a clear blend of fiction and fact in Narayan's novel. Gandhi is an historical figure whose life has been well documented, and he did hold meetings similar to those in Malgudi, Narayan's fictional town. To have Gandhi as such an important character in the novel is a significant departure from the generally accepted criteria of historical novels, particularly those in the tradition of Scott, whose historical figures normally remain in the background, leaving the fictional characters to perform on the centre stage.

Narayan points out early in this novel, as Rao did in *Kanthapura*, that the followers of Gandhi often went against Indian tradition. Sriram first sees Bharati when she is collecting money for Gandhi's fund. He 'had never been spoken to by any girl before' (p. 19), and this is an indication that Bharati is breaking away from her traditional role, which is confirmed by the *jaggery* merchant who comments: 'I saw a girl jingling a money box. Even girls have taken to it . . . She has something to do with Mahatma Gandhi' (pp. 20–1). Sriram's willingness to follow Bharati, and therefore Gandhi, suggests that he, too, is prepared to break with tradition.

Narayan uses the meeting in Malgudi to present and explain the major principles of Gandhi's philosophy and his campaign against the British. One of the first things we learn is that 'there were a lot of volunteers clad in white *khaddar*' (p. 21), and this immediately sets the Mahatma's followers apart. Then Gandhi himself tells the crowd about his campaign: 'At the outset Mahatma Gandhi explained that he'd speak only in Hindi as a matter of principle. "I will not address you in English. It's the language of our rulers. It has enslaved us"' (p. 23). And he goes on to emphasise that the way to defeat the British is through 'spinning on the *charka* and the practice of absolute Truth and nonviolence' (p. 24).

Gandhi's actions in Malgudi also mirror aspects of his overall campaign. Thus, he leaves the beautifully prepared house of the Chairman of the municipality to stay in a sweeper's hut. The Chairman's preparation of his house, 'Neel Bagh', for Gandhi's arrival is wonderfully comic, exposing the lip service many Indians paid to the National Movement as they sat carefully on the fence. Thus the Chairman substitutes *khaddar* hangings for the usual gaudy chintz ones, and the portrait of George V makes way for 'pictures of Maulana Azad, Jawaharlal Nehru, Sarojini Naidu, and Motilal Nehru, C. Rajagopalachari and Annie Besant' (p. 39). This picture gallery, made up of 'all the available portraits of our national leaders' (p. 39) enables Narayan to introduce the important historical figures of the movement. The Chairman is not alone in such behaviour, and when Sriram later travels around the villages, his conversation with the timber contractor further highlights this aspect of the time:

> 'Ah, Mahatmaji. I gave five thousand rupees to The Harijan Fund. I have a portrait of him in my house. The first face I see is his, as soon as I get up from bed.'
> 'Do you know what he means by nonviolence?'
> 'Yes, yes, I never missed a day's lecture when he came to Malgudi.'
> 'You must also have attended an equal number of Loyalist Meetings, I suppose.'
> The contractor bowed his head shyly. He muttered: 'After all, when the Collector comes and says, 'Do this or that,' we have to obey him. We cannot afford to displease government officials.'
> 'How much have you given to the War Fund?'
> 'Only five thousand. I'm very impartial; when the Governor himself comes and appeals how can we refuse? After all we are businessmen.' (p. 100)

Narayan uses comedy to make a serious comment on the times.

Narayan outlines Gandhi's beliefs and the way he conducts his campaign because they are an important part of the age he is writing about. The events which involve the fictional characters, and the comedy that surrounds Sriram's behaviour, can only be understood against this background. Once this is established, Narayan can move Gandhi into the background as a character, and allow the truly fictional characters to take over.

The 'Quit India' campaign is portrayed through Sriram's activities in the villages surrounding Malgudi. Narayan dates the beginning of this campaign, and thus the period of the novel, quite specifically: 'The Mahatma had in his famous resolution of August 1942 said: "Britain must quit India," and the phrase had the potency of a *mantra* or a magic formula' (p. 94). Indeed a resolution was confirmed by the All India Congress Committee on 8 August 1942, but according to Jim Masselos, 'Quit India' was: 'a term coined by an American journalist in place of Gandhi's "orderly British withdrawal"'.[4] But what Narayan writes is true to the myths of the age, and that Gandhi said 'Britain must quit India' has become, with the passage of time, truth of a kind.

This campaign is set against the backdrop of the earlier stages of the National Movement's struggle. Thus the reader learns that Bharati's father 'died during the 1920 Movement' (p. 52), and that the father of Gorpad, another of Gandhi's followers, 'died ten years ago, facing a policeman's gun' (p. 67). Gandhi's own long involvement is shown by reference to the Dandi Beach Salt March of 1930 (also referred to by Rao in *Kanthapura*):

Do you remember Mahatma's March to Dandi Beach in 1930? He walked three hundred miles across the country, in order to boil the salt water on the beach of Dandi and help anyone to boil salt water and make his own salt. (p. 111)

Sriram's lecture, here, to the shopman in one of the many small villages he visits is, perhaps, a rather awkward way of establishing historicity – akin to Masters's awkward questioning in *Nightrunners of Bengal*. Such references do, however, show the long-term and total commitment of Gandhi and his followers, and emphasise the difference between those who have genuinely, through conviction, supported the movement over the years, and Sriram, who takes up the cause because he loves Bharati.

This difference is further illustrated through the jail terms Bharati and Sriram serve. Bharati is jailed as a political prisoner, but Sriram's commitment to the movement is not strong enough to persuade him to go to jail. Ironically, once Bharati is in jail, he drifts into the company of Jagadish, an INA sympathiser, whose influence leads to Sriram being jailed for derailing trains. Again Narayan is commenting on the times here. Without Bharati to guide him Sriram falls into bad ways: similarly, with Gandhi in jail in 1942 the Independence movement was deprived of the leadership of the only man who could really control it, and incidents such as those Sriram is involved in were commonplace.

Narayan deliberately gives a wide view of the Independence Movement. In *Kanthapura* Rao made it clear that not everyone supported Gandhi; in *Waiting for the Mahatma* Narayan shows that there are many who are not prepared to support the 'Quit India' campaign, as the village teacher articulates: I don't want to see Britain go. I am not one of those who think that we'll be happier when Hitler comes, perhaps with the help of people like you' (p. 97). And thus Narayan also draws attention to the Second World War, which brought yet another element into the struggle. It is the war that Gopal blames for the famine facing India:

> 'See what the British have done to our country: this famine is their maneuvering to keep us in enslavement. They are plundering the forests and fields to keep their war machinery going, and the actual sufferer is this child.' . . . 'Everyone is engaged in this war. The profiteer has hoarded all the grain beyond the reach of these growers. The war machine buys it at any price. It's too big a competitor for these poor folk.' (pp. 82–3)

Yet ironically, it is money which comes from the military pension paid as a result of the death of his father in the British Army in World War One, that allows Sriram to lead his dilettante lifestyle.

Further, Narayan outlines the view of the INA and the conflict between those who followed Gandhi's strict campaign of non-violence and those like Jagadish who followed Chandra Bose, and preferred to resort to any means to force out the British.

Although it is very much in the background in this novel, Narayan does not neglect to remind the reader of the power of the adversary, the British Raj. Thus at the first of the Mahatma's meetings in Malgudi, 'pulled obscurely to the side was a police van with a number of men peering through the safety grill' (p. 22). Similarly, the Collector, 'who was the custodian of British prestige' (p. 34), is present at the municipality committee meeting at which the arrangements for

Gandhi's visit are made, and he is in a position to censor the Chairman's speech of welcome: 'The Collector had taken the trouble to go through the address before it was sent for printing in order to make sure that it contained no insult to the British Empire' (p. 36). In an attempt to provide an all round picture of the age, Narayan shows another side of the British presence in India when Sriram visits the Mathieson Estates. Here the owner of the plantation informs Sriram that 'it is just possible I am as much attached to this country as you' (p. 106). During this conversation Mathieson refers to Cripps's offer, and Sriram's unvoiced reply, 'it is just an eyewash' (p. 105), echoes the sentiments of the Indian response to the offer.

The reader's first view of an independent India coincides with Sriram's release from prison, thus maintaining Sriram's role as our guide. (And this is, of course, another reason why Sriram cannot become too committed to any particular aspect of the struggle.) Sriram's release from prison symbolises the birth of the new nation in which 'buildings hung with the tricolor flags, the *Charka* in the middle' (p. 210). But Narayan does not glorify the new nation, and uses Sriram's continued imprisonment to avoid showing the Independence celebrations which were ignored by Gandhi:

'On the fifteenth of August when the whole country was jubilant, and gathered here to take part in the Independence Day festivities, do you know where Bapu was? In Calcutta where fresh riots had started. Bapu said his place was where people were suffering and not where they were celebrating. He said if a country cannot give security to women and children, it's not worth living in. He said it would be worth dying if it would make his philosophy better understood.' (p. 231)

Through Jagadish, now back at his photographic business, Sriram discovers the details of the Independence Day Celebrations, and Narayan raises the question of whether or not iconography, in this instance photography, can tell a 'true' story: '"Here is a complete history of our struggle and the final Independence Day Celebration." . . . Sriram looked through the album which in effect was a documentary of the independence movement' (pp. 215–16).

If the pictures tell a story of Independence which is unfamiliar to Sriram, they tell a story which is familiar to the reader. Narayan is reminding us that this is Jagadish's documentary of Independence, and that it is only one aspect of the truth. Because the photographs are of such places as the ruined temple, and of such figures as Jagadish himself, we know that this documentary evidence cannot be historical truth; the places and people are fictional.

It is also through Jagadish that Sriram learns about the communal rioting: 'Are you aware of what has been going on in East Bengal? Hindus versus Muslims. They are killing each other. Are you not aware of anything?' (p. 219). Thus the celebration of the new nation is tempered by sadness, just as the marriage of Sriram and Bharati will be saddened by Gandhi's death. Sriram's journey to Delhi by train, where he is going to meet Bharati who is working on a refugee children's camp, brings home the full menace of the violence that is staining India.

In *Waiting for the Mahatma* Narayan successfully captures the mood of the times within the Indian communities, but it is questionable whether he provides a fully-rounded picture in a novel where the British are all but excluded. However, it is true that there was little real evidence of the British presence in many small towns and villages. As Sriram comments in one village; 'Your *sircar* have not given you even a police station!' (p. 97).

At the end of the novel Gandhi's death is told in an apparently faithful description – except that again, it could not have happened exactly as Narayan describes it, because Sriram and Bharati are fictional characters and could not have been the last people the Mahatma spoke to before walking out into the gardens at Birla House. This is the clearest meeting of fact and fiction in the novel, although the fictional protagonists, Sriram and Bharati, regularly share the stage with the largely factual figure of the Mahatma. In this sense Narayan's novel is somewhat experimental; however, it is not a bold experiment. Narayan uses the language and traditions of the English novel (and this is ironical when one considers what Gandhi had to say about English being the language of the British, which had enslaved India). Raja Rao, on the other hand, experiments more boldly in *Kanthapura*, where he uses the language of the rulers, but influenced by the traditions of India.

In Paul Scott's *Raj Quartet*, unlike *Waiting for the Mahatma*, actual historical figures are very much in the background. This does not mean though that its sense of history is in any way diminished. Writing about the *Raj Quartet* George Woodcock has suggested that it 'comes as near to history as fiction can approach'.[5] Often Scott achieves a sense of history in ways frequently seen in fiction; at other times he achieves it in quite unusual ways.

The opening paragraph of *The Jewel in the Crown* draws the reader into the past, reminds us of the present and invites us into the world of fiction:

Imagine then, a flat landscape, dark for the moment, but even so conveying to a girl running in the still deeper shadow cast by the wall of the Bibighar Gardens an idea of immensity, of distance, such as years before Miss Crane had been conscious of standing where a lane ended and cultivation began: a different landscape but also in the alluvial plain between the mountains of the north and the plateau of the south.

It is a landscape which a few hours ago, between the rainfall and the short twilight, extracted colour from the spectrum of the setting sun . . .

This is the story of a rape, of the events that led up to it and followed it and of the place in which it happened. There are the action, the people, and the place; all of which are interrelated but in their totality incommunicable in isolation from the moral continuum of human affairs. (*Jewel*, p. 9)

The effect of the opening lines is similar to that created by the opening lines of both *The Siege of Krishnapur* and *A Passage to India*. And whilst it skilfully transfers the reader into the world of India by conveying the Indianness of the landscape, this opening also transfers the reader into the world of fiction – 'This is the story . . .'. The passage shows the difference between East and West by establishing the alien nature of the British presence on the landscape; the civil lines which stand out from the Indian landscape clearly do not belong.

At the outset of *The Jewel in the Crown* Scott establishes the period and the political and historical climate of his work:

In 1942, which was the year the Japanese defeated the British army in Burma and Mr. Gandhi began preaching sedition in India, the English then living in the civil and military cantonment of Mayapore had to admit that the future did not look propitious. (*Jewel*, p. 10)

The date is announced, and important events of that time are alluded to, but significantly, the events to which Scott refers, the Japanese victory in Burma, and Gandhi's 'sedition', are directly

related to the events of Scott's novels and affect the lives of his
characters. Scott's historical references, unlike Kaye's, do enhance
his story. References to the date, which show the passage of time,
and to historical details which place Scott's fictional events in an
historical context and within a particular political climate, continue
throughout the four novels. Thus there are references to the presence
of US troops in India, Wingate's Chindits in Burma and to Hiroshima. Scott pays attention to minor historical details also; for example, Karim Muzzafir Khan, who joins the INA, is the son of Subedar
Muzzafir Khan Bahadur, VC; in fact, soldiers of the Indian Army
became eligible for the VC after 1912, and a number of awards were
made to Indians serving in the First World War.

The historical event which Scott appears to be suggesting lies at
the root of the other historical events which occur in British India
during the course of this work is the Congress vote of 8 August 1942,
which passed Gandhi's 'Quit India' motion. Gandhi, Nehru, Bose,
Mountbatten, Wavell, Cripps and a whole host of others are referred
to at intervals by Scott's characters. However, none of these figures
plays a role in the *Raj Quartet* in the way Gandhi does in *Waiting for
the Mahatma* or even, albeit an offstage role, in *Kanthapura*. In this
respect Scott follows his namesake, Sir Walter, whose leading characters were never leading historical figures of the age. The problems
facing the Indian political figures of the time are played out around
the fortunes of the Kasim family, just as the problems of the British
are played out in the lives of the Layton family.

Apart from the many direct references to particular historical
events or figures, a general historical picture of the period is carefully
established. Sister Ludmila, whom some said 'was related to the
Romanovs; others that she had been a Hungarian peasant, a Russian
spy, a German adventuress, a run-away French novice' (*Jewel*, p. 124),
is a reliable voice. She is neither British nor Indian, and like the
white-Russian emigré, Count Bronowsky, appears to observe events
with a detached objectivity that no other character consistently
achieves. It is in Sister Ludmila's testimony in *The Jewel in the Crown*
that the harshest account of British–Indian relations in Mayapore in
1942 is voiced:

> The British Raj could do anything. The province was back under
> the rule of the British Governor because the Congress ministry
> had resigned. The Viceroy had declared war. So the Congress
> said, No, we do not declare war, and had gone from the ministry.

Anything that offended was an offence. A man could be imprisoned without trial. It was even punishable for shopkeepers to close their shops at an unappointed time. To hear of these things, to read of them, to consider them now, an element of disbelief enters. At the time this was not so. (*Jewel*, p. 134)

These many historical references all point to the importance of the war. After the First World War, Britain had the opportunity, and indeed had promised, to give India Dominion status in return for her wartime support. It could be argued that Britain, and the British in India, were now suffering the consequences of that broken promise, just as the rape can be seen as the result of an earlier, metaphorical rape of the country by the British. Daphne herself is in India because her brother has been killed in the war, and many important developments are related to the war. It is during 'War Week' that Daphne and Hari talk and are observed by Merrick, and it is because his friend Colin Lindsey, who is in India because of the war, ignores him that Hari gets drunk and comes into open conflict with Ronald Merrick. Hari (like Sriram in *Waiting for the Mahatma*) is imprisoned under the Defence of India Act rather than put on trial for the rape of Daphne Manners, an anomaly which creates suspicions about Merrick and suggests misuse of the Act. The war leads to Merrick's transfer from the police to the army, though the move raises the question of whether Merrick was allowed to move as a reward for his handling of the Kumar case, or whether he was moved out of the way as a punishment. Brigadier Reid criticises Indians for not helping in the war effort, but from an Indian viewpoint, why should they? India, to all intents and purposes, was already occupied by the British, and the question became, who is the worst enemy, the British or the Germans and the Japanese?

The Henry Moore drawings of people in the underground during the Blitz, which hang on Merrick's living-room wall when Daphne visits him, are of interest. It may not be particularly accurate, historically, that drawings of the Blitz, which occurred in 1941, should be on the wall of an Anglo-Indian living-room in 1942, but this does not matter – the drawings show the British homeless and defenceless; it is the iconography, not the historicity, which is vital here.

The regular dating in the *Raj Quartet* is of particular importance because, unlike many novels with a strong sense of history, it is not wholly chronological. In *The Jewel in the Crown* the same story is repeated a number of times, on each occasion from a slightly different point of view, until a whole picture is built-up – the picture from which the events of the next three novels stem. *The Day of The Scorpion* and *The Towers of Silence* essentially cover the same period, although the opening of the latter precedes the opening of the former by some three years, building on the events of *The Jewel in the Crown* and preparing the way for the events of *A Division of the Spoils*. Thus, to echo Guy Perron's words, we see the events as they emerged rather than as they occurred, and as they impinged on individual consciousnesses (in much the same way, for example, that we see events unfold in Lawrence Durrell's *Alexandria Quartet* [1957–60], though there are differences). This lack of linearity in the *Raj Quartet* is no accident; as Kermode explains in *The Sense of an Ending*, structure is never innocent. Scott's *Raj Quartet* is structured around the all-encompassing question of 'what is truth?' Throughout the novels there are questions about who said what and who did what, which remain unanswered. And Scott is clearly thinking in terms of postmodernist structure when he writes of Teddie Bingham 'who in the early months of 1942 enters the page as it were in the margin'.[6]

The structure is one of the more experimental methods Scott employs to achieve a sense of history in the *Raj Quartet*. The first book, *The Jewel in the Crown*, has the style of a documentary novel, with an implied narrator/historian collecting material which he carefully edits. It is a useful device to give the impression of realism and one which goes back as far as such writers as Defoe, Swift and Richardson, but which is now used self-consciously and moves away, quite deliberately, from the all-knowing narrator of so many historical novels. The implied presence of this shadowy figure collecting the historical material also has the effect of placing the reader in a seat opposite Lady Chatterjee, Sister Ludmila, and so on, as they each tell their stories. Scott's novel, then, reconstructs the lives of Miss Edwina Crane, Daphne Manners and Hari Kumar, from a series of letters, diaries, interviews and first-person recollections. And because of this documentary style the reader is left with the impression that the events described happened, or if we insist on recalling that the events are fictional, that events such as Scott describes could have happened as he describes them. In other words, they are fictionally true. If *The Jewel in the Crown* provides the historical skeleton of one event, the three volumes which follow it provide the flesh and blood of fiction. The traditional third-person narrator is adopted for a large part of these three novels, and it is only in the final book that Scott once more returns, albeit at intervals, to the documentary style of the first book with the recollections of Guy Perron and Sarah Layton, the two most sympathetic characters in the *Raj Quartet*, and the characters whose views are closest to those of the author. Scott takes the opportunity of reminding the reader of the structure of his work when Perron, who is, significantly, an historian, comments: 'in trying to give an impression of my idea of what happened, I have filled the story out with some imaginative detail'.[7] Earlier, too, Scott has portrayed the author in the role of the historian when Robin White writes to him with these words: 'I gather that your concern with this affair arose from a reading of Brigadier Reid's unpublished book, which came into your hands as a result of your known interest in this period of British-Indian history'(*Jewel*, p. 335). And there are other historians in the *Raj Quartet*, too. Major Tippet tells Mohammed Ali Kasim that he is 'a historian really'[8] and that he is writing a monograph on Premanagar Fort, and Merrick's best subject at school was history.

The central incident of the novel, the rape of Daphne Manners in the Bibighar Gardens in Mayapore, is never shown, only recalled, but it is this fictional event, along with the Second World War, which acts as an historical anchor throughout the series of novels. The fictional rape is tied to documented history not only by context, but by a number of strongly suggestive names which hint at the many layers of the British–Indian experience which underlie the actions of the present. The name Mayapore (*maya* = illusion, *pore* = town) suggests another level of fictionality or, in an Indian context, perhaps of truth,[9] as well as contrasting with Chillingborough, which suggests something cold (indeed, 'cold' adjectives are frequently applied to the British, whilst 'warm' adjectives are associated with India or Indians), and Sarah Layton, significantly, draws 'a red ring round her Indian relatives on the family tree and a blue ring round her English relatives. . . . There was a warming preponderance of red crayon on the tree' (*Scorpion*, p. 89). The location of the rape in the Bibighar Gardens, is intended to remind the reader of the Bibighar where Nana Saheb is said to have ordered the slaughter of European women and children during the Mutiny: 'The Europeans seldom went, except to look and sneer and be reminded of that other Bibighar in Cawnpore' (*Jewel*, p. 146). Scott is always very deliberate in his choice of names, as he makes clear through Guy Perron towards the end of the *Raj Quartet*. Guy says:

'Most names have meanings. My name means wide. On the
other hand it might mean wood. So you'd better go on calling me
Perron which is probably just the place where we lived once. And
I shall call you Edward after all. Ronald means the same as Rex or
Reginald. It means someone with power who rules. Edward means
a rich guard.' (*Division*, p. 503)

And, of course, Daphne, too, is equally carefully chosen.

Similarly, the Chillianwallah Bagh where Hari lives in Mayapore
sounds almost identical to the Jallianwallah Bagh which was the
scene of Dyer's infamous action in Amritsar. As Allen Boyer explains:
'By matching the Bibighar Gardens with the Bibi-ghar, and the
Chillianwallah Bagh with the Jallianwallah Bagh, Scott links the
transactions of his characters with the events of history'.[10] Further, the
attack on Miss Crane, the elderly missionary teacher, recalls the
attack on a missionary woman in Amritsar in 1919, just as Brigadier
Reid's actions in response to the unrest in Mayapore recall General
Dyer's actions in Amritsar. As the narrator tells us, 'there was a
rather sordid little joke going round among Mayapore Indians that if
you spelt Reid backwards it came out sounding like Dyer' (*Towers*,
p. 84). The matriarchal Mabel Layton has always been troubled by
Dyer's actions and in her dreams she mutters what Barbie Batchelor
hears as 'Gillian Waller', which is really Jallianwallah, but which the
reader knows could also refer to Chillianwallah. (Indeed the resur-
rection of Jallianwallah [or Chillianwallah] as 'Gillian Waller' recalls
the wonderful muddle which led to the renaming of Mrs Moore as
'Esmiss Esmoor' in *A Passage to India*.) Thus Scott skilfully uses fictional events to firmly establish the novel in the broad context of
Anglo-Indian history, and reminds us, as Sister Ludmila reminds the
author-figure who is collecting the material, 'that a specific historical
event has no definite beginning, no satisfactory end' (*Jewel*, p. 133).

The rape is used by Scott as a recurring metaphor for what the
British were doing to India. This is spelt out by Daphne in her
journal:

There is that old, disreputable saying, isn't there? 'When rape is
inevitable, lie back and enjoy it.' *Well, there has been more than one
rape.* I can't say, Auntie, that I lay back and enjoyed mine. But Lili
was trying to lie back and enjoy what we've done to her country.
(*Jewel*, p. 462)

Kenneth Burke makes a similar suggestion about the 'assault' on Adela Quested in *A Passage to India* when he writes: 'in this book the embarrassments of *empire* invariably have counterparts in *sexual* embarrassments, be they between members of the same or opposite sexes'. He then adds the following footnote:

> All sociopolitical relationships are expressible in terms of intimate, personal relationships – and these in turn are reducible to analogous sexual relationships. For instance, a general condition of conflict between classes can be stated in terms of private conflicts between individuals. And these in turn might be 'dramatized' by expression in some such sexual terms as seduction, rape, or sadism.[11]

Whilst the rape is the central incident in the *Raj Quartet*, the most obvious symbol which recurs throughout the four novels is the picture which once hung on the wall in Miss Crane's Muzzafirabad schoolroom:

> a semi-historical, semi-allegorical picture entitled *The Jewel in Her Crown*, which showed the old Queen . . . surrounded by representative figures of her Indian Empire: Princes, landowners, merchants, money-lenders, sepoys, farmers, servants, children, mothers, and remarkably clean and tidy beggars. The Queen was sitting on a golden throne, under a crimson canopy, attended by her temporal and spiritual aides: soldiers, statesmen and clergy. The canopied throne was apparently in the open air because there were palm trees and a sky showing a radiant sun bursting out of bulgy clouds such as, in India, heralded the wet monsoon. Above the clouds flew the prayerful figures of the angels who were the benevolent spectators of the scene below. Among the statesmen who stood behind the throne one was painted in the likeness of Mr. Disraeli holding up a parchment map of India to which he pointed with obvious pride but tactful humility. An Indian prince, attended by native servants, was approaching the throne bearing a velvet cushion on which he offered a large and sparkling gem. (*Jewel*, pp. 26–7).

During the course of the novel the painting (see Plate 4) is interpreted by various characters as a simple allegory in which India is offered to Queen Victoria, and as an illustration of *Man-bap*.[12] However it has a far greater symbolic meaning. The picture may show the jewel being presented to Queen Victoria, but the jewel, presumably the Koh-i-Noor diamond, was actually stolen, just as India was stolen. Like the attack on Daphne Manners, the picture is a metaphor for the rape of India. Miss Crane perhaps realises this when she takes down the picture and locks it away after she sees how the soldiers look at her native servant Joseph when they visit her following the assault on herself and the rape of Daphne Manners. The picture, which in the course of the quartet passes from Miss Crane to Barbie Batchelor, to Ronald Merrick, and then to Susan's child, Edward Bingham, suggests that the British were taking everything from India and keeping it for themselves; that the British were plundering the country. This recurring metaphor is skilfully linked to the central incident of the novel, and thus everything in turn is related to the attitudes expressed by the painting. There is also the suggestion that the rape of a British woman by a group of Indians is, symbolically, a response to the British rape of India; it is a way a culture can get its own back. The rape of Daphne Manners, then, is an inversion of the British rape of India, rather than a parallel with it.

The Jewel in Her Crown, a significant leitmotif, is not the only picture referred to in the *Raj Quartet*; indeed references to pictures pervade all four novels, and it is apparent that Scott thinks in images or pictures. Bronowsky, for example, says 'I am trying to get a picture' (*Scorpion*, p. 205) when he asks Merrick about Kumar. At a linguistic level it is a metaphor to which Scott is thoroughly attached; much of his diction is in iconographical terms – Susan says that she 'used to feel like a drawing that anyone who wanted to could come along and rub out' (*Scorpion*, p. 352). And pictures are also used in allegorical terms; Barbie Batchelor writes in one of her unposted letters to Helen Jolley:

> My poor Edwina sat huddled by the roadside in the rain, holding that dead man's hand. That, I continually see, was significant. For me that image is like an old picture of the kind that were popular in the last century, which told stories and pointed moral lessons. I see the caption, 'Too Late.' (*Towers*, p. 208)

The titles of the four novels add to the sense of assault conveyed by the painting, *The Jewel in Her Crown*. The title of the first novel, *The Jewel in the Crown*, refers to India, and to the fact that it is governed by Britain. *The Day of the Scorpion* takes its title from an incident where a scorpion is placed inside a ring of fire and scorched to death, and which is almost repeated when Susan, in her grief, places her young son in a similar fiery ring. This fire image, which suggests the meeting of East (the scorpion) and West (the fire) and is only destructive (Miss Crane becomes *sati* in the woodshed, and Teddy Bingham and Ronald Merrick are horribly burnt), is in marked contrast to the Indian image of Shiva, in the form of Nataraj, dancing in a circle of cosmic fire which suggests not only destruction but also creation. Further, the ring of fire suggests imprisonment, which is the organising motif of this novel. Mohammed Ali Kasim, Hari Kumar and Colonel Layton are all imprisoned like the butterflies in the French lace, and even Sarah Layton is imprisoned by duty to her family, just as the British themselves are imprisoned in India, clinging to an idea that they know is over. *The Towers of Silence* is a novel about communication:

> Because it is to be talked to that I want above anything. I want to create around myself a condition of silence so that it may be broken, but not by me. But I am surrounded by a condition of Babel. To this, all my life, I have contributed enough for a dozen people. And He stops His ears and leaves us to get on with it. (*Towers*, p. 196)

It is a novel full of silences: Barbie goes silent at the end of the novel, and there is always the question of who is being silent about what in the Kumar affair. The towers of silence are where the Parsees place their dead to be consumed by the vultures, which suggests sacrifice, and also, metaphorically, places the British in the position of the vultures, greedily consuming India. *A Division of the Spoils* refers to the partition of India; the fact that India is referred to as Britain's 'spoils' evokes an image of plunder that has resulted from something taken by force, which again suggests the rapes of Daphne and India.

All this points to the gulf that divides East and West, which has been apparent in all the fiction discussed so far. The idea of bridges, which was central to the fiction discussed in the last chapter, plays an important role in the *Raj Quartet* also. A bridge party of the kind that was so unsuccessful in *A Passage to India* is found in *The Day of the Scorpion*. Sarah Layton's aunt and uncle, the Graces, have to call on the Purvises because: 'They're having a bridge party – Indians, not cards – and want to muster forces for after dinner when it gets tense and embarrassing because everybody's said everything twice'

(*Scorpion*, p. 424). Sarah has never been to a bridge party however, which suggests that such efforts to bridge the gap between East and West are still relatively rare – at least officially. It has always been possible for individuals to step onto the bridge temporarily, as long as one foot is kept on the British side of the gulf, as is the case when Sarah and her escort, Major Clark, spend their evening 'across the so-called bridge' (*Scorpion*, p. 430). In *The Jewel in the Crown* Miss Crane and Daphne Manners are, ironically, the two characters who make genuine attempts to cross that bridge. Hari, brought up to think like an Englishman, finds himself, on his return to India, uncomfortably stranded between two cultures. This is illustrated by his clothing:

> Few of the clothes he had brought from England were of any use to him. His aunt had helped fit him out with shirts and trousers run up by the bazaar tailor. The trousers he wore today were white and wide-bottomed. With them he wore a white short-sleeved shirt, and carried a buff-coloured sola topee. Only his shoes were English; and those were hand-made and very expensive. (*Jewel*, p. 246)

But the English and Indian areas of Mayapore are clearly defined, and literally separated by a river. It may be possible to build temporary bridges, but not to bridge the gulf permanently on Indian soil. Miss Crane realises this when she reaches out her hand to her dead colleague, Mr Chaudhuri – a gesture Ronald Merrick misinterprets as *Man-bap*, but which Barbie Batchelor explains to Sarah was in fact despair – religious despair rather than political despair. Daphne Manners understands the impossibility of bridging gaps too, and this must, at least to a degree, explain her refusal to tell the truth after the rape.

The division between the cultures is emphasised on a human level through the ill-fated relationship between Hari Kumar and Daphne Manners. The separation of their worlds is made poignantly clear; the deserted Bibighar was:

> the one place in Mayapore where [they] could be together and be utterly natural with each other. . . .
> The club was out. There was the other club, what they call the Indian Club, but Hari wouldn't take me there because there *I* would have been stared at. . . . The English coffee shop was out.

The Chinese Restaurant was out. . . . Even the poor little fleapit cinema in the cantonment was out because I wouldn't have had the nerve to try to take Hari into the sacrosanct little 'balcony' and he wouldn't have made me sit on a wooden form in the pit. (*Jewel*, pp. 392–3)

Thus Hari and Daphne stand on opposite banks of the cultural gulf and there is no bridge between. Sister Ludmila elucidates this clearly:

It is curious. But there has always been this special connexion between the house of the singer and the house of the courtesans. Between the MacGregor House and the Bibighar. It is as though across the mile that separates them there have flowed the dark currents of a human conflict, even after Bibighar was destroyed, a current whose direction might be traced by following the route taken by the girl running in darkness from one to the other. A current. The flow of an invisible river. No bridge was ever thrown across it and stood. You understand what I am telling you? That MacGregor and Bibighar are the place of the white and the place of the black? To get from one to the other you could not cross by a bridge but had to take your courage in your hands and enter the flood and let yourself be taken with it, lead where it may. This is a courage Miss Manners had. (*Jewel*, pp. 150–1)

Daphne's choice to keep the child she believed to be Hari's shows her refusal to swim back to the Anglo-Indian bank, just as in *A Passage to India* Adela Quested leaves the Anglo-Indian side for good when she refuses to give evidence against Aziz (the parallel between Daphne and Adela is quite marked), and Olivia's flight after her abortion, in *Heat and Dust*, severs her contacts with Anglo-India. Evidence of this can be seen in the change in the attitude of the other memsahibs:

Poor Miss Manners. How short a time it took for her to become 'that Manners girl'. Perhaps before Bibighar she had also sometimes been called this. But immediately after Bibighar her name was spoken by Europeans with the reverence they might have used to speak of saints and martyrs. But now. That Manners girl. And that ugly comment – 'Perhaps she enjoyed it.' (*Jewel*, p. 161)

The relationship between Hari Kumar and Ronald Merrick is a further exploration of the East–West conflict. As Hari tells Rowan when he is finally re-examined in prison:

> [Merrick] said for the moment we were mere symbols. He said we'd never understand each other if we were going to be content with that. It wasn't enough to say he was English and I was Indian, that he was a ruler and I was one of the ruled. We had to find out what that meant. (*Scorpion*, p. 307)

Merrick is in the master role because he is English, and Hari is in the servant role because he is Indian – but in this particular case there is more to their relationship than can be explained by a simple East–West or master–servant relationship.

> Place Merrick at home, in England, and Harry Coomer abroad in England, and it is Coomer on whom the historian's eye lovingly falls; he is a symbol of our virtue. In England it is Merrick who is invisible. Place them there, in India, and the historian cannot see either of them. They have wandered off the guideline, into the jungle. But throw the spotlight on them and it is Merrick on whom it falls. There he is, the unrecorded man, one of the kind of men we really are (as Sarah would say). Yes, their meeting was logical. And they had met before, countless times. You can say they are still meeting, that their meeting reveals the real animus, the one that historians won't recognize, or which we relegate to our margins. (*Division*, p. 302)

Thus in the Merrick–Kumar relationship the question of British class differences is also raised, as Patrick Swinden has observed:

> ... what Merrick is beating and humiliating in Kumar is not only the envious Indian for whom he feels contempt, but the contemptuous English public school boy for whose class, accent and perfect manners he feels the deepest, though un-self-acknowledged, envy.[13]

Kumar has had all the advantages of a British upper-class education; Merrick has not. Yet in India Merrick can aspire to mix with a class of people who would not have given him the time of day in England;

the reverse is true of Hari, as it was to a degree of Gandhi himself. Indeed, this is true of Hari to such an extent that he feels like a foreigner in his own country, just as Sarah and Susan Layton felt out of place in England when they were left there to attend school, and the Anglo-Indian children in Elizabeth Cadell's *Sun in the Morning* (1951) feel like foreigners in England when they are trapped there by the First World War.

The relationship between Merrick and Kumar also explores a homosexual–heterosexual conflict. Merrick, a repressed homosexual, initially takes an interest in Daphne because of their mutual interest in Kumar. As Sister Ludmila suggests: 'It was Kumar whom Merrick wanted. Not Miss Manners. And it was probably her association with Kumar that first caused Merrick to look in her direction' (*Jewel*, p. 165). This is confirmed by Daphne herself in the journal she addresses to her aunt, Lady Manners: '[he] took notice of me because he saw me go up to Hari and talk to him' (*Jewel*, p. 406).

Apart from the homosexual implications there is also a sense of Merrick not wanting the conquered to enjoy the spoils of the conqueror. Merrick could come to terms with a white woman being raped by an Indian, a member of the ruling/conqueror class being raped by a member of the lower/conquered class, but what he could not accept was the thought of Hari Kumar and Daphne Manners meeting on terms of equality – of Daphne *giving* herself to Hari – which is why Merrick singles Hari out for such cruel treatment. As Max Beloff suggests: 'Even when social constraints were a little loosened the reluctance to contemplate the sexual involvement of British women and Indian men remained a rooted one'.[14] Further, Edward Said has pointed out that India is always presented as feminine whilst the English are presented as male, thus justifying India's colonisation by the English. To go against this, as Hari's relationship with Daphne does, undermines the whole business of colonisation, as Daphne herself recognises:

I felt as if they saw my affair with Hari as the logical but terrifying end of the attempt they had all made to break out of their separate little groups and learn how to live together – terrifying because even they couldn't face with equanimity the breaking of the most fundamental law of all – that although a white man could make love to a black girl, the black man and white girl association was still taboo. (*Jewel*, p. 379)

Hari has broken the code, and by attempting to cross boundaries he is threatening the whole fabric of Anglo-Indian society.

The relationship between the past and present and the importance of hindsight is always kept in view in this work. There are many references to the present which ranges from 1964 in *The Jewel in the Crown* to 1970 in *A Division of the Spoils*. This sense of a conscious recalling of the past is seen when Lily Chatterjee says, 'Yes, I remember Miss Crane' (*Jewel*, p. 76), which suggests that a train of thought is sparked off by first remembering the name.

The importance of history in relation to the present is outlined in a rather different light in *The Towers of Silence* through the figure of Barbie Batchelor. Though she may not be a central player in the history Scott is creating, her role is nevertheless important and cannot be ignored. Her attitude towards her trunk full of memorabilia from her missionary teaching days is put into words for her by her reading of Emerson:

> 'The trunk is a very different kettle of fish. Unlike a writing-table, unlike one's clothes, one's *shoes*, it is of no use. But it *is* my history. And according to Emerson without it, without *that*, I'm simply not explained. I am a mere body, sitting here. Without it, according to Emerson, *none* of us is explained because if it is my history then it is yours too and was Mabel's.' (*Towers*, pp. 279-80)

Barbie's copy of Emerson is another of the leitmotifs Scott uses in the *Raj Quartet*; her copy passes to Guy Perron, who takes up the history in the fourth volume. Historical fiction necessarily involves major historical events and figures, but it must also be concerned with the whole of its period, and minor figures like Barbie add verisimilitude. As Emerson expounds in the phrase which first attracted Barbie to his work, 'Man is explicable by nothing less than all his history' (*Towers*, p. 76). It is certainly a line that Scott has paid heed to in the *Raj Quartet*, and another example of the postmodernist interest in intertextuality.

Scott's references to newspapers or newspaper articles, fictional or actual, are also a means by which he adds historicity to his subject. When the story of the assaults on Edwina Crane and Daphne Manners are told once more in *The Towers of Silence* we are able to see the effects of those incidents on another group of people. On this occasion Scott introduces the story headed 'ENGLISH WOMEN ATTACKED', as an article '*From the Ranpur Gazette: August 15th, 1942*' (*Towers*, pp. 52–4). Though the report and the *Ranpur Gazette* itself are, of course, fictional, the effectiveness of Scott's means of reporting is not diminished. The date is clearly re-introduced, and the appearance of documented fact, so carefully constructed in *The Jewel in the Crown*, is re-enforced.

This gathering of documentary information, and the importance of the present, are underlined when the author-figure, as he looks around the Mayapore Gymkhana Club where he is talking to Lily Chatterjee, refers to an English woman who is 'turning over the pages of a none-too-recent issue of the *Sunday Times* Magazine – today's fashionable equivalent of *The Tatler* or *The Onlooker*' (*Jewel*, p. 173). Scott has already told the reader that the 'now' of his visit to Mayapore is 1964, and this reference to *The Sunday Times* Magazine, first published only two years earlier in 1962, supports this. In other words he establishes the present as carefully as he does the past.

Just as in *The Jewel in the Crown* there is an obvious parallel between Scott and the historian figure who gathers the documentary evidence presented in that novel (and like this historian figure, Scott himself returned to India in 1964 to research his work[15]), so there is a parallel between the author and Guy Perron who is an academic historian when he returns to India. Indeed, the account of Perron's earlier exit from India (and his escape from Merrick) is similar to the account Scott gives of his own 'escape' from Singapore back to Calcutta in 1945:

> There, handed a posting-order that would have kept me in that modern apology for a Romantic Eastern Port for the remaining months of my service, I knew I was homesick in quite a different way – for the sight and smell of an arid Indian plain. Twisting the arm of an old friend who was in a position to produce another posting-order and lose the first in a foolproof and therefore totally impenetrable filing system, I hopped a plane for Rangoon, and without waiting there as my friend advised, hopped another for Calcutta.[16]

Perron re-appears in the story in June 1947, and the date is significant:

> On June 4 [Mountbatten] held a press conference (a feature of his viceroyalty which some old hands thought unnecessarily showy) and in answer to a question confirmed that this hastening

through of legislation in Whitehall meant that Government would transfer power not next year but this year. He said, 'I think the transfer could be about the fifteenth of August.' (*Division*, p. 455)

Scott has immediately introduced both a date and a major historical event, and both dates and events are of consequence as Perron and the editor of 'a popular Indian-controlled English-language newspaper' (*Division*, p. 456) whose office he is visiting, look at a series of cartoons by Halki, the span of which, from late August 1945 to 5 June 1947, covers roughly the same period as the events of this volume of the *Raj Quartet*.

Each cartoon that Perron picks out represents an important event in the final years before Independence; Scott's words, 'The next significant cartoon . . .'(*Division*, p. 457) could as justifiably read 'the next significant event . . .'. The most detailed cartoon, which occupies a whole page of the newspaper and three pages of Scott's novel, is a response to Mountbatten's announcement of the division of power:

Halki had worked throughout June 4 and drawn a picture of an immense Gothic building, or rather a structure which the architect had planned as one only to be frustrated (one had to imagine) over certain details of land acquisition. The attempt to create an illusion of a single façade, although admirably conceived and executed, hadn't quite worked, although it took several moments of close study of Halki's exemplary drawing to discern this. (*Division*, pp. 464–5)

Halki's cartoons, including those described in the opening pages of *A Division of the Spoils* which were published under an earlier pseudonym, provide a vivid synopsis of the major events of the period, and, not surprisingly, this climax to the series of cartoons described coincides with the climactic event of the period. There are many ways of recording history in fiction; Scott's use of cartoons is both simple and effective. It is a form of iconography which can also be found in Manohar Malgonkar's *The Princes* and Salman Rushdie's *Midnight's Children*.

Paul Scott acknowledged the tremendous influence of *A Passage to India* on Anglo-Indian novelists in general and on himself in particular, when he said: 'I recognise that the ground I need to tread if writing about Anglo-India bears permanent impressions of a certain person's footprints and that to plant your own there is to invite comparison'.[17] The comparison I want to consider here is not so much between Forster and Scott as between the attitudes of the Anglo-Indian characters in the two periods twenty years apart. The obvious similarities suggest that although the two historical periods are clearly definable, the character of Anglo-Indians did not change markedly over a generation.

The conflict within the Anglo-Indian community of the 1920s, illustrated in the conflict between the Turtons and Burtons on the one hand and Fielding on the other, is still apparent in the *Raj Quartet*. The attitudes of the Turtons and Burtons can be seen in such characters as the Trehearnes and Rankins; the attitudes of Fielding are found, more deeply-rooted and less naive, in such characters as Sarah Layton and Guy Perron. And both Edwina Crane and Barbie Batchelor, like Mrs Moore in *A Passage to India*, suffer a loss of religious faith when they realise that India and its problems are too much for their Jehovah.

Adela Quested's desire to see the real India is less naively stated and more successfully realised by Daphne Manners, but with greater consequences both for herself and for Hari Kumar. Adela's imagined assault in the Marabar caves becomes for Daphne a very real assault, and Aziz's suffering is minor compared to the cruelty Hari must face, first at the hands of Ronald Merrick (who shares the same first name with Ronnie Heaslop), and then under the Defence of India Act which allows him, unlike Aziz, to be imprisoned without trial. Further, Daphne, like Adela, refuses to give the Anglo-Indians the public revenge they desired: 'it was only gradually that they realised they were going to be denied public revenge' (*Jewel*, p. 165). Mrs Moore, Adela's prospective mother-in-law, who knows all along that Aziz is innocent, but does nothing concrete to save him, is paralleled in Scott's novels by the figure of Lady Manners, Daphne's aunt, who for quite some time does nothing to secure Hari's release, although she is sure of his innocence. Also, the friendship between Hari Kumar and Colin Lindsey, which did not survive on Indian soil, recalls the opening conversation between Hamidullah, Aziz and their friends in *A Passage to India*, and indeed, the closing words of that novel.

The hurried Club-meeting in response to the attacks on Miss Crane and Daphne Manners suggests that the attitudes which prompted a similar meeting in Forster's Chandrapore after the

'assault' on Adela Quested still prevail. What is important is that
whilst these attitudes have survived twenty years, there have been
noticeable changes too; the members now include Indian officers
and their wives. But whilst they may have been allowed to join the
Club they have not been wholly accepted:

> At this point an Indian officer from General Rankin's staff,
> Major Chatab Singh, known affectionately as Chatty (which he
> was) got on his feet. . . .
> People laughed at his jokes, which were not too clever. Had
> they been so the suspicion might have arisen that Chatty har-
> boured bitter thoughts inside that neatly turbanned head.
> (*Towers*, p. 55)

Another aspect of the Bibighar affair which recalls *A Passage to India*
is the Indian memory of the incident: 'But out of it, out of all its
mysteries, to them there seemed to be at least one thing that emerged,
perhaps not clearly, but insistently, like an ache in an old wound that
had healed itself. That Daphne Manners had loved them' (*Jewel*,
pp. 167–8). This response is certainly reminiscent of the Indian
memory of Mrs Moore. And over the whole incident hovers the
belief that 'if poor Miss Manners had not been such an "innocent"
about India this distressing business would never have arisen' (*Jewel*,
p. 314). Her innocence, like Adela's naivety, led her to ignore the
boundaries between East and West, and the consequences in each
book further strengthened the resolve of Anglo-Indians to keep
themselves apart from the 'real India'.

* * *

R.K. Narayan and Paul Scott are representatives of the majority of
Indian and British writers who treat Independence in their fiction;
one may present the period from an Indian viewpoint, and the other
with a particular interest in how Independence affected the lives of
the British in India, yet essentially they both see Independence in
terms of another, philosophical, conflict between East and West. But
there was another side to the medal of Independence; the futures of
the Eurasian community and the princely states were also stakes in
the game, and like pawns in a game of chess, their fates were being
decided by others whose moves were determined for their own
profit.

John Masters's *Bhowani Junction*, although, like the majority of British novels about Independence, concerned more with the end of British rule in India than with the birth of Indian rule, is important because it portrays the problems facing the Eurasian community as Independence approached. Manohar Malgonkar's *The Princes*, however, unlike the majority of Indian novels about Independence, is concerned less with the birth of Indian rule than with the end of the rule of the princes.

In the opening paragraphs of *A Passage to India*, E.M. Forster describes Chandrapore as a city divided into *three* distinct parts:

> Houses belonging to Eurasians stand on the high ground by the railway station. Beyond the railway -- which runs parallel to the river – the land sinks, then rises again rather steeply. On this second rise is laid out the little Civil Station, and viewed hence Chandrapore appears to be a totally different place. It is a city of gardens. It is no city, but a forest sparsely scattered with huts. It is a tropical pleasance, washed by a noble river. The toddy palms and neem trees and mangoes and peepul that were hidden behind the bazaars now become visible and in their turn hide the bazaars. (p. 31)

Yet it was only when, as Allen J. Greenberger suggests, the British in India 'were finding a conflict between their constant reiteration that England was home, their love for India, and their growing realization that they had a place in neither country',[18] that some British writers turned their attention to the third group, the Eurasians.

John Masters is one of those writers and this is not surprising when one recalls that he is the very type Greenberger was referring to, having been born in India and having spent much of his life there. In the opening paragraphs of *Bhowani Junction*, Masters, like Forster, describes a city divided into three distinct communities:

> There are really three separate Bhowani's – the Railway Lines, the cantonments, where the English live, and the city, where God knows how many thousand Indians are packed in like sardines.[19]

Unlike Forster's description Masters's words also suggest the prejudice against Indians which was common in the Eurasian community. And in the opening section, narrated by the Eurasian Patrick

Taylor, further evidence of this prejudice is clearly exposed; Indians
are referred to as 'Wogs', whilst in contrast England is fondly called
'Home'. The irony of this is seen on the walls of Mr Jones's parlour:
'There were pictures of the King Emperor, the Queen Empress, and
old Sergeant Duck, and several paintings – a deer in a fog, two dogs
with a salmon, and others by famous painters' (p. 11). The paintings
of the English countryside depict scenes wholly unfamiliar to most
Eurasians, and rather than establishing their relationship with England, these paintings show the gulf which separates the Eurasians
from that country. In fact, because the Indian landscape is familiar,
the suggestion is that India is 'Home', as Victoria is fully aware
when she snaps at Patrick: 'Don't call England "home". It's not *our*
home, is it?' (p. 23). *The Monarch of the Glen* (Plate 5), to many the
epitome of Victorian art, is probably the deer in a fog that hangs on
Mr Jones's parlour wall.

   Masters is showing from the outset the dilemma facing the Eurasian
community as Independence approaches and they begin to realise
that their position in the gulf between East and West is no longer a
tenable one. Victoria, who has been away from the Eurasian community, serving as a WAC subaltern in Delhi, sees this more clearly
than most:

> She said, 'I've been four years among only Englishmen and
> Indians. Do you realise that they hardly know there *is* such a thing
> as an Anglo-Indian community? Once I heard an old English
> colonel talking to an Indian – he was a young fellow, a financial
> adviser. The colonel said, "What are you going to do about the
> Anglo-Indians when we leave?" "*We*'re not going to do anything,
> Colonel," the Indian said. "Their fate is in their own hands. They've
> just got to look around and see where they are and who they are
> – after you've gone."' (p. 26)

From here on the novel focuses on Victoria's attempts to do just that
– to look around and see where she is and who she is, and it is this
individual quest for identity, which Masters uses to symbolise the
Eurasians' search for identity, that leads Victoria to explore the
various sides of her character through her relationships with Patrick,
with the Indian Ranjit Singh Kasel and with the Englishman Rodney
Savage. These relationships examine the options that were open to
the Eurasians as Independence became an inevitability: to remain as
they were, represented by her relationship with Patrick; to embrace

the new India, seen in her relationship with Ranjit; or to leave India and try to make a new home in England (or America, or Canada, or Australia) which is the option her relationship with Rodney offers.

Victoria is dissatisfied with her relationship with Patrick because she is aware that there are alternatives, whereas Patrick, like the majority of Eurasians, will not even consider change: 'Victoria talked as if we Anglo-Indians could change, but we couldn't' (p. 26). This refusal to consider change is seen in Patrick's attitude towards his old school, St Thomas's:

> This business of St Thomas's explained exactly what I felt. The Presidency Education Trust, which was over a hundred years old, was a group of English businessmen who had got up funds to help give a good education to us Anglo-Indians and our children. Mind, we paid too, as much as we could. In 1887 the Trust built St Thomas's, a boarding school for boys, at Gondwara. Besides St Thomas's they ran day-schools in Bombay, Calcutta, and Cawnpore. What the Trust was saying to us now, in 1946, was this: 'St Thomas's doesn't pay its way. It only survives because the Provincial Government gives it more help from provincial funds than it's really entitled to, considering the number of boys it educates. An Indian government will come to power soon. Is it likely that they will continue to give special help to the education of Anglo-Indians? Of course not! So sooner or later you'll have to sell out. But there's a boom on now, and *now* is the time to sell St Thomas's. With the money, you'll be in a position to keep the day-schools open, at least, whatever happens.'
>
> All that made sense, I suppose, but what those Englishmen in Bombay didn't realize was that we *couldn't* sell St Thomas's, be-cause it was in our hearts. It, the idea of it, was part of us. Without it we'd just be Wogs like everybody else. They might just as well have said we couldn't afford trousers or topis, or told us to turn our skins black instead of khaki. (pp. 26–7)

The attempts Victoria makes to rise above the prejudice her com-munity practises towards the Indians brings her into closer contact with Patrick's Indian assistant in the railway office, Ranjit Singh Kasel. Significantly, however, it is the actions of the Englishman, Lieu-tenant Macauley, who tries to rape her, which lead to her more intimate relationship with Ranjit. Rather than being attracted by Ranjit, she is initially forced towards him by Macauley, just as the

Eurasians, rather than being attracted by India, were pushed in that direction by the British.

Victoria's decision to wear a sari, or as Mr Surabhai, the local Congress leader, puts it, 'to don the national garb' (p. 183), shows her attempt to embrace India. Yet despite this, Victoria is aware that 'However close [she] got to Ranjit there was always a thing like a very delicate gauze screen or curtain hanging down between [them]' (p. 224), and it soon becomes apparent that neither she nor Ranjit will be able to break down those final barriers. On the surface she may look Indian, but inside she is, and will remain, Eurasian.

Ranjit is a lapsed Sikh, who wishes to return to his religion, and wants Victoria to join him; again there is a parallel with the Indian historical situation. India, which has allowed its identity to be overshadowed by British rule, wishes to adopt a new, national identity, and the Eurasian community could be a part of that identity if it wished – though at the cost of losing its own identity. Victoria attempts to go through the ceremony of becoming a Sikh, but flees when the time comes for her to be given a new name. She could travel so far with him, but to adopt a new name would be to give up her own, significantly that of the first Queen Empress of India, and lose her identity. She is prepared to embrace a new India ruled by Indians, but she cannot stop being Eurasian. The fact that Ranjit lets her go, and that the ceremony proceeds without her, shows that the Indians will proceed with or without the Eurasians beside them. As Victoria explains: 'It was awful of me to run away and leave him. But he didn't *need* me, however much he loved me – and I thought he did love me, in his fashion. He didn't need me; he did need the Guru Panth' (p. 262).

Victoria's relationship with Rodney Savage is intended to show the relationship between the Eurasian community and the British community in much the same way her relationship with Ranjit explored the relationship between the Eurasians and Indians. There is no gauze screen or curtain hanging between Victoria and Rodney; their relationship is basically a sexual one. What the relationship does suggest is that the two communities can successfully meet on the surface, but that beyond the surface, or beyond the physical relationship, they have nothing in common. Victoria and Rodney both realise this after they have been on their excursion into the jungle. Intended to bring them closer together, it does in fact show that there is no strong bond between them. To use Masters's own metaphor, they can meet in the same room, but they cannot live together in it.

Victoria returns to Patrick, who, despite all his shortcomings is one of her own kind. As Patrick suggested at the beginning of the novel: 'We couldn't become English, because we were half Indian. We couldn't become Indian, because we were half English. We could only stay where we were and be what we were' (pp. 27–8).

However, whilst Victoria must be who she is, and the Eurasians must be who they are, they must also be willing to accept change. Thus, Masters resolves the conflict over St Thomas's in the only way that will secure its future, and which suggests the only way the Eurasians can secure theirs – by accepting the inevitable and by being prepared to compromise:

> [Kasel] said he couldn't promise what a Congress government in Delhi or in the province would do later, but we weren't talking about that. He thought that the school should be left going, so that such a Congress government could be free to make it fit into their plans, perhaps by enlarging it instead of abolishing it. I didn't like that idea much, about Indian boys being able to go to St Thomas's too, but after all it would be better than no one going. (p. 395)

It is implied that this future lies not in their own hands, but in the hands of the British and the nationalists. St Thomas's fate will finally be decided by the school's British governors and the new Congress government, not by the Eurasians themselves.

Thus, even the problems facing the Eurasians are ultimately a part of the conflict between East and West, and it is here that, although he attempts to be fair to both sides, Masters shows that his sympathies are with the British. The Indians he presents fall into two categories, good and bad. The good Indians, Ranjit Singh Kasel and Mr Govindaswami in particular, are those who co-operate with the British, whilst the bad Indians are those like K.P. Roy who violently oppose the Raj. Between these extremes are figures like the Congress leader Surabhai, who opposes the British, though not in the way Roy does, and who is presented as a rather comic or foolish character.

Similar divisions are evident in *Waiting for the Mahatma*, but Narayan's portrayal of the various sides of the National Movement is not so simplistically presented as a clear-cut division between good and bad.

Bhowani Junction is interesting because it examines the plight of the Eurasians at the time of Independence, and therefore probes an area of Indian history frequently ignored by both British and Indian writers. Like *Nightrunners of Bengal* and *The Far Pavilions* it has much in common with the romantic adventure tradition, yet does, nevertheless, offer a valid sense of history. Masters may not be a great writer, but he does know and love India. *Bhowani Junction* demonstrates once more that adventure novels are part of the Anglo-Indian experience, and the better ones do add to our understanding of Indian or British-Indian history.

In spite of its sympathetic intentions, according to Geoffrey Moorehouse '*Bhowani Junction* irritated [Eurasians] no end'.[20] This may well be because apart from showing the problems facing the Eurasians, Masters also shows their prejudices and shortcomings, and often presents them in a comical light.

Just as *A Passage to India* and *Bhowani Junction* begin with descriptions that show the division between the three communities within British India, *The Princes* (1963) begins with a look at the map of India which shows, not the division between the communities within British India, but the division between British India and the princely states:

The map was red and yellow. The red was for British India; the yellow for the India of the princes: the Rajas and the Maharajas, the Ranis and the Maharanis, the Nawabs, the Rawals, the Jams.

For more than a hundred years, the red and the yellow had remained exactly as they were. Then the British left, and in no time at all, the red had overrun the yellow and coloured the entire map a uniform orange. The princely states were no more.[21]

The Princes quite definitely describes an Indian India, yet it has much in common with the presentation of Independence in British novels; rather than celebrating the birth of India, it is mourning the passing of the princely states.

Both Masters's *Bhowani Junction* and Malgonkar's *The Princes* are first-person narratives, and this intimate voice is used to provide a reliable yet sympathetic guide to the Eurasian community and the world of the princes, respectively. In *Bhowani Junction* Masters shares the narrative between Patrick Taylor, Victoria Jones and Rodney Savage, providing a wider perspective than a single first-person narrator could offer. His narrators are from the Eurasian and the British communities, but not, significantly, from the Indian community; the reader must rely on Victoria's excursion into the Indian room for his or her knowledge of that world. In choosing Abhayraj as his narrator, Malgonkar has selected the limited viewpoint of someone born into a feudal system, 'the world of princely India, remote from the twentieth century' (p. 20). Abhayraj though, like Dr Shankar, the narrator of Mulk Raj Anand's *Private Life of an Indian Prince* (1953), represents 'the voice of sanity, which is pitted against the reactionary and medieval attitudes of the rulers themselves'.[22]

Malgonkar is attempting to tell the story of the lives of the Indian princes set against the changing world, as Independence approached. Thus, much time is spent describing the daily life of the Maharajas, 'the days of silk turbans and egret plumes and brocade robes and velvet slippers and the glittering life that went with them' (p. 13). He is trying to capture the feeling of the last days of the princes, rather than the age in a wider historical sense.

Like many historical novels, *The Princes* is full of composite characters, whom Malgonkar uses to show the essence of the princely 'type'. The Maharajas in both *The Princes* and *Private Life of an Indian Prince* are intended to be representatives of the five hundred or so princes who ruled states of varying sizes immediately prior to Independence. This is clearly seen when Abhayraj describes the people who were with him at the Princes' College at Agra, in a description which, all sport and no culture, emphasises the Britishness of the princes:

> Jumbo Kanil, the present Maharaja of Rajgoli, was with me. He was called Kanil Minor then. His elder brother, who won the posthumous V.C. in the Aracan, was called Kanil Major. Perhaps my closest friend was the Maharaja of Ninnore, Snappy Baindur, who broke my nose in the welterweight championship during my final year at school. He joined the Air Force during the war, and some years later was nearly, in the official phrase, derecognised as Maharaja, but was lucky to be let off with a warning. The Nawab of Waranda was our star pace bowler, although no one who sees the Nawabsahib today, with all those rolls of fat and his glazed, drink-sodden eyes, would think of him as a thin and wiry youth with the grace of a panther and a spark of genius in his fingers, or imagine that he could ever have run the four-forty in

sixty seconds. Ranjit Singh, the Raja of Joida, was there too during
my time, the one who scored the first century against the M.C.C.
touring side and then died in a polo accident. Sandy, the Maharaja
of Usoda and String, the Raja of Pusheli were in the hockey eleven
with me, and the Thakur of Konshet was my doubles partner at
tennis. (p. 83)

Whilst there may not be a Ranjit Singh, Raja of Joida, for example,
there was a famous Indian cricketer by the name of Ranjitsinhji who
was the Maharaja Jam Saheb of Nawangar.[23] The captain of the Indian cricket team which toured England in 1946 was the Nawab of
Pataudi.[24] Further, the Maharaja in this novel, whilst one cannot say
he is based on a particular person, is a true enough picture to cause
people to speculate about his real identity, and is at least fictionally
true, as this extract from an interview with Malgonkar illustrates:

J.Y.D.:   E.M. Forster in *Hill of Devi* describes one of the
               princes of India. This prince or Maharaja reminds
               me of your prince in *The Princes*. (He had an
               English tutor, a concubine, a feud with the Deccan
               Brahmins, etc.) Are the characters in *The Princes*
               drawn from real life?

Malgonkar: It is surprising that you should mention it, because
               I also know the very same prince of that very same
               state very well. The prince that E.M. Forster knew
               died soon after Forster's visit. And his son, who
               became Maharaja after him is a great friend of mine
               and I am friendly with him today. So I couldn't take
               liberty with the characters and lie about my friend's
               father. But I am familiar with the state and what-
               ever comparisons you see are perhaps real; I may
               have drawn something from my experience, which
               is also E.M. Forster's experience.[25]

And as is so often the case, those events which appear the most
fictitious are firmly based on fact. The story of the Bedar's treasure in
the Patalpat fort is based on the famous Jaipore treasure:

Malgonkar: I am afraid my parallel was with the Jaipore treas-
               ure. In fact, anyone who has visited Jaipore and

> stayed in the Palace was shown their fort which is
> on a hilltop. Well, the Jaipore treasure is believed to
> have been, and was, where the prince or maharaja
> visited only once in his lifetime and could take out
> whatever he wanted.[26]

Malgonkar is deliberately showing an aspect of this period of history not treated by most novelists.

He does, however, firmly root his story in its historical period. As in the Scott tradition of the historical novel, real historical figures are in the background of his story. There are regular references, both general and specific, to Gandhi, Nehru and the National Movement on the one side, and to Wavell, Mountbatten and the British on the other. In Anand's *Private Life of an Indian Prince*, historical figures are again in the background; one, however, briefly steps onto the main stage – Sardar Patel, who was the Deputy Prime Minister in the late 1940s and the man responsible for overseeing the accession of the princely states to the Indian Union.

Throughout *The Princes*, Abhay's growth is set within the framework of verifiable rational events. Thus the reader learns that 'The days of [Abhayraj's] boyhood were also the days of Mr. Gandhi's nation-wide agitation for self-rule' (p. 65), and that 'The year Charudutt [Abhay's half-brother] left for Kitchener College at Delhi, the anti-salt tax campaign was in full swing' (p. 69).

Such references to Gandhi also allow Malgonkar to show the princes' attitude towards the nationalists:

> My father had banned all the nationalist papers such as the
> *Chronicle* of Bombay and the *Hindustan Times* of Delhi, and had
> promulgated ordinances in the state to keep in step with the
> Viceroy's ordinances legalizing preventive detention, and indeed
> had kept well ahead of the British parts of India in the race for
> repressive legislation. He bustled about energetically, trying to
> make 'examples' of people associated with the agitation. He dis-
> missed a clerk in his octroi department because he had seen the
> man's son wearing the white khaddar cap. And once he was so
> enraged by a group of people shouting 'Inquilab-zindabad', which
> meant 'long live the revolution', after his car had passed, that he
> had all of them rounded up and sent to prison for three weeks.
> (p. 65)

Similarly, when Abhayraj talks to Kanakchand, his Untouchable schoolfriend and later a nationalist agitator, about the salt tax he tells the reader: 'I was quite taken aback to hear Kanakchand refer to Mr. Gandhi as the Mahatma, the great man. My father always spoke of him as "that man Gandhi"' (p. 69). In *Private Life of an Indian Prince*, Anand illustrates not only the attitude of the princes towards the Congress Party, but also the attitudes of the Congress Party towards the princes.

The Second World War allows Malgonkar to show the selfish nature of the loyalty of the princes to the British crown:

> For the whole week, as the talk of war gathered momentum, my father had been busy exchanging wires and emissaries with his friends amongst the princes, and between them they had worked out the wording of the telegram they were going to send to the Viceroy the moment the actual declaration of war came out.
>
> I was with my father in the billiard room when we heard Neville Chamberlain's broadcast telling the world that we were at war with Germany. My father sent for his secretary and dashed off the agreed telegram to the Viceroy, ordered another whisky and soda and resumed his interrupted game. As far as he was concerned, he was done with the war: he had demonstrated his loyalty, he had formally placed 'the entire resources of the state' at the disposal of the Viceroy. (p. 133)

Abhayraj's immediate decision to apply for a commission in the army demonstrates that *his* loyalty, too, is based on selfishness – his desire to get away from home.

Malgonkar makes reference to a number of newspapers and periodicals in his novel, using them to specify the period. The shortages of the war, made clear in the presents Abhayraj buys for Minnie – such as nylon stockings and Chanel No. 5 – are emphasised in a passing comment on *Strand*: '... the packet of photographs lay on the coffee table beside the previous day's *Statesman* and the latest issue of the *Strand* magazine now shrunk to pocket size because of the paper shortage' (p. 168).

His reference to *Home and Outdoors* serves a number of purposes:

> Today, nineteen years afterwards, Kamala looks entirely different from the girl I married, for she has learnt to make the best of her looks, and the years have given her features more definition

and a look of refinement. In a certain light, she might even be called beautiful. Washington Bond, the society photographer from *Home and Outdoors* who came to India to do a series on the homes of the Indian princes, has posed her with her face turned slightly upwards and to the left and called her one of the loveliest amongst the Maharanis – not that Kamala is any longer a Maharani. (p. 230)

The novelist is making effective use of hindsight, viewing the past from the present, clearly established, here and elsewhere, as 1963. The passage also indicates that there is enough distance in time for some degree of objectivity, yet the events are recent enough to give verisimilitude to the fiction that these are the memories of a first-person narrator.

In *Bhowani Junction* and *The Princes*, respectively, Masters and Malgonkar look at areas neglected by most of the writers who choose to write about Independence. Perhaps none of the writers discussed in this chapter present a fully-rounded picture of the age, but each has much to offer to our understanding of the period, and together they do provide the reader with a vivid sense of the historical sequence leading up to the independence of India.

6

Partition

Muslims said the Hindus had planned and started the killing. According to the Hindus, the Muslims were to blame. The fact is, both sides killed. Both shot and stabbed and speared and clubbed. Both tortured. Both raped.[1]

The early taste of freedom was a bitter one, washed down by the blood of half a million newly-free Indians and Pakistanis. The violence of the time could not be ignored by anyone writing about the period, and thus Paul Scott includes scenes of communal violence in the final volume of his *Raj Quartet*, notably an attack on a train, in which one of the protagonists, Ahmed Kasim, is murdered along with hundreds of others. This brief period of history has interested mainly Indian and Pakistani writers. Bapsi Sidhwa's novel *The Bride* (1983), though not a 'partition novel', does describe the violence of this period, which is the starting point for the later events of the novel. Similarly, Balachandra Rajan's *The Dark Dancer* (1959), although again not a 'partition novel', includes an horrific attack on a refugee train, as does Manohar Malgonkar's *A Bend in the Ganges* (1964). Indeed attacks on refugee trains are so common in the literature of Partition that they almost become a leitmotif for the period.

None of these novels is, however, primarily concerned with Partition; the main interest of each lies elsewhere, in the problems facing a young England-returned Indian on the eve of Independence (*The Dark Dancer*), the horror of tribal traditions (*The Bride*), or the history of a much wider period (Scott's *Raj Quartet*). Two novels in which the primary focus is on the historical events surrounding the partition of the Indian sub-continent into two countries, India and Pakistan, are Chaman Nahal's *Azadi* (1975), which won the Sahitya Akademi Award in 1977, and Kushwant Singh's *Train to Pakistan* or *Mano Majra*.[2] Neither of these novels is concerned with the East–West encounter which has been a feature of much of the fiction so far discussed in this study. They record a level of violence similar to that found in the Mutiny fiction: yet beneath the violence these novels speak more than anything else of humanity – they are optimistic novels, at least on an individual level.

Chaman Nahal's *Azadi* is concerned in particular with the plight of Hindu and Sikh refugees who are forced to leave their homes in Sialkot in the Punjab when it becomes part of the newly-formed Pakistan. Through the family of Lala Kanshi Ram, a Hindu grain merchant, we see the older generation being suddenly robbed of the comfort of a hard-earned old age, and in Arun, his son, we see the younger generation robbed of a fruitful start in life. The leading characters are all fictitious, but the events Nahal describes are those that did happen to thousands of similar families, Hindu and Sikh or Muslim, fleeing eastwards or westwards across the Punjab in the weeks following Independence. And in the background there are a number of historical characters – Gandhi, Nehru and Jinnah – though there is fictional licence in Nahal's account of a meeting the Mahatma addressed in Sialkot in 1929. As Nahal tells us in his brief 'Author's Note', 'The account of Gandhi's tour of the Punjab . . . is entirely fictitious'.[3] Though it is not historically true, this account is, like the meeting Gandhi addresses in R.K. Narayan's *Waiting for the Mahatma*, fictionally true.

The novel is clearly dated throughout, from the opening sentence, 'It was the third of June, 1947' (p. 13), to the closing scenes on the day of Gandhi's assassination in Delhi on 30 January 1948. During the eight months the novel covers, a number of important historical dates are carefully cited. The first of these is that which opens the novel, the date of Mountbatten's address to the nation which first confirmed the fact of Partition, and from which stemmed the terrible events Nahal describes in *Azadi*, followed by the announcement 'in a press conference that the date of freedom would be advanced from January 1948 to August 1947' (p. 91). Both these events are also referred to in Scott's *Raj Quartet* where he describes the cartoons drawn by Halki in response to the announcements. These and the many other dates place the events which overtake Lala Kanshi Ram in their historical context. The story of the fictitious characters is at the heart of this novel, and through the juxtaposing of the fictional story with the clear historical signposts, Nahal shows the consequences those political decisions had on the lives of the common people.

An even broader historical context is established in the novel through references to historical events which pre-date freedom and

Partition. Arun, Lala Kanshi Ram's son, his Muslim friend Munir and Bill Davidson, the English sergeant who has befriended them, discuss the political events that occurred in the years leading up to 1947, and thus draw those events to the reader's attention:

> Arun and Munir had first met Davidson in 1945. Gandhi was released from prison in 1944, but Nehru was still inside at that time, and the Quit India resolution of 1942 was very much alive in the mind of every Englishman. Through the following two years, through the arrival of Wavell as the Viceroy, the release of Nehru and the other Congress leaders, the Simla Conference of 1945, the British Parliamentary Mission and the British Cabinet Mission of 1946, the two Indians and their English well-wisher had reviewed all the events, and Bill Davidson maintained all along the Indian leaders were pushing things too fast. (p. 121)

And Nahal does not ignore the mixed feelings that existed towards the British in the years immediately prior to Independence. Lala Kanshi Ram himself views them with a mixture of hatred and respect:

> He hated them for what they had done to his country and wanted azadi. . . .
> But deeper down, he also admired the British – in any case he enjoyed the safety of the British Raj and hugged it lovingly. All said and done, the British had brought some kind of peace to this torn land. (p. 18)

This final statement is particularly poignant in the light of the events Nahal is about to describe in this novel.

Earlier periods of the struggle are also recalled in the relationship of Lala Kanshi Ram and Chaudhri Barkat Ali, the fathers of Arun and Munir, whose backgrounds, despite their different faiths, are similar. Chaudhri Barkat Ali recalls the meeting he and Lala Kanshi Ram attended to hear Gandhi speak in 1929, the Champaran agitation of 1917, and the Mutiny of 1857. The fact that Chaudhri Barkat Ali's and Lala Kanshi Ram's attendance at the meeting in 1929 is only fictionally true, whereas the Champaran agitation (amongst the indigo workers in Bihar) and the Mutiny are historically true, does not lessen the novel's historicity in any way; rather it helps to integrate the fictional story with the historical one.

The presence of Lala Kanshi Ram and Chaudhri Barkat Ali at the Sialkot meeting during Gandhi's fictional tour of the Punjab in 1929 allows Nahal to show that not all Indians saw Gandhi in the same light. Many were not interested in Gandhi as a freedom fighter:

> Before Gandhi could say a word, before he was even properly introduced, half the gathering at Ramtalai got up to leave. It was the women who were leaving. . . . When Gandhi showed up and they had seen him, they felt no need to stay there longer. They were not interested in politics, nor in Gandhi's speeches. For them Gandhi was a mahatma, a religious figure, and they had come only to pay homage to a saint. (p. 104)

Even the two friends respond differently; Chaudhri Barkat Ali is overawed by Gandhi's speech, whereas Lala Kanshi Ram is rather more reserved:

> Comparing him with the English sahibs he had seen, he regretfully reminded himself the man was not even dressed properly for the occasion. Seventy thousand persons had assembled here to greet him and he had come half naked! (p. 105)

Similarly, Nehru's speech, which followed the Viceroy's, and accepted the fact of Partition, was met with dismay and criticism for their leader that is rarely recorded:

> [Nehru's] people were indulgent of him, the crowds would laugh at his temper and dismiss his angry words. . . .
> This day he said no abrupt words to them. He sounded meek and gentle, he sounded in sorrow. And in spite of that he could win no sympathy from this group gathered in the mirror-studded living room of Bibi Amar Vati. (pp. 64–5)

Yet most surprising of all is the mixed reception with which the Punjabi refugees in the Delhi camp greet the news of Gandhi's assassination. Mixed with the mute disbelief are the words of Bibi Amar Vati: 'It's good he is. He ruined us' (p. 362). But it is in response to Gandhi's death that Nahal attempts to enunciate the real meaning of Independence:

For the first time Lala Kanshi Ram became aware of a blessing azadi had brought them. The crowds in the bazaar were thick. Some shops were closed, but many were still open. Groups of people stood all over in the bazaar, and each face was blank. They were all refugees from West Punjab and there was not a man in that crowd who had not suffered in the riots. Yet they all looked crestfallen, as if this death was a personal loss. Some did speak in the vein of Bibi Amar Vati, blaming everything on Gandhi. Most stood quiet with pursed lips, afraid of bursting into tears. Those who talked, talked in hoarse asides. As soon as a news bulletin came on, all noise died down. After the news bulletin, they resumed talking in subdued tones.

What impressed Lala Kanshi Ram was the pride with which each man stood. He would be blind if he didn't see that. He thought of the pre-independence days, before the nation was free. How self-conscious the people were then! An Indian leader dying and the crowd feeling openly for him? It was unthinkable. They sorrowed and they came out on the roads, but there was no dignity in it. They were afraid of persecution at the hands of the British, they were afraid of violence, they were afraid of their own people who might betray them. And in reaction to those fears, they went into excesses. They wept too loudly or they shouted too loudly. Today the men stood in pride – evenly balanced, firm, sure of themselves. Unlike the past, there was no leader urging them to demonstrate their feelings. The feelings had their own recourse. Lala Kanshi Ram raised his head with pride and stretched back his shoulders. He was unrestricted now, he was untrammelled. (pp. 368-9)

This passage, however, seems rather artificial, and cannot be accepted wholeheartedly. Having extended his narrative into the refugee camps of Delhi, this is clearly an attempt to put some optimism into it. But despite Lala Kanshi Ram's awareness of a new pride in the Indian people, he is also aware, as is Nahal, that these people are housed in refugee camps, and that all over India and Pakistan, refugees are living in similar camps going through the long and heart-rending process of re-settlement.

Nahal draws attention to the bitter reality of the situation facing the Punjabi refugees. Having fled the religious and communal violence that swept the Punjab after the announcement of Partition, they then had to face the prejudice that was practised towards Punjabis by the people of Delhi, evident particularly in their search for housing: 'The native people in Delhi seemed so afraid of the Punjabis. The moment they gave out their identity, the door was shut on them. "Punjabis? Never! You're too quarrelsome"' (p. 351).

Nor do Lala Kanshi Ram and Arun fare any better at the Refugee Office or the various offices of the Area Custodians of evacuee property where they find that the power given to the officers, many of them Punjabi refugees themselves, has thoroughly corrupted them:

> 'It takes a thousand rupees to put the sahib in a good mood,' whispered one of the clerks at the Bara Tuti office to Lala Kanshi Ram. Lala Kanshi Ram recoiled at the information. That would leave him with only a thousand. At each different office, some clerk of the government passed the same information on to him. (pp. 347–8)

This aspect of freedom stands in marked contrast to Lala Kanshi Ram's memory of the British Raj, under which the English Superintendent of Police would not even accept *dalis* (gifts of baskets of fruit or bottles of Scotch whisky) sent to him on occasions like Diwali. Nahal is questioning the reality of Independence and exactly what it means to those forced out of their homes and off their land.

At the heart of this novel, though, is the question of humanity. There is no doubt that Part Two, 'The Storm', which recounts the attack on the refugee camp and the ordeal of the convoy of refugees who walk to the borders, demonstrates a loss of humanity. The height of inhumanity is perhaps the parade of Hindu women who had been abducted by the Muslims:

> The procession arrived. Arun counted them. There were forty women, marching two abreast. Their ages varied from sixteen to thirty, although, to add to the grotesqueness of the display, there were two women, marching right at the end of the column, who must have been over sixty. They were all stark naked. Their heads were completely shaven; so were their armpits. So were their pubic regions. Shorne of their body hair and clothes, they looked like baby girls, or like the bald embryos one sees preserved in methylated spirit. Only the breasts and the hips gave away the age. The women walked awkwardly, looking only at the ground.

They were all crying, though their eyes shed no tears. Their faces were formed into grimaces and they were sobbing. Their arms were free, but so badly had they been used, so wholly their spirits crushed, their morale shattered, none of them made any attempt to cover themselves with their hands. (p. 296)

But even amidst this grotesque and sickening display there are signs of humanity. Firstly there is Arun's reaction to the spectacle: 'he sat down on the shop-front where he and Suraj were standing and he wanted to throw up' (p. 298). More significantly, there is the reaction of the Muslim hakim in front of whose shop Arun sits:

The hakim sahib had covered his face with his hands and was rocking a little and he was saying, 'Allah, Allah, Allah!' And then he knelt on his knees, raised his arms and spread his hands before him as while saying namaaz. There was the look of infinite pain on his face. His thin, frail eyelids rested on his eyes as if they would never open again. And moving his outstretched hands, like begging alms, he murmured in Punjabi, 'Rabbul-Alamin, for-give these cruel men. And, oh, my Allah, oh Rabbah, protect these women!' (p. 298)

The violence was not one-sided though, and Nahal makes this clear in *Azadi* through skilful use of fictional techniques. Having shown the horror quite vividly as it affected the lives of his leading characters during their exodus from Pakistan, he effectively mirrors each atrocity they have endured with one on the Indian side of the border which they witness or hear of as they continue their journey eastwards. This time it is Muslim homes that have been burnt, Muslim shops that have been looted, and in Amritsar it is a group of Muslim women who are subjected to the degradation that Arun had pre-viously seen in Pakistan:

Arun thought of the afternoon in Narowal when Suraj and he were together. He saw the dome of the Golden Temple in the background and wondered if any Sikh out there was weeping for these women. (p. 327)

Nahal does not need to describe the horror a second time; the mirror technique successfully recalls all the horror of the earlier incident on the other side of the border. Similarly, the trainload of massacred Muslims that delays their journey on to Delhi mirrors the massacre of Hindu and Sikh refugees near Wazirabad which included Lala Kanshi Ram's daughter and son-in-law. Nahal places the burden of responsibility as much on the Indians as on the Pakistanis when he writes: 'Indians soldiers stood guard with their machine guns, but they were only a facade – like their counterparts in Pakistan. They had failed to protect the Muslims' (p. 328).

Lala Kanshi Ram's realisation of this is significant: 'I can't hate the Muslims anymore. . . . What I mean is, whatever the Muslims did to us in Pakistan, we're doing it to them here! . . . Every single horror' (p. 338). Only through the understanding and humanity that Lala Kanshi Ram displays here is there any hope for the future, just as in *Nightrunners of Bengal* the future depended on the humanity of people like Rodney Savage and Sir Hector.

Martin Levin, writing in the *New York Times Book Review*, suggests that *Azadi* is 'full of lessons that will never be learned'.[4] But this is perhaps unfairly pessimistic. Lala Kanshi Ram does learn the lesson and so does Arun. In a novel full of horror, these are bright lights indeed.

Although Kushwant Singh's *Train to Pakistan* does not contain many specific historical signposts, it nevertheless, like *Azadi*, captures the feeling of its age. The action of the novel is not simply set against the historical background, as it is in *Azadi*; rather the historical period, which Singh clearly defines, is set against a timeless geographical background, as are the events of J.G. Farrell's *The Siege of Krishnapur* and E.M. Forster's *A Passage to India*. In *Train to Pakistan* this timeless background is established through descriptions of the landscape, the weather, the eloquent description of the monsoons (pp. 108–11), the endless rhythm of the seasons which is at the very heart of village life.

Against this background *Train to Pakistan* is very much the story of Partition and the communal slaughter which remains today as the major image of that period. It is also a story of dacoity, through which Singh comments on the nature of the Indian police, and through the arrival of Iqbal in Mano Majra Singh includes the activities of the communists in this period. Finally, it is the story of the villain Juggut Singh, *budmash* number ten on the police register, whose story gives the novel a human and sympathetic quality (as do the stories of Moorthy in Raja Rao's *Kanthapura* and Sriram in R.K. Narayan's *Waiting for the Mahatma*) which is such an important characteristic of this type of fiction. Thus, in his three central characters, Juggut Singh, Iqbal and Hukum Chand the magistrate (all, incidentally, single adult males), Singh is able to present three different points of view of Partition, none of which is a simple Hindu–Muslim comparison.

These various aspects of the novel are skilfully woven together into a whole which portrays the horror of the period with sympathy, and attempts to understand rather than condemn.

In the opening sentence Kushwant Singh immediately sets *Train to Pakistan* in its historical perspective: 'The summer of 1947 was not like other Indian summers' (p. 9). This establishes the date, and introduces a note of foreboding. Singh then goes on to give the context of the period; the communal riots in Calcutta, and in the Punjab and Northwest Frontier Province Sikhs and Hindus fleeing East and Muslims fleeing West.

From this view of the wider conflict Singh takes the reader to the tiny Punjabi village of Mano Majra which he uses as a microcosm. Whereas Nahal, in *Azadi*, attempts to show the history of the period on a large scale, Singh uses the smallest of scales and suggests that if the reader understands the part he or she will also understand the whole. Mano Majra is representative of thousands of small villages dotted along the newly-created border between India and Pakistan; the villagers are representatives of the millions of peasants – Sikh, Hindu and Muslim – who were caught up in the bloody events which followed Partition:

> By the summer 1947, when the creation of the new state of Pakistan was formally announced, ten million people – Muslims and Hindus and Sikhs – were in flight. By the time the monsoon broke, almost a million of them were dead, and all of northern India was in arms, in terror, or in hiding. The only remaining oases of peace were a scatter of little villages lost in the remote reaches of the frontier. One of these villages was Mano Majra. (p. 10)

Once Singh has shifted the focus of his story to Mano Majra, he takes time to establish the harmony within the village, where Sikhs and Muslims live side by side as they have done for generations. The importance of the railway is also emphasised. The railway is the very heartbeat of Mano Majra; it is the whistle of the early morning express which wakes the village, the midday express which signals a rest period for the villagers, and,

> When the goods train steams in, they say to each other, 'There is the goods train'. It is like saying goodnight. . . . By the time it leaves, the children are asleep. The older people wait for its rumble over the bridge to lull them to slumber. Then life in Mano Majra is stilled, save for the dogs barking at the trains that pass in the night.
> It had always been so, until the summer of 1947. (pp. 13–14)

The repetition of the date (it is the third mention of 'the summer of 1947' in six pages) sits uneasily with the peaceful picture of Mano Majra, and prepares the reader for the events which are to follow.

As the summer of 1947 progresses, the train-regulated lives of the villagers are gradually disrupted: 'Since partition of the country . . . the trains were often four or five hours late and sometimes as many as twenty. When they came, they were crowded with Sikh and Hindu refugees from Pakistan or with Muslims from India' (p. 44). However, few of these refugees get off the train in Mano Majra, and the horror that is slowly gripping the countryside remains little more than a rumour in Mano Majra.

One person who does get off the train in Mano Majra is a young man named Iqbal: 'He could be a Muslim, Iqbal Mohammed. He could be a Hindu, Iqbal Chand, or a Sikh, Iqbal Singh. It was one of the few names common to the three communities' (p. 48). In Mano Majra, a Sikh village, he is content to be known as Iqbal Singh; he is, in fact, a communist agitator, Comrade Iqbal, who has been sent to turn the villagers against the government in Delhi.

By introducing the communists, the police and the Sikh extremists, Singh also shows how some groups complicate the issues by using the political unrest for their own ends. In this he is far more effective than Nahal, whose villain, Abdul Ghani, the hookah-maker, is a rather cardboard character, though the opportunism of Captain Rahmat-Ullah Khan in Nahal's novel is well handled. Singh is able, through Iqbal, to introduce some humour into what could so easily have been a very bleak novel. It is Iqbal who is out of touch with his countrymen in the villages, rather than the government in Delhi as he suggests. He carries with him an air mattress to place over his charpoy, water purification tablets and toothpaste, the latter a marked contrast to the *keekur* twig the villagers such as Meet Singh use to brush their teeth. He also produces 'a tin of sardines, a tin of Australian butter and a packet of dry biscuits' (p. 47); Meet Singh watches 'with disgusted fascination' as he eats 'fish complete with head, eyes and tail' (p. 49).

Through the contrast between Iqbal and the villagers Kushwant Singh reveals much about the lives of the peasants at this time. Their questions, 'What is all this about Pakistan and Hindustan?' and 'Babuji, tell us, why did the English leave?' (p. 61), show how little the lives of the villagers have been touched by British rule or by the National Movement, and how unnecessary the Partition riots really are. This ignorance of the villagers is emphasised by Bhabani Bhattacharya too, in his novel *So Many Hungers!* (1947), set in Bengal during the last stages of the Second World War.

Iqbal's arguments do not carry much weight with the villagers; to them freedom means very little; 'Freedom is for the educated people who fought for it. We were slaves of the English, now we will be slaves of the educated Indians – or the Pakistanis' (p. 62). The villagers' ignorance of the outside world is also a good reason for Singh to include little in the way of wider historical perspective, though Gandhi, whose name had spread to every village in the sub-continent, is mentioned on two occasions which shows the awe in which the great man is held by the villagers.

The increasing violence is represented by further disruption to the trains, and to the lives of the villagers:

> Trains became less punctual than ever before and many more started to run through at night. . . . Goods trains had stopped running altogether, so there was no lullaby to lull them to sleep. Instead, ghost trains went past at odd hours between midnight and dawn, disturbing the dreams of Mano Majra. (pp. 92–3)

But it is only when the railway delivers a train-load of corpses to Mano Majra that the village is finally and irreversibly touched by the horror that is all around it. The arrival of this train places the thin end of the wedge between the two communities:

> When it was discovered that the train had brought a full load of corpses, a heavy brooding silence descended on the village. People barricaded their doors and many stayed up all night talking

in whispers. Everyone felt his neighbour's hand against him, and thought of finding friends and allies. (p. 137)

It is not, however, the knowledge of the terrible violence alone which drives the wedge between the two communities who had lived together as brothers for generations. Rather, the wedge is driven between them by the careful plans of the magistrate, Hukum Chand, who believes that if the Muslims leave Mano Majra there will be no trouble.

The naivety of this attitude is soon seen. Even after the Muslims have left Mano Majra for the refugee camp in Chundunugger further signs of the trouble reach the village in the form of corpses carried by both the railway and the river, the heartbeat and life-blood of Mano Majra.

It also comes in the form of extremist Sikhs who counsel the villagers in hatred and violence: 'for each Hindu or Sikh they kill, kill two Mussulmans' (p. 171). This kind of talk, the very opposite of Gandhi's teaching, caused much of the hatred. Meet Singh's voice of reason, 'what have the Muslims here done to us for us to kill them in revenge for what Muslims in Pakistan are doing?' (p. 171), goes unheard against the young Sikh agitator's vitriolic attack, and a number of villagers are persuaded to help attack a trainload of Muslims bound for Pakistan.

Meet Singh's final protest that 'The train will have Mano Majra Muslims on it' (p. 173) is ignored, and the magistrate, although aware of the impending attack, will do nothing concrete to prevent the slaughter, rationalising that the possibility of four or five hundred Muslims being slaughtered on the train is better than thousands being massacred in the camp. His only attempt to prevent the slaughter is to release Iqbal and Juggut Singh in the hope that one or other of them may be able to persuade the villagers to call off the attack.

Singh is critical here of both Iqbal and the Magistrate. Iqbal is quick to suggest Meet Singh should do something to stop the attack, but when in return Meet Singh suggests Iqbal should speak to the villagers, pointing out that after all that was his reason for coming to the village, he sings a different song: 'Bhaiji, when people go about with guns and spears you can only talk back with guns and spears. If you cannot do that, then it is best to keep out of their way' (p. 193). Hukum Chand and Iqbal, faced with the problem of the anti-cipated attack on the refugee train are rendered impotent by their intellectual grasp of the situation. Like Forster, Singh appears to be suggesting that the Indian situation, in this instance Partition, is too complex, the possibilities too tangled, the differences between right and wrong too blurred, for a rational decision to be reached. Thus Hukum Chand and Iqbal simply fail to act. And like Forster, Singh appears to distrust intellectual attempts to understand India.

In the end it is the uneducated Juggut Singh, known by everyone as a *budmash*, a rogue or bad lot, who, through simple heroism, prompted by his love for the Muslim girl Nooran, saves the train, albeit at the cost of his own life. It is ironic that it should be Juggut who gains the reader's sympathy; his petty dacoity pales into insignificance compared to the behaviour of others around him. Kushwant Singh, like Nahal, Masters, Farrell and Forster, is suggesting that hope only exists through the humanity of individuals. Juggut Singh's sacrifice shows that love and humanity can win against all the odds.

Singh concludes his novel with further illustrations of the three points of view held by his central characters. Juggut's instinctive sacrifice is in sharp contrast to Iqbal's whisky-induced sleep and Hukum Chand's tearful prayers, and indeed it is described immediately after the chilling stories of inhumanity that Hukum Chand, in his despair, recalls:

> There was Sundari, the daughter of Hukum Chand's orderly. She had made her tryst with destiny on the road to Gujranwala. She had been married four days and both her arms were covered with red lacquer bangles and the henna on her palms was still a deep vermilion. She had not yet slept with Mansa Ram. Their relatives had not left them alone for a minute. She had hardly seen his face through her veil. Now he was taking her to Gujranwala where he worked as a peon and had a little room of his own in the Sessions Court compound. There would be no relatives and he would certainly try it. He did not seem particularly keen, sitting in the bus talking loudly to all the other passengers. Men often pretended indifference. No one would really believe that she wanted him either – what with the veil across her face and not a word! 'Do not take any of the lacquer bangles off. It brings bad luck,' her friends had said to her. 'Let him break them when he makes love to you and mauls you.' There were a dozen on each of her arms, covering them from the wrists to the elbows. She felt them with her fingers. They were hard and brittle. He would have

to do a lot of hugging and savaging to break them. She stopped day-dreaming as the bus pulled up. There were large stones on the road. Then hundreds of people surrounded them. Everyone was ordered off the bus. Sikhs were just hacked to death. The clean-shaven were stripped. Those that were circumcised were forgiven. Those that were not, were circumcised. Not just the foreskin: the whole thing was cut off. She who had not really had a good look at Mansa Ram was shown her husband completely naked. They held him by the arms and legs and one man cut off his penis and gave it to her. The mob made love to her. She did not have to take off any one of her bangles. They were all smashed as she lay in the road, being taken by one man and another and another. That should have brought her a lot of good luck! (pp. 202–3)

Atrocities like this can only be prevented by the love and humanity of people like Juggut. The irony of the phrase 'The mob made love to her' is a reminder of other imagined or real rapes, in *A Passage to India*, and Scott's *Raj Quartet*, and recalls Nahal's description of the procession of women in *Azadi*, already discussed. The sudden, dramatic impact of Singh's passage, and the superb way he handles the scene, showing Sundari's thoughts about the consummation of her marriage being interrupted by the castration of her husband followed by her own brutal rape, is more effective than Nahal's somewhat didactic, though intensely moving, passage.

Further, this passage introduces once more the glass bangles, which have been a recurrent image in *Train to Pakistan*. At the beginning of the novel Malli and his dacoits throw a package of glass bangles over Juggut's wall:

There was a muffled sound of breaking glass in the courtyard.

'O Juggia,' he called in a falsetto voice, 'Juggia!' He winked at his companions. 'Wear these bangles, Juggia. Wear these bangles and put henna on your palms.'

'Or give them to the weaver's daughter,' one of the gunmen yelled. (p. 19)

The bangles which are intended as an insult to Juggut, a sign of his weakness, are in fact a symbol of his love and humanity, just as the bangles Sundari wears are a sign of love. The breaking of the bangles, which should be a further symbol of love and passion is in both cases inverted, becoming a symbol of the lack of love and humanity evident at this time.

Juggut Singh is of great importance to the novel; he is the kind of figure whom the writer of fiction can bring to history and in so doing add sympathy and understanding. Juggut Singh's love for Nooran is skilfully handled, without any of the sentimentality that overshadows the unlikely love stories of John Masters's novels, and to some extent those of Manohar Malgonkar. Unlike those love stories, Juggut Singh's love for Nooran never interferes with the historical purpose of Singh's novel, but enhances it.

Train to Pakistan is a novel about a particular time, despite the absence of frequent historical signposts of the type found in many of the novels discussed. It is also about a particular place, a regional novel, which raises once more the question of Indian identity. In neither *Train to Pakistan* nor in *Azadi* is this simply a question of religion, as the British appear to have viewed it. Indeed, this failure on the part of the British to see beyond the simple Hindu–Muslim question is taken up by Nahal in *Azadi*. On his first meeting with Arun and Munir, Bill Davidson expresses his surprise at their relationship:

> 'Are you two good friends?' he asked.
> Munir and Arun gave no reply, but looked at each other and shook hands with broad smiles.
> 'How is that? A Hindu and a Muslim?'
> 'Do you find that so odd?' asked Arun.
> 'It is not very common, is it?'
> 'That's what you have been told by the government. You should visit the villages and see for yourself. What you've seen is only towns. In every village you'll find hundreds of others like us.'
> (pp. 120–1)

In the same novel, the strong sense of regional identity is shown in the difference in looks between Punjabi and Kashmiri women, and by Lala Kanshi Ram's interest in the vibrant Punjabi language with its glorious expletives. In *Train to Pakistan* too, Singh uses the idiom of the Punjabi villagers to give his characters a strong regional identity, as Shakti Batra has illustrated in an essay entitled 'Two Partition Novels'.[5] In the large town of Sialkot, Lala Kanshi Ram's identity is further defined by wealth and by status in business terms, whereas in the village of Mano Majra, Singh shows that identity is very much a matter of position in the age-old village hierarchy. Whilst it is, therefore, partly dependent on religion (the Sikhs as landowners, the Muslims as their tenants), it is not wholly determined by it. Juggut Singh, for example, is a *budmash* because his father, and *his* father before *him*, have been. Identity, then, is also related to the size of the city or village of one's origin.

The essential difference between these two novels is that *Azadi*, which quite overtly seeks to give the reader a great deal of factual information about the period, tends to be didactic, whilst *Train to Pakistan* is more dramatic, and less linear. The time-sense of *Azadi*, to use Nicholas Berdyaev's three basic categories for defining time-history (cosmic time, historical time and existential time), is historical or linear.[6] Time and history in Nahal's novel could be represented by a horizontal line which plots the history of Partition. In *Train to Pakistan*, Singh uses cosmic time, which is essentially cyclic, and suggests the endless recurrence of things: the monsoons, the trains, even the lives of his characters. Indeed, the fact that Nooran is carrying Juggut's child emphasises this sense of cosmic time.

Further, Singh's novel follows a more complex group of characters in a plot which involves much more moral decision than Nahal's. *Train to Pakistan* stops at the height of one successful individual action, and therefore ends with impact and optimism. *Azadi*, on the other hand, covers a longer period of time and follows its main characters into the sombre state of refugee life, thus giving the reader far more information about the period, but at the same time losing impact towards the end.

Both authors, however, treat the horror of the period with sympathy, and the various elements of the novels are woven together into a whole that seeks to understand rather than to condemn. The optimism of each lies in its portrayal of the love and humanity of individuals in the face of the horror which engulfs them.

7

The End of
the Old Order

*What galled him most, and this he did talk about, was that history would
now be revised and rewritten. All dictatorships meddled with history.*[1]

Although the British Raj officially came to an end on 14 August 1947,
not all the British left India. Those who remained did so for a variety
of reasons: some to serve in the army of the newly-independent
India, others to work in the administration of that country, still
others to work in the commercial sector, for both Indian and foreign
companies. Some stayed because they loved India and knew no
other country, others, because they realised the money they had and
the pensions they would be entitled to would not keep them in the
same comfort in England as in India.

Those who chose to stay on were, like Tusker and Lucy Smalley in
Paul Scott's *Staying On*, the last sahibs and memsahibs, the last
remnants of the Empire, but they were not the last foreigners to be
drawn by India and to inhabit the fiction of India. India, and all that
it meant to the British imagination, the myths of a fabled land,
remained as a legacy for a new generation. These latter were the
travellers of the 1960s and 1970s who were drawn to India for a
variety of reasons, spiritual, cultural, or simply for what Indians call
'the dreaming drugs'.[2] Lucy, during her stay with Tusker in the
princely state of Mudpore says 'This is the *real* India',[3] the India, that
is, of palaces, peacocks and gorgeous clothes. It contrasts with Mrs
Bhoolabhoy's version of the 'real India' in the same novel: 'there are
many western tourists in search of the real India as well as hippies
who have found it and are having sex' (p. 195), and with the 'real
India' that Adela Quested sought in *A Passage to India*, yet this is,
paradoxically, the India of most English people's imaginations. Lucy's
is the concrete manifestation of the British sense of the exotic, or
'otherness', which has kept India at the forefront of the British
imagination for so long.

A number of novelists, like David Walker in *Harry Black* (1956) and John Masters in *To the Coral Strand* (1962), have dealt with the subject of those who chose to stay on after Independence. In Anita Desai's novel *Baumgartner's Bombay* (1988), as in *Staying On*, the life of the central character is drawing to a close, and as in *Staying On* we see much of his history in a series of flashbacks which parallel Lucy's letters to Sarah Layton, and her imaginary conversations with Mr Turner. Baumgartner's past, however, is very different from that of the Smalleys. He has always been an outsider, having come to India in the 1930s to escape the Nazis. As a German in India during the war he is interned, despite being a Jew. This is a side of India that has not been explored by Britons or Indians writing about the period, and indeed Desai's interest in this subject is probably due, at least in part, to her own half-German heritage. Baumgartner, then, is neither a member of the old order, nor the new. But none of these novelists treat the subject of those who chose to stay on after Independence more poignantly than Paul Scott does in *Staying On*.

As the last of the sahibs, Lucy and Tusker are what Ruth Prawer Jhabvala, in her collection of stories, *A Stronger Climate* (1968), identifies as the 'sufferers'. Jhabvala's collection is divided, thematically, into two parts, 'seekers' and 'sufferers'. The 'seekers' are all young Europeans who came to India in search of something, whilst the 'sufferers' are all elderly Europeans who have stayed on after Independence, and are forced to live out their remaining days in India. In 'the only love letter [Lucy] had had in all the years she had lived' (p. 233), Tusker explains his own decision to remain in India: '. . . it seemed to me I'd invested in India, not money which I've never had, not talent (Ha!) which I've only had a limited amount of, nothing India needed or needs or has been one jot the better for, but was all I had to invest in anything. *Me*' (pp. 231–2). Tusker's own investment reflects the investments of so many British families who lived and worked in India, who were born there, or died there. They had, quite literally, invested their lives in the country. The question raised by Paul Scott in *Staying On* is essentially the same as that asked by Stevie Smith in *The Holiday* (1949):

So this is the other side of the question, of the famous old bogey-question of England-in-India, yes, this is the other side of that. And how can we leave India when we have these loving memories, how can we do it?[4]

In *Staying On*, as he did in the *Raj Quartet*, Paul Scott uses the structure of his novel to add to its sense of history. Here, it is a circular structure, in which the conclusion to the story is given in the opening sentence:

> When Tusker Smalley died of a massive coronary at approximately 9.30 a.m. on the last Monday in April 1972 his wife Lucy was out, having her white hair blue-rinsed and set in the Seraglio Room on the ground floor of Pankot's new five-storey glass and concrete hotel, the Shiraz. (p. 5)

As Janis Tedesco explains, this means that 'there is no advancement of plot, no surprise tragedy to which a series of episodes builds'.[5] Thus more attention can be paid to details, to how the conclusion is reached, rather than to what the conclusion will be. The interest of the story shifts from a desire to know the outcome of the plot, to a desire to understand why. This is the case with much historical fiction. The reader may often know the outcome of a particular event. A reader may well bring to Farrell's *The Siege of Krishnapur*, for example, the knowledge that, if it follows the course of the Siege of Lucknow, there will be some survivors. Scott's structure gives the reader that same knowledge at the beginning of *Staying On*, and in so doing ensures that the whole is viewed from a position of hindsight.

This circular structure, apart from controlling the novel as a whole, is repeated on occasions within the novel. Mr Bhoolabhoy, for example, wakes to find himself still in Lila's bed one morning, and recalls the events of the previous day to explain why he should find himself there. Similarly, the conversation between Mr Bhoolabhoy and Lila, his wife, about the letter that must be sent to give notice to the Smalleys, occurs both at the beginning and end of the novel, since this letter is the catalyst to Tusker's fatal heart attack. These incidents reinforce the overall pattern in which the reader knows the result and is forced to wait for the cause.

Staying On can justifiably be seen as an epilogue to the *Raj Quartet* as the Smalleys are minor figures in the quartet, and the years 1942–47 play an essential part in the later novel. The letters exchanged between Lucy and Sarah Layton (now married to the historian, Guy Perron), after Lucy hears of Colonel Layton's death, bring the reader, as well as Lucy, up to date with events and characters from the *Raj Quartet*, as Yasmine Gooneratne has noted.[6]

But, more than this, these details also re-establish the Smalleys as part of that earlier period. They may be living in Pankot in the 1970s, but they are still very much a part of the 1942–47 era of Pankot's history; they belong, in other words, more to a period which has finished than to the one which is continuing. Thus in many respects the novel is an elegy for a lost age: the loss of the Empire, the end of the Raj, the end of the way of life they knew, for the Smalleys. Through these references to the Layton family history and other 'historical' events from within his own fiction Scott also establishes *Staying On* in a fictional historical context.

Within the novel, Tusker's library book, on which he is making notes, '"A Short History of Pankot" by Edgar Maybrick, BA, LRAM. Privately Printed' (p. 84), is viewed as the official history of Pankot. The history of this time and place in India is inextricably entwined with the Smalley's own personal history; yet nothing which is important to Tusker appears in Maybrick's book. The details of Tusker's and Lucy's life are not in it, the Pankot Rifles, the Regiment to which Tusker was attached in Pankot, is mentioned in only one paragraph, and Smith's Hotel is not mentioned at all. And even the 'facts' it does contain may be wrong: 'He's got the date of the Church right but is out by a year over the installation of the organ, according to Billy-Boy' (p. 88), which invites a comparison between memory and the errors that can become accepted as 'official history'. Similarly, Tusker questions Maybrick's details of the last burial in Pankot, and Lucy admits that what she refers to as 'Mr Maybrick's charming little book' (p. 95), is wrong about the date of Mabel Layton's death. What Maybrick's book lacks is human interest, as his dry, dull account of Mabel's death shows, when compared with the interesting details Lucy recalls. And the notes Tusker makes on the library book are full of personal interest.

The Smalleys' lives are shown to be very individual, yet very ordinary lives (unlike the extraordinary life of Saleem Sinai in *Midnight's Children*). In fact all the characters in *Staying On* are so deliberately ordinary, even Ibrahim, the faithful retainer, that they become almost archetypal in their ordinariness. Tusker and Lucy, as pukka sahib and memsahib, are representative of thousands like themselves. Nothing appears to happen in terms of plot, or historical importance, yet so much does happen; in *Staying On* history is seen as the outcome of *character* rather than *event*. In addition, the shifting point of view of the novel offers a variety of perspectives, all individual. Ibrahim, for example, remembers the Raj through the

Moxon-Greifes, the family with whom his father was in service, a different perspective from either that of Lucy or Tusker.

Despite the strong links Scott establishes between the Smalleys and an earlier period, *Staying On* is firmly set in the early months of 1972. Lucy, during one of her imaginary conversations with the historian, Mr Turner, recalls the short war between India and Pakistan which took place in December 1971:

> It's ironic and perhaps sad don't you think, Mr Turner, that in the wars between India and Pakistan, the one just over, for instance, the opposing generals are often old class-mates, some of them even once subalterns together in the same regiment. I've heard that described as a good thing because if one general knows another well he knows how his mind works but I think that cuts two ways and might almost be a guarantee of stalemate, although it didn't work out that way last December. (p. 155)

(Such a situation occurs in Manohar Malgonkar's *Distant Drum*.) Immediately after this war Zulfikar Ali Bhutto replaced Yahya Khan as prime minister of Pakistan, and Mujibur Rahman became the first prime minister of the newly-created Bangladesh; it is quite natural that both men should be referred to in conversation by guests at the Menektaras' Holi party:

> Mrs Srinivasan and Mrs Mitra were talking about Mr Bhutto, the new prime minister of Pakistan. 'He's only a grocer's son,' Mrs Srinivasan was saying, 'so what can you expect? And what is Mujhib? Anyway I am tired of Bengal. It has never been anything but a trouble to us. Like Ireland to the English, isn't it, Lucy?' (p. 176)

References are also made to the sterilization campaign which 'offered a free transistor to every Indian having a vasectomy' (p. 31), which also helps to establish the novel in the early 1970s. In *Staying On* though, the campaign does not receive the harsh criticism that it attracts in Nayantara Sahgal's *Rich Like Us* (1985) or Salman Rushdie's *Midnight's Children*.

Staying On is also set in its historical period through references to the British political situation of the time. Early in the novel, for example, we learn that during their Monday evening get-togethers, Tusker passed on a variety of information to Mr Bhoolabhoy, including 'why Prime Minister Heath was married to a boat' (p. 8). Ted Heath was prime minister of Britain from June 1970 to February 1974.

The presence of the English 'Hippie' in Pankot is also a sign of the times, though not so specific. It is this new breed of foreigner that writers like Jhabvala treat so well in novels such as *A New Dominion*.

Rather more interestingly, Scott helps evoke the age through the use of old gramophone records and film titles. Thus the period of Lucy's youth is recalled through references to some of the films she saw at that time, old silents like *The Big Parade* and *Seventh Heaven*. The 1970s is similarly established. On Monday evenings, whilst Tusker is being convivial with Mr Bhoolabhoy, Lucy usually goes to the New Electric cinema, accompanied on the journey by Ibrahim, who sees the film from the cheap seats before attending her home. After Tusker's first illness they resume their Monday evening entertainment:

'So yes, Ibrahim, let us tonight both go to the pictures. Do you know what is on?'
'Repeat showing, Butch Cassidy, Sundance Kid. Paul Newman, Robert Redford.'
'Yes, of course. We saw it last year, but such good actors.' (p. 72)

Butch Cassidy and the Sundance Kid was released in 1969, and it is perfectly in keeping with this release date that the film should have been first shown in Pankot in 1971. Scott's choice of *Butch Cassidy and the Sundance Kid* to help convey the period of his novel is suggestive in itself; the film and Scott's novel have some common themes. *Butch Cassidy and the Sundance Kid* is the story of two outlaws whose lives span the eras of the fast-fading old West and the beginning of the modern era, just as the lives of Tusker and Lucy Smalley span the eras of the old Raj and the beginning of the modern era of Indian history. Moreover, the film is prefaced by the words, 'Not that it matters, but the following story is true'. Whilst *Staying On* may not be true, it would be difficult to argue that the novel is not true to the stories of those who stayed on, and whose lives have been documented in various history texts, memoirs and photographs. The photographs Lucy rummages for in the bottom drawer of the chest in her bedroom are part of the history of Pankot, just as the photographs of Lucy taken for Father Sebastian's magazine article will become history, too. And in keeping with the sense of history in the novel as a whole, these photographs present history in terms of people rather than events.

Staying On is further placed in time through references to Independence and Partition. In the letter to Lucy, Sarah Layton recalls the train journey to Ranpur, 'when the train was stopped and people were killed' (p. 93), and Mrs Bhoolabhoy, a member of the new order of Indian business entrepreneurs, is poised to join a consortium which will see the end of Smith's:

> All the businessmen concerned in these enterprises had come from the Western Punjab in 1947 when it became part of Pakistan at the time of Independence and Partition, and had arrived in India penniless, they said. Mrs Bhoolabhoy's first husband was believed to have come from there, having 'lost his all' in the riots between Muslims and Hindus. It was agreed by the servants both at Smith's and the Shiraz that you could hardly find a Western Punjabi, once destitute, nowadays not making a packet. 'Bloody immigrants,' Ibrahim sometimes called them. (pp. 18–19)

This reference, apart from establishing the novel in a period far enough after Partition for the Punjabis to be rich once more, also shows the prejudice against these people, so evident in Nahal's *Azadi*. It contrasts these 'Bloody immigrants' with the English, who have been in Pankot (and India) so long, and in such a position, that they would never be considered by Ibrahim as 'immigrants', and yet in a sense, of course, they are. Further, the wealth of these 'immigrants' contrasts sharply with the relative poverty of Tusker and Lucy who have to struggle to make ends meet.

Similarly, comparisons with the past, usually the five years between 1942 and 1947, help to establish a sense of distance from that earlier period:

> The hut where Ibrahim slept lay behind the corrugated iron garage which was a comparatively new construction. As a bungalow The Lodge had always been diminutive, the servants' quarters correspondingly so: six or seven men, women and boys had once had accommodation here, just sufficient for a modest bachelor establishment in the days of the *raj*. Then, there had been several huts and a cookhouse. Only the hut in which Ibrahim slept remained in good repair. The others had fallen into ruin

and of the cookhouse there was nothing left except a few blackened bricks. (p. 20)

The contrast between the six or seven servants of the days of the Raj, and the single servant of the 1970s is clear. And as Patrick Swinden explains, 'we have to know not merely about their past, but about how their past informs their present'.[7]

This contrast between the two periods is highlighted in the two Pankot hotels, Smith's and the Shiraz. The former is a symbol of the old order, the latter of the new. Tusker and Lucy feel at home in the dining room of Smith's, but somewhat out of place in that of the Shiraz. When Scott writes 'But for Smith's now it all seemed to be coming to an end' (p. 12), he could as easily have been writing of the last survivors of that earlier period as of the hospitality symbol of those days. The Shiraz casts a shadow on Smith's that is metaphorical as well as literal, and it blocks out the view of Smith's from East Hill, just as the present is gradually blocking out memories of the past. When she thinks about the past and the days of the English in India, Lucy concludes, 'that was at another season and in a distant country' (p. 223), which recalls the opening line of L.P. Hartley's novel *The Go-Between*: 'The past is a foreign country: they do things differently there'.[8] And Lucy recognises that she and Tusker are already relics of that 'distant country' when she ironically suggests to Tusker that they:

> 'should write to Cooks' . . . 'and ask them to put us on the tourist itinerary. After the Taj Mahal, after the rock temples of Khajarao, after Elephanta, after Fatehpur Sikri, after the beach temple at Mahabalipuram and the Victoria Monument in Calcutta, the Smalleys of Pankot.' (p. 89)

The loss of the Empire, and more particularly the loss of the way of life that people like the Smalleys knew, is one theme of *Staying On*. Closely linked to this is what David Rubin terms the theme of eviction.[9] The Smalley's eviction from Smith's parallels the end of the Empire and the effective eviction of the British from India, whilst Susie's eviction from her salon highlights the loss of security, particularly job security, which faced the Eurasian community when India gained her Independence. The suggestion is that the end of the old order is regressive rather than a step forward. The wisdom of the historical events portrayed is also questioned by Father Sebastian's choice of text for his first sermon in Pankot:

Father Sebastian had preached beautifully, taking as his text verses 17 and 18 and part of 19 from chapter two of Ecclesiastes: 'Therefore I hated life, because the work that is wrought under the sun *is* grievous unto me: for all is vanity and vexation of spirit. Yea, I hated all my labour which I had taken under the sun: because I should leave it unto the man that shall be after me. And who knoweth whether he shall be a wise *man* or a fool?' (p. 129)

Whilst much of Scott's novel is concerned with a past which is rapidly coming to an end, Father Sebastian's sermon looks to the future and questions whether the directions the present is taking are wise or foolish. The death of Tusker similarly mirrors the death of the Raj, or the closing down of the old order, and the fate of Lucy, left alone 'amid the alien corn, waking, sleeping, alone for ever and ever' (p. 255), mirrors the situation of those who, twenty-five year earlier, stayed on.

Whereas *Staying On* is very much an epilogue to the period of Indo-British history which came to an end in 1947, Nayantara Sahgal's *Rich Like Us*, set in New Delhi one month after the declaration of the Emergency in 1975, is a novel of post-Independence India. Unlike the characters in *Staying On*, those in *Rich Like Us* are anything but archetypal. The new times create new types; entrepreneurs replace the old-fashioned merchants (and the contrast between Mrs Bhoolabhoy and Mr Bhoolabhoy reflects this too). The ambiguous title, *Rich Like Us*, draws attention to the value of the complex and fertile Indian culture, despite the poverty of ideals suffered during the Emergency.

The leading characters of the novel are all fictional, but in the background there are a number of historical figures – Indira Gandhi, Sanjay Gandhi and Jayaprakash Narayan – who add a note of historical authenticity. Interestingly, however, these people, although easily identifiable, are never actually named. Mrs Gandhi is usually referred to as 'Madam', or occasionally as 'the P.M.' or as 'the Supremo'; Sanjay loses even more of his own identity when he becomes 'Madam's son', 'the P.M.'s son' or 'the Supremo's son'; and Jayaprakash Narayan is always referred to as 'J.P.', the initials by which he was known throughout his long and distinguished political career. Thus the historical characters remain shadowy figures, whose decisions are seen to affect the lives of the fictional characters in the story. Sahgal shows the consequences of the Emergency through these fictional lives. Rose's beggar, for example, is a ubiquitous reminder of the fate of the peasant classes who are not otherwise represented in the novel. History, in the making of which the poor can take no part at a conscious level (unlike Sonali, Ravi or Dev), simply passes over them.

Rich Like Us is dated from an early point. The Emergency is referred to on the second page of the novel, and the date of the declaration of the Emergency, 26 June 1975, echoes throughout in the same way that 8 August 1942, the date of the beginning of Gandhi's Quit India campaign, echoes through *The Jewel in the Crown*.

The events which occur in the novel's present are frequently signposted by references to 26 June. This is true, for example, of the events which lead to Sonali's demotion, and effective dismissal from the civil service:

Instructions were that files had to move fast and on that morning, one month after June 26th, I wrote a brief rejection in the wide margin of the proposal on my desk. I had had plenty of time to study it and there was no other decision I could make. It was a preposterous proposal, requiring the import of more or less an entire factory. Policy did not allow foreign collaboration in industry except under a complicated set of regulations, although essential items the economy needed that we couldn't produce for ourselves were exempt from the list. There were a number of those but a fizzy drink called Happyola wasn't one of them. When the visiting representative of the company came into my office, I told him so.

Facing me across my desk, he looked taken aback.

'I understood there were changes in policy.' (p. 25)

That final line is a reference to the Emergency, and Sonali, in rejecting the proposal which has been sanctioned from above, fails to act pro-Emergency. Her swift dismissal is a direct consequence: 'The logic of June 26th had simply caught up with me' (p. 28).

The consequences of not actually supporting the Emergency are also seen in the treatment meted out to Kishori Lal. His allegiance to the Jan Sangh is described as 'positively dangerous since the emergency had marked his political party out for surveillance and put all its leaders and crowds of its workers in jail' (p. 74). His arrest and subsequent beatings show the brutal side of the Emergency first-hand.

Further, the fact that he is known to his friends as K.L. means that his arrest and brutal mistreatment remind the reader of the arrest of that other man of initials, J.P., and is another means of blending the fictional stories with the historical period in which they are set.

Similarly, Dev's rise to importance during the Emergency in many ways mirrors Sanjay Gandhi's rise to political power, so much that at times the fictional character of Dev and the historical figure of 'Madam's son' appear to merge. In this novel it is Dev who is seen to play a visible role in the organisation of the youth camps, which recall the camps organized by Sanjay Gandhi and his re-organization of the Youth Congress. Dev comes to play an important part in the motor car manufacturing firm that was controlled by 'the P.M.'s son', and his wife, Nishi, is active in the sterilization campaign which was also conducted, ruthlessly, by Sanjay Gandhi. Through Dev, another side of the Emergency is seen. Whilst talented people like Sonali lose their jobs, and honest men like K.L. lose their liberty, the fortunes of untalented and dishonest characters like Dev increase dramatically.

Dev is shown to be incompetent in the handling of the once-successful family garment business from the outset of the novel, yet, because he can afford the necessary bribes, he quickly rises to a position of importance as the leader of the New Entrepreneurs, and a key figure in the Happyola business which cost Sonali her job. And finally he is rewarded with an appointment as a Cabinet Minister.

But Sahgal is aware that the present cannot be understood without first understanding the past. Thus Rose, Ram's Cockney wife and Dev's stepmother, becomes a major character in the novel, and with her blatantly working-class background, she offers a point of view which is unusual if not unique in Indo-Anglian fiction.

Her first meeting with Ram is initially signposted in relation to the present, thus linking the two periods: 'they had met in a chocolate shop in London forty-three years ago' (p. 34). The year 1932 is further established by reference to Ram and Rose having been to see 'Jean Harlow in *Red Dust*' (p. 35), a film which was released in that year.

And just as it is necessary to look back at 1932 to understand the present of this novel, so it is necessary to look back further to understand 1932. Thus the references to 1919 explain the attitude of Ram's father to the British in general and to Rose in particular:

the real reason, Rose discovered, was the order passed in his town when he was a boy that Indians had to crawl on their bellies if they wanted to pass a white person on that particular stretch of road. It was where an English missionary called Miss Sherwood had been dragged off her cycle and beaten up in 1919. So a whipping frame had been set up there and six boys had been tied to it and flogged, and Ram's father, who refused to crawl, had been whipped too. (p. 38)

Similarly, Rose's murder is only fully understood in relation to an even earlier past, that of Sonali's great-grandmother who was burned as an involuntary *sati*, and was thus murdered, too. And it is significant that Sonali discovers the truth about her great-grandmother from her father's trunk, which gradually reveals the past to her. At the bottom of this trunk Sonali finds 'a small manuscript marked, in Papa's hand, "Written by my father in 1915"' (p. 119). The manuscript, found in her father's trunk, written by *his* father, is actually written about *his* father. Thus the past is recalled through four generations. In a fictional sense, this is an historical document, and Sahgal also introduces real historical documents into her novel in the form of the Puckle Circular, which Sonali also finds in her father's trunk, and which, Sahgal tells us in her acknowledgements, is an original document. Thus within her father's trunk, which reveals both real and fictional historical documents, history and fiction are carefully blended, as they are throughout the novel. The past discovered in the trunk, like the past which pervades this novel, and *Staying On* too, is a past made up primarily of the memories of people. Even the ruined tomb where the beggar, and perhaps Rose also, senses comfort, represents a past of people rather than events.

There are, nevertheless, many historical events between 1932 and 1975 which are signposted, including the demand for a separate Muslim country, a demand which first gained momentum in the early 1930s, the arrest of Gandhi on his return from the Round Table Conference in London in 1932, Partition, the Mahatma's assassination and the Naxalites who were active in Bengal in the early 1970s. There are also references to events from world history, such as the abdication of Edward VIII, the bombing of Hiroshima and Nagasaki and the Soviet Union's intervention in Hungary in 1956.

However, the most interesting thing about the treatment of this period, which includes a spell of confident British rule, as well as

Independence, Partition and twenty-seven years of Indian self-rule, is that it is presented as a basically continuous period of Indian history. The achievement of Independence and the bloody division of the sub-continent are not dwelt on, and the suggestion is that in the forty-three years between 1932 and 1975 , and despite these upheavals, nothing really changed. This was true, for example, of the civil service, whose 'passage from British-trained to Indian-trained machine' was 'accomplished without a creak' (p. 24). It is only as 1975 draws near that all this changes.

Nineteen seventy-five, not 1947, Sahgal suggests, signalled the end of the old order, despite the death of Ram's father in Lahore shortly after the announcement of Partition. Thus as the Emergency is declared Sonali's father, Keshev Renade, an old friend of Ram's, who had served proudly in the ICS (Indian Civil Service) dies; Ram, who has been successful in his business ventures, without political patronage, has a stroke which leaves him paralysed and unconscious, reflecting a country which is in a state of suspended animation due to the Emergency; and K.L. is imprisoned and beaten. Indeed illness is a metaphor for the time, as Sonali, too, suffers an attack of hepatitis which strikes on the very day that she loses her position in the civil service. Further, Ram is clearly a symbol of the old order, whilst his son, Dev, is a symbol of the new order which the Emergency fosters. Ram's collapse is both literally and symbolically brought on by the dishonesty of his son. The old order does not give way gracefully to the new, rather it is brought to an abrupt end by the dishonesty of the new order.

In many respects the fortunes of Ram's family and friends, which are at the centre of the novel, reflect the fortunes of the country as a whole. Rose, for example, is greeted with a mixture of acceptance and antagonism when she arrives in India. Ram's westernized friends, including his Muslim friend Zafar, welcome her to her new home in Lahore, whilst Ram's father, and, of course, his first wife, Mona, do not want her and do not accept her. To Ram's father she is a representative of the British who had oppressed Indian for two hundred years, and to Mona she is an intruder who disrupts her marriage and almost causes her to become *sati*. It is only when each is forced to view Rose on an individual level, and in so doing recognise her humanity, that she is accepted. Partition sees the death of Ram's father, reflecting the loss of home and identity (which in this novel, as in so many of the Indian novels treated, is linked to place) forced on so many refugees, and results in Mona and Rose living in sep-arate homes for the first time. It is Partition, rather than Rose's arrival, which splits the family for good, just as it was only in 1947 that the British finally split the sub-continent along religious lines that may well have been no stronger than the regional ties which were ignored. Ram's marriage to Rose is, of course, a marriage of East and West; his continued interest in English women, particularly Marcella, both pre- and post-Independence reflects the position of westernized Indians before and after 1947. The affair that had lasted for over two hundred years did not simply end with Independence.

The narrator of *Rich Like Us*, which varies between the third-person, the first-person and an omniscient one, further underlines the consequences of the Emergency. The opening chapter, although essentially an omniscient point of view, describes the evening from the perspective of Mr Neuman, the foreign businessman being entertained by Dev and Nishi. The atmosphere, like the room itself, is sterile and anonymous, and in this respect it is a reflection of the Emergency. It contrasts with the sections of the novel where the point of view is either Rose's or Sonali's, which are warm and personal in comparison, and embody the values of the pre-Emergency past.

Once again, hope in this novel is based on love and humanity. Ravi, who is seen as a political opportunist at the beginning of the novel, comes to an understanding about the Emergency by the end. It is Ravi who provides the link between Mr Neuman and the Minister for Industry, and who as 'a bureaucrat of importance in the current set-up . . . and part of the conveyor belt that had delivered the cash to the Minister of Industry' (p. 12) ensures the Happyola factory receives approval, and who, therefore, costs Sonali, his long-time friend and sometime lover, her job.

It is also through Ravi that the change in the civil service is seen. Before the Emergency the lines between politics and administration had been clearly drawn: 'Once upon a time we had thought of the civil service as "we" and politicians as "they", two different sides of the coin. . . . Our job was to stay free of the political circus' (p. 24). However, this clear line is erased gradually in the years leading up to the Emergency when Mrs Gandhi asserts her influence over both the Congress Party and Parliament. Sonali and her father, who together represent the established order of the civil service, witness the beginning of its end as early as 1969:

[Ravi] sprang on to the bonnet of one of the taxis and seated himself there with his right arm draped casually along the roof and, in a voice resonant as bells, asked the assembled taxi drivers to raise three *zindabads* for the nation's supreme leader ... we knew when we heard it that an alien note had been struck, as unexpected as the sight of a civil servant taking time off to make political hoop-la from the bonnet of a taxi. Papa could not have been more astounded if the President himself had bounded out of Rashtrapati Bhavan, jumped on a tricycle and started hawking ice-cream cones, only that would have been merely eccentric. This was prophetic. (p. 151)

Yet through Ravi, Sahgal also offers hope. Having been so thoroughly behind the Emergency, his humanity, when it finally shines through, is all the more important.

His positive answer in response to Sonali's plea that he help Rose by attempting to stop Dev forging his father's signature on bank cheques, is the first sign of his changing attitude towards the Emergency, and the first sign of hope, which culminates in his confession to Sonali that: 'Things have slipped out of control. There are no rules and regulations any more. I never realized it would come to this' (p. 229).

This essential humanity is also displayed by K.L., who refuses to leave the jail whilst the young prisoner he has shared a cell with remains behind, and in Rose's behaviour throughout. It is with Sonali, however, that hope rests in the end: 'Immersed in the past, I was preparing all the while for the future . . .' (p. 234). In this final paragraph Sahgal is repeating the necessity of understanding the past to understand the present, and the future.

The Emergency signals the end of the dream which began for Rose in 1932, symbolised by references to her trip to India as a voyage to Cythera. Soon after her arrival in India, talk turns to 'Pakistan, Cythera, and other mythical places' (p. 66), and Ram's friend Zafar tells Rose that 'Cythera is where you embarked for when you left your native shores' (p. 66). For Rose, Cythera, like India, was 'a real place . . . but it was unreal too' (p. 67).

Years later, in a bookshop in London that she visits with Sonali, Rose finds a picture postcard of:

'L'Embarquement pour l'île de Cythère' by Jean-Antoine Watteau, 1684-1721. The pamphlet below it explained about its style and composition. The voyage was a quest, it said, and Cythera a paradise, an impossible dream, towards which pilgrims journey but never arrive. (p. 181)

Rose keeps it, thereafter, clipped to her dressing-table mirror, to symbolise her relationship with Ram and India. The painting (Plate 6) depicts 'pink and white ladies in powdered wigs and ball gowns reclining languidly on a grass slope beside a river, with sailing ships at anchor nearby' (p. 71); it is a world that was brought to an abrupt end by the French Revolution, just as Rose's world will be brought to an abrupt end by the Emergency. This postcard, with what she describes as 'its invitation to fantasy' (p. 224), Sonali later removes from Rose's dressing-table mirror as a keepsake of her friend.

Sahgal uses other paintings in her novel, too:

The wall above their beds looked sprayed in blood and the obscene splatter framed in teak. Nishi bent forward in her chair, oppressed by the sight. Her mother had telephoned an hour ago with the news that her father had been in jail for a week, and for the past hour Nishi had been unable to move, rooted to the chair facing the blood splatter with the telephone beside it. She had never more than glanced at the painting before. (p. 205)

This abstract, with the red splashes which look like blood, and perhaps like the tiny red handprints left at one time by *satis* on the walls of *sati* gates, suggests the blood which is metaphorically on the hands of Dev and others who support the Emergency. Dev is indirectly responsible for K.L.'s imprisonment, just as he is directly responsible for Ram's stroke and Rose's murder.

There is one more painting, whose title is not given, which is referred to in the manuscript Sonali finds in her father's trunk:

I have seen a painting in an art gallery in England of a group of men with a high round circular window in the stone wall behind them. The painting is severe and undecorated but the textures are palpable. The wall is visibly rough stone, as their clothes are obviously thick and woollen besides being black, and their squarish black hats are made of something stiffer than felt. They are sitting at a table and one is as conscious of the massive shapes beneath the folds of their garments as of the oily gleam of the table's wood. The only light on the canvas pours sharply from the circular window on to their naked faces, but in the dark background one can see the cowled heads of monks. I suppose the painting re-presents some actual incident. It has all the hallmarks of the particular, as of some moment in history recaptured. What I remember vividly is the intentness of those faces, almost garishly lit and unnaturally focused on one person in their midst whose lowered eyelids half cover his eyes. (pp. 132–3)

The composition, as Sonali's grandfather suggests, had much in common with the attention being paid to his mother by the other members of the family after her husband had died. She is the person apparently on trial in the painting, and, judging from the lighting and the staring faces, condemned too. It also suggests the position of those like Sonali, and more particularly Rose, who oppose the Emergency. Mythology, which Ram describes to Rose as 'human behaviour in the raw' (p. 55), also underlies the story of *Rich Like Us*. Ram's name recalls the story of the *Ramayana*, which, in certain respects, parallels the story of *Rich Like Us*. Thus Rose's death is forecast early in the novel:

> In the very end when life became too much even for the long-suffering Sita, she prayed for the earth, her mother, to open up and receive her, which the earth did; i.e., Ram had remarked . . . she died. Or was murdered by society, corrected Keshav, for how voluntary are voluntary deaths, and was it bliss hereafter or earthly hell that drove *satis* to climb their husbands' funeral pyres and be burned alive? Why would a lovely princess cry out for the earth to swallow her if life hadn't become a wilderness? (p. 67)

That wilderness, of course, is the Emergency, and Rose did not cry out for the earth to swallow her, she was murdered by the society bred of the Emergency, just as Sonali's great-grandmother was murdered by the society which supported *sati*. And here, I think, is the clearest link between the Emergency and *sati* to which the abstract painting draws our attention.

Ironically, after sitting on the sofa alone in the middle of the night, Rose thinks about both Cythera and the *Ramayana*, yet ignores their prophetic warnings in her offhand dismissal of the framed calligraphy, the 'writing on the wall': 'Against one wall black ink calligraphy fragile as filigree sprang like gazelles across a page burnished by moonlight, within wide borders decorated with gold leaves and flowers. Fancy putting a frame around handwriting!' (p. 67).

The Emergency, Sahgal appears to be suggesting through her use of paintings and mythology, is something which can only be understood through metaphor. This is vividly suggested during K.L.'s imprisonment:

> he suddenly remembered, as one does irrelevantly sometimes, how the Germans treated Russian prisoners during the war, differently, very differently from other Allied prisoners. And standing before the chief tea drinker he knew without a doubt that Madam was a German and he was a Russian. And now he started to believe it was happening. (p. 174)

But a simple metaphor, whilst able to explain K.L.'s immediate predicament, cannot explain the whole of the Emergency, as O.V. Vijayan recognises in his novel *The Saga of Dharmapuri* (1988). For that, Sahgal has to use surrealism, which she does in the brief description of the surrealist play that K.L.'s young cell-mate is writing in his head:

> First of all the dictator's chariot arrives. Chariot? asked K.L., isn't that rather old-fashioned, or are you setting your play in olden times? I don't know if this will appeal to you, said the boy, but I am making this a surrealist play which you probably won't understand, but the chariot turns into a car and then into a jet plane and through all of this the dictator is arriving, and he steps down to trumpets and fanfare and all the rest, and then instead of a big Heil So-and-so going up, there's this loud taped laughter, a huge barrage of it, that's all, then silence. Next he/she – and by the way one half of the dictator is a he and the other half is a she – this is not a sexist play – tells about what he/she is going to do for the people. Politicians are such bullshitters and this one starts bullshitting. And after every few sentences when he/she stops for applause, there's this loud hilarious Ha! Ha! Ha! instead. And soon you have everyone bloated with laughter, falling over themselves with jollification, and they can't stop laughing while he/she is getting enraged and baffled because every time he/she says 'I shall banish poverty' or 'Watch me remove disparities', there's this colossal raucous cackle. (pp. 187–8)

This suggestion that the reality of Indian politics is too extraordinary to be fully understood in conventional, realist terms, is something which Salman Rushdie explores further in *Midnight's Children*.

8

The Chutnification of History

One day, perhaps, the world may taste the pickles of history. They may be too strong for some palates, their smell may be overpowering, tears may rise to eyes; I hope nevertheless that it will be possible to say of them that they possess the authentic taste of truth . . . that they are, despite everything, acts of love.[1]

Salman Rushdie's novel *Midnight's Children* covers the years from 1915 to 1978, and spans three generations of Saleem Sinai's family, though the main interest of the novel lies in the post-Independence period, which is closely linked to the life of the narrator, Saleem Sinai. In this respect it is something of an autobiographical *Bildungsroman* of epic proportions, probably the first Indian *Bildungsroman*, albeit one in which the author sabotages the very form in which it is written.[2] The shape of his novel, however, owes as much to the Indian oral tradition as it does to the literary traditions of the West. Rushdie himself states that, 'one of the major roots of *Midnight's Children* lies in the oral narrative'.[3] And in this respect the novel shares common ground with Raja Rao's *Kanthapura*. The frequent digressions and summaries Rushdie describes as characteristic of the oral tradition are characteristic of *Midnight's Children*, too. The novel also owes much to the language and form of the Bombay cinema. Rushdie uses film metaphors throughout, and the novel is laced with film titles (including some western film titles, such as *I Confess*). Further, as Michael Harris explains: 'Rushdie takes the language popularized by Hindi cinema with its street-slang, fast pace, melodrama, romance, and action, and fuses it into his narrative to render a surprisingly modern, energetic view of India'.[4] It may be this combination of eastern and western influences that gives *Midnight's Children* its status as a world novel, with universal application to twentieth-century life.

170

J.G. Farrell and E.M. Forster use the Indian situation, particularly the political clash between East and West, to ask questions about British civilization. Rushdie, in contrast, uses *Midnight's Children* as a metaphor for *world* civilization, not just Indian or British civilization. Saleem's childhood is essentially the childhood of any western (English speaking) civilization. His childhood is influenced by the cinema (including western cinema), advertising (the Kolynos Kid), bicycles and even Superman comics. Moreover, he is a middle-class boy living in a city, which gives him the background of most children of the West, too. And, indeed, Saleem *is* half-English, the illegitimate son of William Methwold.

Saleem is shown to be inexorably bound to the wheel of history, his whole existence determined as much by the history of the thirty-two years before his birth as by the thirty-two years after, and this detailed binding to history is only an exaggeration of the postmodernist belief that each individual is created by history, and yet, paradoxically, is creating history. Saleem is created by the history of his times, yet he is also creating his own history as he writes his autobiography; he constructs his own world when he invents his own India.

Midnight's Children is more comprehensive, and of broader historical scope, than any of the other novels in this study. In *Midnight's Children* it is not only that Saleem has become, in himself, a metaphor for India, but that Rushdie has managed to make the relationship between Saleem and India in itself a metaphor for the relationship between any human being and his or her world. When Saleem buries the souvenirs which tie his fate to that of the nation in a battered tin globe, Rushdie has, quite literally and very deliberately, placed Saleem's story of India in a global context (*sic*). And, of course, the tin globe is one more item that links Saleem's childhood to the childhood of any western child of his age. What Rushdie has done in *Midnight's Children*, is to recognise and demonstrate that the Indian situation is the perfect metaphor for characteristically twentieth-century questions about history, language, social and political fragmentation, and creativity. Whereas Narayan's view in *Waiting for the Mahatma*, or Singh's view in *Train to Pakistan*, for example, is microcosmic, Rushdie's view in *Midnight's Children* is most certainly macrocosmic. India, because of its size and complexity, and the fecundity of its myth and culture, is the ideal metaphor for the plight of the individual in history.

The sense of timelessness which was so evident in the opening paragraphs of *The Siege of Krishnapur* and *A Passage to India* is noticeably absent in *Midnight's Children*:

> I was born in the city of Bombay . . . once upon a time. No, that won't do, there's no getting away from the date: I was born in Doctor Narlikar's Nursing Home on August 15th, 1947. And the time? The time matters, too. Well then: at night. No, its important to be more . . . On the stroke of midnight, as a matter of fact. Clock-hands joined palms in respectful greeting as I came. Oh, spell it out, spell it out: at the precise instant of India's arrival at independence, I tumbled forth into the world. (p. 9)

The fairy-tale opening 'once upon a time . . .' is rejected, and in these opening lines Saleem Sinai's fate is tied to the fate of India, as Nehru forecasts in his congratulatory letter which defines Saleem's own tryst with destiny:

> Dear Baby Saleem, My belated congratulations on the happy accident of your moment of birth! You are the newest bearer of that ancient face of India which is also eternally young. We shall be watching over your life with the closest attention; it will be, in a sense, the mirror of our own. (p. 122)

Thus Saleem (false etymology aside) is narrating both history and *his* story. In *Midnight's Children*, as Dieter Riemenschneider observes, 'there is virtually no event which is not given an individual as well as an historical meaning'.[5] Saleem's fictive autobiography is also the autobiography of a nation.

In *Midnight's Children*, Rushdie is quite deliberately re-inventing India as Nehru's letter acknowledges. 'That ancient face' clearly suggests the long history of the country, but at the same time the fact that it is also described as 'eternally young', recognises the fact that India is continually being re-invented. Indeed, Saleem is seen to be 'the newest bearer of that ancient face of India', when the map of India is re-drawn, or re-invented once more, this time by the antagonistic Mr Zagallo in his human geography class:

> 'In the face of thees ugly ape you don't see the whole map of *India*?' . . . 'See here – the Deccan peninsula hanging down!' . . .

'These stains,' he cries, 'are Pakistan! Thees birthmark on the right
ear is the East Wing; and thees horrible stained left cheek, the
West! Remember, stupid boys: Pakistan ees a stain on the face of
India!' (pp. 231–2)

Saleem calls himself an historian and links his own life to the
times: 'It is possible, even probable, that I am only the first historian
to write the story of my undeniably exceptional life-and-times'
(p. 295). This also serves as a reminder of the 'my-life-and-times'
convention (of which *Tristram Shandy* [1759–67], is an extraordinary
example, but the one most relevant to *Midnight's Children*), and of
the possibility of other views from other individuals who are differently linked to history. And in the various Padma episodes we see
Saleem in the process of writing his story/history; we do not see any
of the events as they happen. These episodes, the only present
time passages in the novel, are very limited in a Beckettian or
postmodernist sense. The setting of these sections is restricted to one
room in a pickle factory; the furniture consists of a table, a chair, a
pen and sometimes a bed. The only other person in these scenes is
Padma, who comes and goes without ever explaining where she
has been. Saleem has, in the end, retreated from the large unmanage-
able world to a womb-room world of known reality.

Because Saleem's story continues up to the very moment of writing,
the historical distancing in the novel varies considerably, and the
value of hindsight is lessened as the story progresses. The stronger,
more convincing sections of the novel are the earlier sections, and as
the story gets closer to the present the narrative weakens. Saleem/
Rushdie appears to be aware of this:

Reality is a question of perspective; the further you get from the
past, the more concrete and plausible it seems – but as you approach the present, it inevitably seems more and more incredible.
Suppose yourself in a large cinema, sitting at first in the back row,
and gradually moving up, row by row, until your nose is almost
pressed against the screen. Gradually the stars' faces dissolve into
dancing grain; tiny details assume grotesque proportions; the
illusion dissolves – or rather, it becomes clear that the illusion
itself *is* reality . . . we have come from 1915 to 1956, so we're a
good deal closer to the screen . . . (pp. 165–6)

Just as the screen goes out of focus when one gets too close, so Saleem's narrative loses some of its authority as it nears the present.

Rushdie authenticates his narrative by accurate historical signposts scattered throughout *Midnight's Children*. General Dyer's massacre at Amritsar is well documented in Rushdie's novel, as are the birth of Indian Independence, the language marches in Bombay, the creation of Bangladesh or the declaration of the Emergency. Rushdie links Indian history to world history through references to important world historical events, the dropping of the first atomic bomb on Hiroshima, or the first successful ascent of Mt Everest, for example. At every juncture, Saleem's story is linked to the history of the nation. His grandfather, Aadam Aziz, like Ram's father in Nayantara Sahgal's *Rich Like Us*, is in the Jallianwallah Bagh on 13 April 1919:

> As the fifty-one men march down the alleyway a tickle replaces the itch in my grandfather's nose. . . . As Brigadier Dyer issues a command the sneeze hits my grandfather full in the face. 'Yaaaakh-*thoooo!*' he sneezes and falls forward, losing his balance, following his nose and thereby saving his life. His 'doctori-attaché' flies open; bottles, liniment and syringes scatter in the dust. He is scrabbling furiously at people's feet, trying to save his equipment before it is crushed. There is a noise like teeth chattering in winter and someone falls on him. Red stuff stains his shirt. There are screams now and sobs and the strange chattering continues. More and more people seem to have stumbled and fallen on top of my grandfather. He becomes afraid for his back. The clasp of his bag is digging into his chest, inflicting upon it a bruise so severe and mysterious that it will not fade until after his death. (p. 36)

That bruise which never fades is a testimony to the power of memory on the heart. In India, the memory of Jallianwallah Bagh never faded in the minds and hearts of those who sought Independence.

The moment of India's birth as a nation is recorded faithfully, when Jawaharlal Nehru's famous address is repeated without alteration, but interrupted by the details of Saleem's own birth, each echoing the other:

> '. . . At the stroke of the midnight hour, while the world sleeps, India awakens to life and freedom . . .' And beneath the roar of the monster there are two more yells, cries, bellows, the howls of

children arriving in the world, their unavailing protests mingling with the din of independence which hangs saffron-and-green in the night sky – 'A moment comes, which comes but rarely in history, when we step out from the old to the new; when an age ends; and when the soul of a nation long suppressed finds utterance . . .' while in a room with saffron-and-green carpet Ahmed Sinai is still clutching a chair when Dr Narlikar enters to inform him: 'On the stroke of midnight, Sinai brother, your Begum Sahiba gave birth to a large, healthy child: a son!' (p. 116)

And Saleem's son, who is not his son, but is the grandson of the man who is not Saleem's father, is born on 25 June 1975, the very day the Emergency is declared. Similarly, the day Nadir Khan vanishes from his underground life, divorcing Mumtaz Aziz and leaving her free to marry Ahmed Sinai, the bomb is dropped on Hiroshima: 'Oh yes: something else was happening in the world that day. A weapon such as the world had never seen was being dropped on yellow people in Japan' (p. 61). This reference to global politics suggests once more that *Midnight's Children* is a world novel rather than a local one; just as the story of Saleem's family is linked to Indian history, so it is linked to world history, too.

References to many important historical figures, from Mountbatten, to Nehru, to Yahya Khan and Zulfikar Ali Bhutto, and to dates and place names, further add a sense of authenticity to Saleem's crowded story:

> Let me, then, be perfectly explicit: if Yahya Khan and Z.A. Bhutto had not colluded in the matter of the coup of March 25th, I would not have been flown to Dacca in civilian dress; nor, in all likelihood, would General Tiger Niaza have been in the city that December. (p. 374)

Here Saleem's own story is supported by Rushdie's devious, unverifiable causative links to historical figures, dates and places. Indeed, all the place names in *Midnight's Children* are real, whereas the place names in most of the novels discussed in this study – Bhowani, Krishnapur, Malgudi, Ranpur – are imaginary.

The death of Gandhi is also reported, with apparent accuracy, in the course of Saleem's story. His Uncle Hanif's successful film, *The Lover's of Kashmir*, is interrupted by the announcement of Gandhi's death:

'Ladies and gents, your pardon; but there is terrible news.' His
voice broke – a sob from the Serpent, to lend power to its teeth! –
and then continued. 'This afternoon, at Birla House in Delhi, our
beloved Mahatma was killed. Some madman shot him in the
stomach, ladies and gentlemen – our Bapu is gone!' (p. 143)

Yet shortly afterwards Saleem tells the reader of a mistake:

Re-reading my work, I have discovered an error in chronology.
The assassination of Mahatma Gandhi occurs, in these pages, on
the wrong date. But I cannot say, now, what the actual sequence
of events might have been; in my India, Gandhi will continue to
die at the wrong time. (p. 166)

What is disarming about this apparent confusion or error, is that no
date is given for Gandhi's assassination, and it is therefore impossible for the reader to know if it took place on the wrong date or not.
Ironically, the 'actual sequence of events' is irrecoverable. The point
Saleem (or Rushdie) is making is that he, as *narrator*, does have
the power to alter history, as does everyone else who writes their
versions of history, and he recognises this when he says 'I had
entered into the illusion of the artist' (p. 174), but Saleem as the
protagonist of the story, does not have that power. It would appear,
therefore, that fiction is the only place where one can have 'real'
power. Saleem continues with this question: 'Does one error in-
validate the entire fabric? Am I so far gone, in my desperate need for
meaning, that I'm prepared to distort everything – to re-write the
whole history of my times purely in order to place myself in a central
role?' (p. 166). But the question can be viewed from a different
angle. Could it not be that rather than each historical event having
a fictional counterpart, deliberately placing Saleem at the centre,
each fictional event has an historical counterpart, authenticating
Saleem's story?

In many respects this question is raised once more when Saleem
describes Ayub Khan's seizure of power in Pakistan. Ayub Khan is
a real historical figure, but the events Saleem describes could not
have happened quite as he describes them because, as we know,
Saleem is a fictional character, and could not have been present as
he suggests. However, Ayub Khan's seizure remains fictionally
true, as do the meetings Sriram attends in *Waiting for the Mahatma*
and Lala Kanshi Ram and Chaudhri Barkat Ali attend in *Azadi*.

In other words, whilst the narrative undoubtedly aspires to the condition of truth or reality, it is, ultimately, a fictional truth not an historical truth.

History and myth are closely linked in *Midnight's Children*. Saleem is by night an historian; by day he works in a pickle factory:

> I, Saleem Sinai, possessor of the most delicately-gifted olfactory organ in history, have dedicated my latter days to the large-scale preparation of condiments. But now, 'A cook?' you gasp in horror, 'A khansama merely? How is it possible?' And, I grant, such mastery of the multiple gifts of cookery and language is rare indeed; yet I possess it. You are amazed; but then I am not, you see, one of your 200-rupees-a-month cookery johnnies, but my own master, working beneath the saffron and green winking of my personal neon goddess. And my chutneys and kasaundies are, after all, connected to my nocturnal scribblings – by day amongst the pickle-vats, by night within these sheets. I spend my time at the great work of preserving. Memory, as well as fruit, is being saved from the corruption of the clocks. (pp. 37–8)

By both day and night, then, Saleem is a preserver. In terms of Hindu mythology he is related to the figure of Vishnu. Saleem's opposite, Shiva, is clearly linked to his namesake, Shiva the destroyer, the most powerful of the Hindu pantheon. But Shiva is also Shiva-lingam, the creator, and in this book the father of one thousand and one children. And myth intrudes further. Saleem's son, Aadam, who is really the son of Shiva and Parvati, bears a remarkable resemblance to Ganesh, the son of the gods Shiva and Parvati, and the patron of literature. This leaves Brahma, the creator, unaccounted for, and this is the role which Rushdie himself fulfils in writing *Midnight's Children*. He has created, invented, or re-invented India in the pages of his novel. Other mythologies enter the story too, in the naming of characters. Eve Lilith Burns carries the names of both the Biblical Adam's wives, Eve, and the lesser-known Lilith, who, according to Jewish tradition is the more sensual of the pair, the earth-mother figure. Lilith is also a female demon who lies in wait for children, and slaughters them. This too fits with the character of Eve Lilith Burns, who provides the push that sends Saleem hurtling down the hill into the language marchers. And, of course, allegorical identity is also implied in the names of Mary Pereira, one of Saleem's many mothers, and Joseph D'Costa.

Rushdie establishes a sense of history in a number of ways in *Midnight's Children*, but one of the more interesting is the use he makes of newspaper headlines, a means Bernard Bergonzi describes as, 'an effective if unsubtle way of emphasising the novel's historicity'.[6] Scott makes effective use of newspaper headlines in the *Raj Quartet*, but in *Midnight's Children* Rushdie uses them in a very different way. Saleem cuts words and letters out of the headlines to paste together a letter which warns Commander Sabarmati that his wife is having an affair. Saleem admits to 'cutting up history to suit my nefarious purposes' (p. 259), and to this being his 'first attempt at rearranging history' (p. 260). Dieter Riemenschneider is correct when he writes, 'Saleem's act reveals the absurdity of the historian's claim to render history objectively; rather, history can be bent to serve subjective and individual purposes'.[7] And it is important to note that the headlines Saleem uses are not all political headlines (as Riemenschneider wrongly suggests), but sports headlines, and headlines from human-interest stories, all of which are part of the history of the period, and all of which must be swallowed to taste the whole. Rushdie, too, is cutting up history and pasting it into the pages of *Midnight's Children*. Rushdie's Sabarmati case is another excellent example of the blend of truth and fiction so important in this novel. Whilst the Sabarmati case is fiction, few Indians will fail to recognise it as a thinly-disguised version of the famous Nanavati case which did take place in the 1950s. And by comparing the Sabarmati/Nanavati case to the *Ramayana* – 'If Rama himself were alive, would we send him to prison for slaying the abductor of Sita?' (p. 264) – Rushdie draws attention to the similarities between history and myth: 'And then I had this awful and blasphemous notion which I became convinced was true, which is that the Nanavati case was like a kind of re-staging in the 20th century of the *Ramayana* story'.[8] History, he seems to be suggesting, as well as fiction, can have its origins in myth.

This raises once more the question of the nature of truth. The question is clearly addressed when Saleem confesses his love for his sister, now renamed Jamila Singer: 'although what he was saying was the literal truth, there were other truths which had become more important because they had been sanctified by time' (p. 325). The literal (or historical) truth cannot simply replace another truth, in this case the myth which has been sanctioned by time. Thus Saleem's family are unable to see him any differently after Mary confesses her long-secret crime:

'when we eventually discovered the crime of Mary Pereira, we all found that it *made no difference*! I was still their son: they remained my parents. In a kind of collective failure of imagination, we learned that we simply could not think our way out of our pasts . . .' (p. 118)

The same is true of what Saleem refers to as 'the notorious (and arguably fictional) Black Hole of Calcutta' (p. 187).

And just as it is possible to question myth, so it is possible to question official truth and, of course, historical truth. Writing about the disputed territory of the Rann of Kutch, Saleem tells us that 'the story I am going to tell, which is substantially that told by my cousin Zafar, is as likely to be true as anything; as anything, that is to say, except what we were officially told' (p. 335). Does this mean that what we are officially told is the one thing which is not true?

The nature of official truth is again questioned when Saleem tells us:

And while we drove through city streets, Shaheed looked out of windows and saw things that weren't-couldn't-have-been true: soldiers entering women's hostels without knocking; women, dragged into the street, were also entered, and again nobody troubled to knock. (p. 356)

In other words, there is truth that is never reported. What is reported is only a fragment of the whole truth, and this ties in with Rushdie's view of history.

This idea of history being seen in fragments is important to the style of narration Rushdie gives to Saleem. The opening chapter is entitled 'The Perforated Sheet', and that sheet, through which Aadam Aziz comes to know his future wife bit by bit, is one of the many leitmotifs to be found in this novel. The perforated sheet appears early to provide an important clue to the narrative technique of the novel and to Rushdie's view of history which reflects the postmodern ideology of the whole:

And there are so many stories to tell, too many, such an excess of intertwined lives events miracles places rumours, so dense a commingling of the improbable and the mundane! I have been a swallower of lives: and to know me, just the one of me, you'll have to swallow the lot as well. Consumed multitudes are jostling and shoving inside me; and guided only by the memory of a large white bedsheet with a roughly circular hole some seven inches in diameter cut into the centre, clutching at the dream of that holey, mutilated square of linen, which is my talisman, my open-sesame, I must commence the business of remaking my life from the point at which it really began, some thirty-two years before anything as obvious, as *present*, as my clock-ridden, crime-stained birth. (pp. 9–10)

As Rukmini Bhaya Nair states in response to this passage:

Where the task of historical documentation is immense, meaning-ful patterns can only emerge from selective juxtaposition, partial viewing. Not only does history hang together more coherently when this mode of telling is adopted, it is also rendered more piquant, interesting, loving, true.[9]

India is too large, too diverse, too incomprehensible, to be swal-lowed in one mouthful. The same is true of any individual. Thus Amina Sinai teaches herself to love her husband by falling in love with a bit of him each day.

Similarly, Lifafa Das, the peepshow man, attempts to put the whole world in his peepshow box. But despite his desperate at-tempts to put everything into his box, he can only display his world one picture at a time, in fragments, through the perforated sheet. Life is frustratingly multiple, simultaneous; fiction is inescapably linear in the way it reaches its reader, one page at a time, whatever may happen to time within those pages. Like Lifafa Das, and like Nadir Khan's friend the painter, Rushdie/Saleem is trying 'to encapsulate the whole of reality' (p. 75), and he does 'not believe in shielding his audiences from the not-always-pleasant features of the age' (p. 76). And like Lifafa Das, Saleem can only display his work in fragments. Indeed, the thirty-one pickle jars or the thirty chapters of *Midnight's Children* divide Saleem's life into manageable, swallowable, mouth-fuls, though Rushdie overcomes this apparent linearity by his complexity.

But India is more than the sum of all its parts, and thus one always has the impression that Rushdie is writing about something bigger. In Amritsar, Aadam Aziz realises that Naseem is not the woman he thought from his knowledge of the parts.

In many of the British novels discussed above, such as *A Passage to India*, there has been a tendency to see a simple Hindu–Muslim identity in India. On the other hand, many of the Indian novels, such as *Azadi*, *Train to Pakistan*, or *Rich Like Us*, show that this is simply not the case. In *Azadi* there is a clear Hindu–Muslim opposition in the families of Lala Kanshi Ram and Chaudhri Barkat Ali, but what is striking about these families is that despite their different religions, their lives are essentially the same. In his documentary film, *The Riddle of Midnight*, Rushdie highlights a Muslim tailor and a Hindu sari-seller and shows that whilst in India there is always your opposite, he or she may be no different from you. In *Midnight's Children* Saleem grows up a Muslim in a comfortable, middle-class urban environment; Shiva, like the majority of Indians, grows up a Hindu in difficult, lower-class circumstances. Identity, then, is not simply a matter of religion, but is strongly linked to place, the Punjab, Bengal, Kashmir or wherever, or to the division between village and city. It is also linked to language, as Rushdie shows:

> India had been divided anew, into fourteen states and six centrally-administered 'territories'. But the boundaries of these states were not formed by rivers, or mountains, or any natural features of the terrain; they were, instead, walls of words. Language divided us: Kerala was for speakers of Malayalam, the only palindromically-named tongue on earth: in Karnataka you were supposed to speak Kanarese; and the amputated state of Madras – known today as Tamil Nadu – enclosed the *aficionados* of Tamil. (p. 189)

His 'walls of words' points to the difficulties of any real communication, even for those who speak the same language, and in so doing he identifies one of the major concerns of twentieth-century fiction, philosophy, education. Indeed, his definition of himself as foetus, as a linguistic object, takes to its extreme the postmodernist view that human beings are defined by language:

> What had been (at the beginning) no bigger than a full stop had expanded into a comma, a word, a sentence, a paragraph, a chapter; now it was bursting into more complex developments, becoming, one might say, a book – perhaps an encyclopaedia – even a whole language. (p. 100)

Similarly, his focus on the 1957 language marches in Bombay highlights the division within the state of Bombay between the supporters of the Marathi language and the supporters of the Gujerati tongue.
Here political parties are formed, not along religious lines, but
following language divisions. Rushdie is showing, here and throughout *Midnight's Children*, that the real problem facing India is that
there are six hundred and thirty million versions of India:

> I am not speaking metaphorically; nor is this the opening gambit
> of some melodramatic, riddling, grubby appeal for pity. I mean
> quite simply that I have begun to crack all over like an old jug –
> that my poor body, singular, unlovely, buffeted by too much
> history, subjected to drainage above and drainage below, muti-
> lated by doors, brained by spittoons, has started coming apart at
> the seams. In short, I am literally disintegrating, slowly for the
> moment, although there are signs of acceleration. I ask you only
> to accept (as I have accepted) that I shall eventually crumble into
> (approximately) six hundred and thirty million particles of
> anonymous, and necessarily oblivious dust. (p. 37)

There are, in other words, as many Indias as there are Indians, as
many histories as there are historians.

This sense of multiplicity is vivid when Saleem, like Ashok (in *The
Far Pavilions*) and Kim before him, suffers an identity crisis which
forces him to ask the answer the question of his own identity:

> Who what am I? My answer: I am the sum total of everything that
> went before me, of all I have been seen done, of everything done-
> to-me. I am everyone everything whose being-in-the-world affected
> was affected by mine. I am anything that happens after I've gone
> which would not have happened if I had not come. (p. 383)

For Kim and for Ashok, the question of identity was fundamentally
a question of the individual divided between East and West, but
for Saleem, Rushdie allows no such simple divisions; there are no
such choices in India. As Saleem continues: 'Nor am I particularly
exceptional in this matter; each "I", every one of the now-six-
hundred-million-plus of us, contains a similar multitude. I repeat
for the last time: to understand me, you'll have to swallow a world'
(p. 383). In any twentieth-century context, Indian or other, it is
impossible to see any one life as separate from all others.

This theme of the multiplicity of identity makes it fitting that Saleem should be the child of so many parents. And it is in keeping with Rushdie's view of history that Saleem's real father should be William Methwold, the Englishman who sells the Sinais and several other Indian families their houses at ridiculously low prices, but with two important, if unusual, conditions:

that the houses be bought complete with every last thing in them, that the entire contents be retained by the new owners; and that the actual transfer should not take place until midnight on August 15th. (p. 95)

The father of modern India, Rushdie thus asserts, is the British Raj, which left forever its mark on Indian society. Though the power of the British came to an end on 15 August, the British legacy was inherited by the newly-created nation.

Methwold's great attraction, the parting in his hair, is revealed, shortly before the transfer of the houses, to be no more than a façade; his final gesture is to reveal that the irresistible centre-parting is that of a hairpiece. The power of the British Raj, according to this version of history, was an equally elaborate façade. The colonial confidence J.G. Farrell exposes as so fragile in his description of the buildings in *The Siege of Krishnapur* is again seen in Rushdie's description of Methwold's Estate.

Like J.G. Farrell, Ruth Prawer Jhabvala, Paul Scott and Nayantara Sahgal, Salman Rushdie uses a painting in his novel. Farrell, Jhabvala and Scott, however, all used paintings to describe the attitudes of various characters at particular points in history. Rushdie uses John Everett Millais' painting, *The Boyhood of Raleigh* (Plate 7) to stand in the novel as both a literal and metaphorical presence. As a literal presence it is part of the English furniture of the Methwold houses. This furniture, so unsuitable and irrelevant at first to the Indian ways of life, becomes metaphorical in representing the British culture and habits forced upon India, inappropriate and unused initially, but gradually absorbed by Indians. Thus, for example, Saleem, by imagining the fisherman is wearing a red dhoti, is able to claim the painting and make it Indian. *The Boyhood of Raleigh* is referred to on numerous occasions in the novel: indeed it is one of Saleem's earliest memories, one of the childhood memories which form the imagination, and influence the ways of seeing:

Memory of my blue bedroom wall: on which, next to the P.M.'s
letter, the Boy Raleigh hung for many years, gazing rapturously at
an old fisherman in what looked like a red dhoti, who sat on –
what? – driftwood? – and pointed out to sea as he told his fishy
tales . . . (p. 15)

Like the paintings and the framed calligraphy in Nayantara Sahgal's
Rich Like Us, this painting is a part of 'the writing on the wall', both
literally, hanging next to the prophetic letter from Nehru, and in its
subject.

The subject of the painting is the young Walter Raleigh, listening
to stories of faraway places indicated by the hand of the fisherman-
narrator pointing out to sea. The painting is thus a reminder of the
British past, of the sixteenth-century voyages of exploration, and
the early years of British expansion which led to the Empire. The
painting is also a reminder of the future, using hindsight in much
the same way as it is used, for example, in Farrell's *The Siege of
Krishnapur*. The observer of the Millais painting must know the
future of the adult Raleigh in order to appreciate the meaning of the
painting, the effect on the child's future of stories about the past, just
as the reader of Farrell's novel must know the future history of
Britain in order to understand the meaning of the novel, the effect
upon the British imagination of the 1850s. Similarly, in *Midnight's
Children* the reader knows something about the future, of Saleem
at thirty-two, because of his comments which regularly interrupt
the chronological narrative.

The painting is also linked to Rushdie's narrative method. The
fisherman-narrator, with his back to the audience, is like the story-
teller Saleem, at first scarcely visible to the reader, having only half
an identity, whilst both Padma and the reader are in the position of
the young Raleigh, fascinated and engrossed by the narrator's story.

As the novel continues it becomes clear that the fisherman's
pointing finger, the finger of fate which pointed the young Raleigh
on his way, is also pointing Saleem on his way. The fisherman's
pointing finger links Saleem's story to history, in a chapter aptly
entitled 'The fisherman's pointing finger':

In a picture hanging on a bedroom wall, I sat beside Walter
Raleigh and followed a fisherman's pointing finger with my eyes;
eyes straining at the horizon, beyond which lay – what? – my
future, perhaps; my special doom, of which I was aware from the

beginning, as a shimmering grey presence in that sky-blue room, indistinct at first, but impossible to ignore . . . because the finger pointed even further than that shimmering horizon, it pointed beyond teak frame, across a brief expanse of sky-blue wall, driving my eyes towards another frame, in which my inescapable destiny hung, forever fixed under glass: here was a jumbo-sized baby-snap with its prophetic captions, and here, beside it, a letter on high-quality vellum, embossed with the seal of state – the lions of Sarnath stood above the dharma-chakra on the Prime Minister's missive, which arrived via Vishwanath the post-boy, one week after my photograph appeared on the front page of the *Times of India* (p. 122)

When Saleem writes 'The fishermen were here first' (p. 92), he is speaking both literally, the fishermen were in Bombay long before the British, and metaphorically, as destiny or fate, in terms of the painting. And indeed the finger of fate, or in this case the finger of history, controls other lives besides Saleem's:

. . . the enuretic Zafar Zulfikar. Who became, between April and July, the archetype of all the many disappointing sons in the land; history, working through him, was also pointing its finger at Gauhar, at future-Sanjay and Kanti-Lal-to-come; and, naturally, at me. (p. 334)

There are other fingers at work, too, in this novel, which direct the course of history. Saleem's father's decision to leave Delhi and move to Bombay coincides with another hand pointing the way:

just as he was turning to go he heard a dirty screech in the sky, and, looking up, had time to register that a vulture – at night! – a vulture from the Towers of Silence was flying overhead, and that it had dropped a barely-chewed Parsee hand, a right hand, the same hand which – now! – slapped him full in the face as it fell. (p. 91)

This hand, like the fisherman's hand in the Millais painting, is a right hand. And finally, it is the Widow's Hand which is responsible for the fate of the children of midnight – their mass sterilization and the draining of hope.

Michael Harris suggests that: 'Although many Indian and British novelists have written about India, Rushdie's novel represents a literary landmark in that he has created something distinctly new and dynamic in his reworking of this ancient geographical and cultural subject'.[10] Rushdie does this by breaking away from the traditional form of the historical novel, and turning to what is commonly called fantasy. As Rukmini Bhaya Nair rightly asserts, fantasy in this novel is 'purposeful, it distinguishes the protagonists from millions of others whose stories they represent; fantasy is harnessed in service of the truth, of reality'.[11]

In mixing the recognisably realistic with the fantastic in *Midnight's Children*, Rushdie adopts the form known as magic realism. For Rushdie, as for García Márquez and Grass, his subject demanded it.[12] The recent history of South American politics is so incredible, the Hitler years in Germany so bizarre, that they cannot be understood in normal terms, in a realist novel. The same is true of the period of Indian history that Rushdie deals with in *Midnight's Children*. There is some truth in Richard Cronin's suggestion that: 'The Indian English novel cannot be written by a simple realist, but only by a writer willing to flirt with fantasy, a writer ready to dally with the Bombay talkie'.[13] The elements of fantasy allow him to express, in a literary form, the connections between inner and outer reality, or what Saleem calls the 'eternal opposition of inside and outside' (p. 236). *Outer* reality is to do with verifiable facts; the street names in Bombay, for example, are verifiable facts, and Bombay is a 'real' place. Similarly, within the context of the novel, it is a verifiable fact that Saleem is not the son of his mother and father. However, the *internal* reality of these 'facts' can be almost infinitely modified by the subjective perception of them, by author, or by historian, as well as by characters. Thus it makes no difference that Saleem is not the son of his parents. As Saleem asserts, there is also,

> Memory's truth, because memory has its own special kind. It selects, eliminates, alters, exaggerates, minimizes, glorifies, and vilifies also; but in the end it creates its own reality, its heterogeneous but usually coherent version of events: and no sane human being ever trusts someone else's version more than his own. (p. 211)

In other words, many elements which may appear fantastic or magic in the external world, can be both real and natural in the mind. Thus a reference by Saleem to his father's 'unreal worlds of the djinns' (p. 131) brings together the real world of drink (gin) and the unreal world of djinns. Further, Saleem tells us that the servants 'sold their identities on little pieces of pink paper; and my father turned them into liquid and drank them down' (p. 132). Whilst at first this is an extraordinary statement, it is literally true. And the language Rushdie uses here, 'turned them into', is noticeably the language of the alchemist or magician.

Rushdie's form of magic realism is one which mixes the old 'realist' plot of external action, not only in time, but in the exaggeratedly specific time which is history, with the modernist sense of a moral internal action, or the exaggeratedly unreal action of memory or dream. Rushdie says of *Midnight's Children*:

> Many people, especially in the West, who read *Midnight's Children*, talked about it as a fantasy novel. By and large, nobody in India talks about it as a fantasy novel; they talk about it as a novel of history and politics.[14]

The treatment of time is also very interesting in *Midnight's Children*, and relevant to this discussion of history. Despite its insistence on clock-time, it treats time-history in a variety of ways. Firstly, of course, linear time is evident, despite its many digressions, in Saleem's story of his grandparents and parents. Forward progress is demanded by Padma (who speaks for the reader?): 'But here is Padma at my elbow, bullying me back into the world of linear narrative, the universe of what-happened-next' (p. 38).

What Berdyaev calls cosmic or circular time is clearly seen with the birth of Aadam Sinai. The announcement of his birth is almost an exact repetition of the announcement of Saleem's birth twenty-eight years earlier:

> He was born in Old Delhi . . . once upon a time. No, that won't do, there's no getting away from the date: Aadam Sinai arrived at a night-shadowed slum on June 25th 1975. And the time? The time matters, too. As I said: at night. No, it's important to be more . . . On the stroke of midnight, as a matter of fact. Clock-hands joined palms. Oh, spell it out, spell it out: at the precise instant of India's arrival at Emergency, he emerged. (p. 419)

Like Saleem, his father is not his father, and like Saleem he is myster-iously handcuffed to history, his birth coinciding with the exact birth of the Emergency, just as Saleem's birth coincided with the birth of Independence.

Existential time, time in the mind (Bergson's 'duré') which allows an escape from time-history, is explained in the moral story Mona tells Rose in Nayantara Sahgal's *Rich Like Us*:

> Once a teacher asked his young disciple to fetch him a glass of water and the young man went off to get it, but on the way he met a beautiful girl whom he fell in love with and married. They lived happily together, had three children and cultivated their fields. Before long floods came, and later drought, and they had to work very hard to recover from these calamities, but finally all was well again. Their children were growing fast and in good health, and the whole family was prospering when one day the teacher arrived in the village, looking for his disciple, and said to him, 'Where is that glass of water, my son? I have been waiting half an hour for it.' (p. 208)

In *Midnight's Children* Rushdie allows the linear narrative to assert the authority of time-history, while simultaneously denying, by his use of existential time, that time-history can give a full account of human experience. Existential time is most vividly expressed in the journey through the Sundarbans. As Saleem and his three com-panions approach the jungle, Ayooba kills Father Time and leaves him 'dead in a rice-paddy' (p. 359). Saleem and his companions then enter 'the jungle which is so thick that history has hardly ever found the way in. The Sundarbans: it swallows them up' (p. 359). Once inside the dream jungle they leave behind history, and time, too. Ayooba Baluch cried 'for three entire hours or days or weeks' (p. 361), and they find themselves the victims of the 'time-shifting sorcery of the forest' (p. 368). It is only when they emerge, finally, that time and history return, and the reader learns that their ordeal has lasted for seven months.

Like identity, time-history is not as simple as some novelists and historians would have us believe, and Rushdie shows this with consummate skill in *Midnight's Children*.

Midnight's Children covers a much broader period of history than any of the novels previously analyzed. More complex than any other fiction written about India and more all-encompassing, it tells a multiplicity of stories and offers many versions of history within one novel. But always the versions of history are rooted in documented events. Despite this, however, Rushdie effectively pulls the carpet of truth from under the reader's feet when he begins his final chapter with the oxymoron, 'To tell the truth, I lied' (p. 443). He could as easily be writing about any event in the narrative as about Shiva's death. The reader is forced to agree that 'Nothing was real; nothing certain' (p. 340). In *Midnight's Children*, Rushdie takes fiction and history as far as they have ever been taken together.

9
Epilogue

If you are human you are responsible, responsible in your moment and your context. Who is to say what matters? History plays tricks on us all.[1]

In his article, 'Manohar Malgonkar the Novelist', Ram Sewak Singh begins his final paragraph with the words, 'Lastly, one question remains: whether *A Bend in the Ganges*, a very fine novel, can be read as a document of history too'.[2] It is a question that can be asked about any of Malgonkar's novels, or about any of the novels discussed in this study. The answer in each case must be yes, because consciously (or with the kind of *self*-consciousness we now call self-reflexive), every author I have discussed brings a sense of history to fiction.

It is now generally accepted that one fruitful way of recovering the past is through the work of imaginative writers, and it is evident that the literary works of both British and Indian novelists can tell us a great deal about the history of India. *Kim*, for example, gives us valuable insights into the attitudes towards Empire in the final decades of the nineteenth century, whilst *A Passage to India* is not only a literary exploration of spiritual struggle, but also a useful document which contributes to our understanding of the British in India in the early part of the twentieth century. Those novels which conform to some definition of the historical novel are perhaps even more important as documents of history; they offer insights into particular historical events, and, in addition, record how those events were interpreted at a later stage of history. Thus *The Siege of Krishnapur* adds to our understanding of the Mutiny, tells us about Britain in the 1850s, and carries implications about Britain in the 1970s, too.

Novels like Farrell's show that history is not merely the record of events or personalities; it is the attempt to capture the spirit of a culture, including the games, entertainments and artistic products. Paintings embody the visual and ideological aspects of a particular age, and thus references to them allow the author to immerse the reader more fully in that *Zeitgeist*. The dress, the scenery, as well as the events of historical paintings, are all expressions of the period; but more importantly the paintings used in novels such as *The Siege of Krishnapur* and Paul Scott's *Raj Quartet* are used to show the attitudes of the age. A painting like *The Boyhood of Raleigh*, which Salman Rushdie uses in *Midnight's Children*, has a slightly different function, becoming metaphor as much as synecdoche. Historical fiction wants to convey to the reader how it 'felt' to exist at a particular time; it is able to do this because of the many devices at its command not available to academic studies of history.

This study argues that a number of authors present love and humanity as an answer to the problems of the Mutiny and Partition, to the East–West conflict, as in *A Passage to India*, and to the conflicts within Indian society shown in *Train to Pakistan* and *Rich Like Us*. Forster dramatises through Aziz and Fielding that the legacy of the Mutiny and imperial rule meant there could be no genuine friendship between nations or even between individuals until some future resolution of differences, as the closing lines of *A Passage to India* indicate. In novels such as the *Raj Quartet*, *Indigo* and Santha Rama Rau's *Remember the House* (1956), the England-educated Indian combines both East and West, but the apparent resolution of the East–West conflict causes conflicts of a different kind. Hari Kumar raises once more the question of whether it is possible for an Englishman to be friends with an Indian, and the events of Scott's series of novels seems to agree with Hamidullah in *A Passage to India*, who suggests it is only possible on English soil. Thus the novelist's interest in character works alongside the historian's interest in events, to reveal the effect on individual lives of these periods of struggle.

It also seems clear that, as we move later into the twentieth century, novels which seek to re-create a particular place and a particular time, Lucknow in 1857, or New Delhi in 1975, now, paradoxically, seek to be about the world, not simply about one country. Rushdie's *Midnight's Children* is, of course, the best example of this, but he is by no means alone in his interest in global politics and events. As the past cannot be separated from the present, so it is evident that India cannot be isolated from the influence of the world around it.

In writing about history one must be aware of one's own ideology, and of the shaping-force of one's background. I have not sought to neutralise the influences that have affected my views, but I have tried to be aware of them. Just as there is more than one legitimate way of seeing historical events, so there is more than one set of shaping influences and ideologies that can be brought to the study of any given subject. Like many before me, I, too, have felt the pull of India, and this book is my response to a literary journey through many Indias. Ved Mehta's words in *Walking the Indian Streets* (1963) are an apt conclusion to that journey:

> Shifting images pass before me: Victorian, Civil Service, English India, with tremulous whispers about sex and with smoking-room banter. Political India, with curious legislatures. Intellectual India, with a Sanskrit text. Indias are endless.[3]

Notes and References

1. INTRODUCTORY: FICTION AS HISTORY

1. Raja Rao, *The Serpent and the Rope* (London: Murray, 1960), p. 84.
2. Salman Rushdie, *Midnight's Children* (1981; rpt, London: Picador, 1982), p. 112. All subsequent page references are to this edition and appear parenthetically in the text.
3. Veronica Brady, 'Straddling Two Cultures', rev. of *The Tiger's Daughter*, by Bharati Mukherjee, *CRNLE Reviews Journal*, nos. 1 and 2 (1988), p. 109.
4. Ronald Binns, *J.G. Farrell* (London: Methuen, 1986), pp. 64–5.
5. Manohar Malgonkar, *Distant Drum* (Bombay: Asia Publishing House, 1960), p. 153.
6. See Nicholas Rance, *The Historical Novel and Popular Politics in Nineteenth-Century England* (London: Vision, 1975), pp. 42–4.
7. Linda Hutcheon, *A Poetics of Postmodernism: History, Theory, Fiction* (London: Routledge, 1988), p. 105.
8. Hutcheon, p. 93.
9. Patrick Brantlinger, *Rule of Darkness: British Literature and Imperialism, 1830–1914* (Ithaca and London: Cornell University Press, 1988), p. 12.
10. Richard D. Altick, *Victorian People and Ideas* (New York: Norton, 1973), p. 15.
11. Jerome Hamilton Buckley, *The Triumph of Time* (Cambridge, Mass.: Belknap Press of Harvard University Press, 1966), p. 81.
12. Paul Scott, 'India: A Post-Forsterian View', in *Essays by Divers Hands*, no 36, ed. Mary Stocks (Oxford University Press, 1970), p. 13.
13. Manohar Malgonkar, *A Bend in the Ganges* (London: Hamish Hamilton, 1964), p. 122.
14. Malgonkar, *Distant Drum*, p. 44.
15. Max Beloff, 'The End of the Raj: Paul Scott's Novels as History', *Encounter*, 36, no. 5 (1976), 66.
16. L.P. Hartley, introd. to *The Go-Between* (London: Heinemann, 1953), p. 2.
17. See Sir Walter Scott, *Waverley* (1814; rpt, Oxford: Oxford World's Classics, 1986), pp. 3–5.
18. Hartley, p. 2.
19. Frank Kermode, *The Sense of an Ending* (1967; Oxford University Press, 1968), p. 43.
20. Marc Bloch, *The Historian's Craft*, trans. Peter Putnam (Manchester University Press, 1954), p. 43.
21. Hayden White, *Tropics of Discourse* (Baltimore: Johns Hopkins University Press, 1978), p. 41.
22. E.M. Forster, *Aspects of the Novel* (1927; rpt, Harmondsworth: Penguin, 1966), pp. 52–3.
23. Georg Lukács, *The Historical Novel*, trans. Hannah and Stanley Mitchell (London: Merlin, 1962), p. 39.

24. Hutcheon, p. 114.
25. Avrom Fleishman, *The English Historical Novel: Walter Scott to Virginia Woolf* (Baltimore: Johns Hopkins University Press, 1971), p. 15.

2. THE GREAT REVOLT: 1857

1. Manohar Malgonkar, *The Devil's Wind* (New York: Viking, 1972), p. 136. All subsequent page references are to this edition and appear parenthetically in the text.
2. Unsigned, 'The Indian Mutiny in Fiction', *Blackwood's Edinburgh Magazine*, Feb. 1897, 218.
3. Shailendra Dhari Singh, *Novels on the Indian Mutiny* (New Delhi: Arnold Heinemann India, 1973), pp. 230–46.
4. 'The Indian Mutiny in Fiction', p. 230.
5. Shailendra Dhari Singh, pp. 230–2.
6. O. Douglas [Anna Buchan], *Olivia in India* (London: Hodder & Stoughton, 1912), p. 113.
7. Dinshaw M. Burjorjee, 'The Indian Mutiny in Anglo-Indian Fiction Written after the Second World War', in *Chandrabhaga*, no. 8 (1982), p. 15.
8. John Masters, *Bugles and a Tiger* (1956; rpt, London: Reprint Society, 1957), p. 36.
9. Shailendra Dhari Singh, p. 183.
10. Bhupal Singh, *A Survey of Anglo-Indian Fiction*, (1934; rpt, London: Curzon, 1974), pp. 3–4.
11. Burjorjee, p. 23.
12. Allen J. Greenberger, *The British Image of India* (Oxford University Press, 1969), p. 179.
13. John Masters, *Nightrunners of Bengal* (1951; rpt, London: Sphere, 1977). All subsequent page references are to this edition and appear parenthetically in the text.
14. M.M. Kaye, *Shadow of the Moon* (rev. edn 1979; rpt, Harmondsworth: Penguin, 1980).
15. *The Sunday Times.* Quoted on the cover of the Sphere edition of the novel (London: Sphere, 1971).
16. Bhupal Singh, p. 179.
17. Burjorjee holds a similar opinion. In the second part of his essay 'The Indian Mutiny in Anglo-Indian Fiction Written after the Second World War', *Chandrabhaga*, no. 9 (1983), p. 48, he writes: 'The best Mutiny novel to date is J.G. Farrell's *The Siege of Krishnapur*'.
18. For an account of the Rani of Jhansi's role in the Mutiny see Christopher Hibbert, *The Great Mutiny* (1978; rpt, Harmondsworth: Penguin, 1980), pp. 377–85. The story of the Rani of Jhansi is treated in four early Mutiny novels: *The Afghan Knife* by Robert Armitage Sterndale, FRGS (1879); *The Rane* by Gillean [Major J.N.H. MacLean] (1887); *The Queen's Desire* by Hume Nisbet (1893); and *The Star of Fortune, a Story of the Indian Mutiny* by J.E. Muddock (1895).

19. For a fascinating account of the daily life of an Untouchable see Mulk Raj Anand's novel *Untouchable* (1933).

20. Philip Woodruff, *The Founders*, vol. 1 of *The Men Who Ruled India* (London: Jonathan Cape, 1953), p. 353.

21. See also the portrait of Bulstrode on pp. 188–9.

22. O. Douglas, p. 60.

23. Shailendra Dhari Singh, p. 11.

24. Burjorjee, p. 27.

25. See Georg Lukács, *The Historical Novel*, trans, Hannah and Stanley Mitchell (London; Merlin, 1962) p. 63.

26. J.G. Farrell, *The Siege of Krishnapur* (1973; rpt, Harmondsworth: Penguin, 1979), p. 24. All subsequent page references are to this edition and appear parenthetically in the text.

27. E.M. Forster, *A Passage to India* (1924; rpt, Harmondsworth: Penguin, 1979), p. 31. All subsequent page references are to this edition and appear parenthetically in the text. This similarity has also been observed by Allen J. Greenberger and Edith L. Piness, in their essay 'The Legacy of the Raj: J.G. Farrell's *The Siege of Krishnapur'*, *Indo-British Review – A Journal of History*, 11, no. 1 (1984), 112.

28. Frances B. Singh, 'Progress and History in J.G. Farrell's *The Siege of Krishnapur'*, *Chandrabhaga*, no. 2 (1979), p. 29.

29. Rumer Godden, *Kingfishers Catch Fire* (1953; rpt, London: Reprint Society, 1955), p. 67.

30. William Golding, *Lord of the Flies* (London: Faber, 1954), p. 247.

31. Mary Lutyens, *Effie in Venice* (London: Murray, 1965), p. 21.

32. Alfred Lord Tennyson, 'The Defence of Lucknow', lines 1–6, in *The Works of Alfred Lord Tennyson*, (London: Macmillan, 1932), p. 519.

33. Hibbert, p. 171.

34. Hibbert, pp. 194–5.

35. Charles Ball, *The History of the Indian Mutiny*, 2 vols (London: n.d), vol. 2, p. 337, quoted in Hibbert, p. 370.

36. William Shakespeare, *The Merchant of Venice*, ed. W. Moelwyn Merchant (Harmondsworth: Penguin, 1967), III. i. 63–6.

3. THE PERIOD OF THE GREAT GAME

1. Rudyard Kipling, *Kim* (1901; rpt, London: Macmillan, 1985), p. 285. All subsequent page references are to this edition and appear parenthetically in the text.

2. J.G. Farrell, *The Hill Station* (London: Weidenfeld & Nicolson, 1981), p. 41. All subsequent page references are to this edition and appear parenthetically in the text.

3. Philip Woodruff, *The Guardians*, vol. 2 of *The Men Who Ruled India* (London: Jonathan Cape, 1954), pp. 27–8.

4. John Spurling, 'As Does the Bishop' [an appreciation], in *The Hill Station* (London: Weidenfeld & Nicolson, 1981), p. 160.

5. Ronald Binns, *J.G. Farrell* (London, Methuen, 1986) p. 84.

6. Spurling, p. 154.
7. Paul Theroux, 'An Interrupted Journey', *Sunday Times*, 26 April 1981, p. 42.
8. Binns, p. 83.
9. See Jeffrey Meyers, *Disease and the Novel, 1880–1960* (New York: St. Martin's Press, 1985) for many twentieth-century European parallels.
10. Richard D. Altick, *Victorian People and Ideas* (New York: Norton, 1973) p. 209.
11. Spurling, pp. 156–7.
12. Spurling, p. 157.
13. Altick, p. 200.
14. See for example, J.M.S. Tompkins, *The Art of Rudyard Kipling* (London: Methuen, 1959), pp. 29ff., where the author compares *Kim* and *Huckleberry Finn*, and Norman Page, *A Kipling Companion* (London: Macmillan, 1984), p. 153.
15. Angus Wilson, *The Strange Ride of Rudyard Kipling* (London: Book Club Associates, 1977), pp. 75–6.
16. K. Bhaskara Rao, *Rudyard Kipling's India* (Norman: University of Oklahoma Press, 1967), p. 140.
17. Angus Wilson, introd. to *Kim*, by Rudyard Kipling (1981; rpt, London: Macmillan, 1985), p. x.
18. Bhaskara Rao, p. 157.
19. See Page, p. 151.
20. Wilson, *The Strange Ride of Rudyard Kipling*, p. 90.
21. Bhaskara Rao, p. 159.
22. Edward W. Said, '*Kim*, The Pleasures of Imperialism', *Raritan*, 7, no. 2 (1987), 27.
23. Bhupal Singh, *A Survey of Anglo-Indian Fiction* (1934; rpt, London: Curzon, 1974), p. 83.
24. M.M. Kaye, *The Far Pavilions* (1978; rpt, Harmondsworth: Penguin, 1979), p. 874. All subsequent page references are to this edition and appear parenthetically in the text.
25. Edmund Wilson, 'The Kipling that Nobody Reads', *The Wound and the Bow*, rev. edn (1952; rpt, London: Methuen, 1961), p. 110.

4. BRIDGES

1. E.M. Forster, *A Passage to India* (1924; rpt, Harmondsworth: Penguin, 1979), p. 49.
2. Stallybrass, introd. to *A Passage to India*, pp. 12–13.
3. Scott. 'India: A Post-Forsterian View', in *Essays by Divers Hands*, no. 36, ed. Mary Stocks (Oxford University Press, 1976), p. 125.
4. Santha Rama Rau, *A Passage to India* [a play from the novel by E.M. Forster] (London: Edward Arnold, 1960), p. 7.
5. Stallybrass, introd., *A Passage to India*, p. 25.

6. Frank Kermode, *Essays on Fiction 1971–82* (London: Routledge & Kegan Paul, 1983), prologue, p. 14.
7. E.M. Forster, 'Prefatory Note (1957) to the Everyman Edition', in *A Passage to India*, p. 317.
8. Philip Gardner, introd. to *E.M. Forster, The Critical Heritage* (London: Routledge & Kegan Paul, 1973), p. 2.
9. Ramlal Agarwal, 'Forster, Jhabvala and Readers', *Journal of Indian Writing in English*, 3, no. 2 (1976), 25.
10. Ruth Prawer Jhabvala, *Heat and Dust* (1975; rpt, London: Futura, 1983), p. 2. All subsequent page references are to this edition and appear parenthetically in the text.
11. See Ruth Prawer Jhabvala, 'Disinheritance', *Blackwood's Edinburgh Magazine*, July 1979, p. 8.
12. The links which intertwine these stories, and the links between *A Passage to India* and *A New Dominion*, are quite deliberate, but not germane to the present discussion.
13. Charles Allen, *Raj: A Scrapbook of British India 1877–1947* (London: Deutsch, 1977), p. 18.
14. The boredom of the Indian upper classes is the subject of Satyajit Ray's film *The Chess Players* (India, 1978). *The Chess Players* is an allegorical film set in Oudh in 1856, which revolves around the annexation of that state by the British. The film focuses on the indolent noblemen whose games of chess parallel the games of Empire being played by the British.
15. Christine Weston, *Indigo* (1944; rpt, London: Reprint Society, 1946), p. 270.
16. Salman Rushdie, *'Midnight's Children* and *Shame'*, *Kunapipi*, 7, no. 1 (1985), p. 7.
17. Rushdie, *'Midnight's Children* and *Shame'*, pp. 7–8.
18. Raja Rao, *Kanthapura* (1938; rpt, Bombay: Oxford University Press, 1947), p. 112. All subsequent page references to this edition and appear parenthetically in the text.
19. Ediriwira Sarachchandra, 'Illusion and Reality: Raja Rao as Novelist', in *Only Connect: Literary Perspectives East and West*, ed. Guy Amirthanayagam and S.C. Harrex (Adelaide and Honolulu: Centre for Research in the New Literatures in English & East–West Center, 1981), pp. 108–9.
20. C.D. Narisimhaiah, 'Raja Rao's *Kanthapura*: An Analysis', in *Fiction and the Reading Public in India*, ed. C.D. Narisimhaiah (University of Mysore, 1967), p. 63.
21. Presumably Rao's reference to Saradamma's novel *The Red Pyre* (pp. 144–5) is a means of further establishing the age in a literary context. I have been unable to trace this novel – perhaps because the title given here is a translation of a work in an Indian language. Saradamma is a South Indian name.
22. Sarachchandra, p. 108.
23. Geoffrey Moorehouse, *India Britannica* (1983; rpt, London: Paladin, 1986), p. 119.

5. SWARAJ

1. Paul Scott, *The Jewel in the Crown* (1966; rpt, London: Granada, 1980), p. 427. All subsequent page references are to this edition and appear parenthetically in the text.
2. A.V. Krishna Rao, 'Identity and Environment: Narayan's *The Guide* and Naipaul's *A House for Mr Biswas*', in *Inventing Countries: Essays in Post-Colonial Literatures* (Wollongong: SPACLALS, 1987), p. 168.
3. R.K. Narayan, *Waiting for the Mahatma* (Michigan State University Press, 1955), p. 52. All subsequent page references are to this edition and appear parenthetically in the text.
4. Jim Masselos, *Indian Nationalism: An History* (New Delhi: Sterling Publishers, 1985), p. 207.
5. George Woodcock, 'The Sometime Sahibs: Two Post-Independence British Novelists of India', *Queen's Quarterly*, 86 (1979–80), 49.
6. Paul Scott, *The Towers of Silence* (1971; rpt, London: Granada, 1979), p. 46. All subsequent page references are to this edition and appear parenthetically in the text.
7. Paul Scott, *A Division of the Spoils* (1975; rpt, London: Granada, 1979), p. 261. All subsequent page references are to this edition and appear parenthetically in the text.
8. Paul Scott, *The Day of the Scorpion* (1968; rpt, London: Granada, 1979), p. 32. All subsequent page references are to this edition and appear parenthetically in the text.
9. There is a relationship between illusion and truth in Hindu philosophy. Samkara explains that 'a person may mistake a rope for a serpent. The serpent is not there, but it is not entirely an illusion, for there is the rope'. K.M. Sen, *Hinduism* (Harmondsworth: Penguin, 1981), p. 83. This relationship is also explored in *Kim* during Kim's early training with Lurgan Sahib.
10. Allen Boyer, 'Love, Sex and History in *The Raj Quartet*', *Modern Language Quarterly*, 46, no. 1 (1985), 68.
11. Kenneth Burke, 'Social and Cosmic Mystery: *A Passage to India*', in *Language as Symbolic Action: Essays on Life, Literature, and Method* (University of California Press, 1966), p. 226.
12. *Man-bap* is usually translated as meaning 'I am your father and mother' – the supposed relationship between the Raj and India.
13. Patrick Swinden, *Paul Scott: Images of India* (London: Macmillan, 1980), p. 89.
14. Max Beloff, 'The End of the Raj: Paul Scott's Novels as History', *Encounter*, 36, no. 5 (1976), p. 67.
15. Paul Scott, 'India: A Post-Forsterian View', in *Essays by Divers Hands*, no. 36, ed. Mary Stocks (London: Oxford University Press, 1976) p. 115.
16. Scott, 'India: A Post-Forsterian View', p. 116.
17. Scott, 'India: A Post-Forsterian View', p. 113.
18. Allen J. Greenberger, *The British Image of India* (Oxford University Press, 1969) p. 185.

19. John Masters, *Bhowani Junction* (1954; rpt, London: Sphere, 1983), p. 9. All subsequent page references are to this edition and appear parenthetically in the text.

20. Geoffrey Moorehouse, *India Britannica* (1983; rpt, London: Paladin, 1986), p. 144.

21. Manohar Malgonkar, *The Princes* (London: Hamish Hamilton, 1963), p. 13. All subsequent page references are to this edition and appear parenthetically in the text.

22. Saros Cowasjee, introd. to *Private Life of an Indian Prince*, by Mulk Raj Anand (London: Bodley Head, 1953), p. 13.

23. Moorehouse, p. 179.

24. Moorehouse, p. 17.

25. James Y. Dayananda, 'Manohar Malgonkar on His Novel *The Princes: An Interview*', *Journal of Commonwealth Literature*, 9, no. 3 (1975), 23.

26. Dayananda, p. 27.

6. PARTITION

1. Kushwant Singh, *Train to Pakistan* (1956; rpt, New Delhi: Ravi Dayal, 1988), p. 9. All subsequent page references are to this edition and appear parenthetically in the text.

2. The original title of the novel is *Train to Pakistan*. *Mano Majra* is the US title.

3. Chaman Nahal, Author's Note in *Azadi* (New Delhi: Arnold-Heinemann India, 1975). All subsequent page references are to this edition and appear parenthetically in the text.

4. Martin Levin, rev. of *Azadi*, *New York Times Book Review*. Quoted on the cover of the Arnold-Heinemann edition of the novel.

5. Shakti Batra, 'Two Partition Novels', *Indian Literature*, 18. no. 3 (1975), 83–103.

6. See John Henry Raleigh, 'The English Novel and the Three Kinds of Time', *Sewanee Review*, 62, no. 3 (1954), 244.

7. THE END OF THE OLD ORDER

1. Nayantara Sahgal, *Rich Like Us* (London: Heinemann, 1985), p. 157. All subsequent page references are to this edition and appear parenthetically in the text.

2. See Heather Wood, *Third Class Ticket* (1980; rpt, Harmondsworth: Penguin, 1984), p. 26.

3. Paul Scott, *Staying On* (1977; rpt, London: Granada, 1980), p. 86. All subsequent page references are to this edition and appear parenthetically in the text.

4. Stevie Smith, *The Holiday* (1949; rpt, London: Virago, 1979) p. 100.

5. Janis Tedesco, '*Staying On*: The Final Connection', *Western Humanities Review*, 39, no. 3 (1985), 199.

6. Yasmine Gooneratne, 'Paul Scott's *Staying On*: Finale in a Minor Key', *Journal of Indian Writing in English*, 9. no. 2 (1982), 1–2.
7. Patrick Swinden, *Paul Scott: Images of India* (London: Macmillan, 1980), p. 105.
8. L.P. Hartley, *The Go-Between*, (1953; rpt, London: Heinemann, 1963), p. 9.
9. David Rubin, *After the Raj: British Novels of India Since 1947* (Hanover and London: University Press of New England, 1986), p. 154.

8. THE CHUTNIFICATION OF HISTORY

1. Salman Rushdie, *Midnight's Children*, (1981; rpt, London: Picador, 1982), p. 461.
2. Salman Rushdie, '*Midnight's Children* and *Shame*', *Kunapipi*, 7, no. 1 (1985), p. 9.
3. Salman Rushdie, '*Midnight's Children* and *Shame*', p. 8.
4. Michael Harris, '"Transformation without End": Salman Rushdie's India', *Meridian*, 5, no. 1 (1986), 21.
5. Dieter Riemenschneider, 'History and the Individual in Salman Rushdie's *Midnight's Children* and Anita Desai's *Clear Light of Day*', *Kunapipi*, 6, no. 2 (1984), 58.
6. Bernard Bergonzi, 'Fictions of History' in *The Situation of the Novel*, 2nd edn (London: Macmillan, 1979), p. 232.
7. Riemenschneider, p. 63.
8. Rushdie, '*Midnight's Children* and *Shame*', p. 12.
9. Rukmini Bhaya Nair, 'The Voyeur's View in *Midnight's Children* and *Shame*', *ACLALS Bulletin*, 7th Series, no. 1 (1985), 62.
10. Harris, p. 15.
11. Nair, p. 63.
12. Rushdie appears to be acknowledging the influence of Grass when he names Aadam Aziz's German friend Oskar, presumably after the protagonist of Grass's *The Tin Drum*.
13. Richard Cronin, 'The Indian English Novel: *Kim* and *Midnight's Children*', *Modern Fiction Studies*, 33, no. 2 (1987), 205.
14. Rushdie, '*Midnight's Children* and *Shame*', p. 15.

9. EPILOGUE

1. Santha Rama Rau, *Remember the House* (London: Gollancz, 1956), p. 227.
2. Ram Sewak Singh, 'Manohar Malgonkar the Novelist', *Indian Literature*, 13, no. 1 (1970), 130.
3. Ved Mehta, *Walking the Indian Streets* (1963; rev. edn 1971; rpt, Harmondsworth: Penguin 1975), p. 115.

Select Bibliography

The bibliography lists all works mentioned in this study, and others which, though not cited directly, were of value in preparing the book.

PRIMARY SOURCES

Ackerley, J.R, *Hindoo Holiday*. 1932; rpt, Harmondsworth: Penguin, 1985.
Anand, Mulk Raj, *Untouchable*. 1933; rpt, Harmondsworth: Penguin, 1986.
—— *Coolie*. 1936; rpt, Harmondsworth: Penguin, 1945.
—— *Private Life of an Indian Prince*, 1953; rev. edn London: Bodley Head, 1970.
Ballantyne, R.M. *The Coral Island*. 1857; rpt, London: Nelson, n.d.
Bates, H.E. *The Scarlet Sword*. 1950; rpt, Harmondsworth: Penguin, 1980.
Bhattacharya, Bhabani. *So Many Hungers!* Bombay: Hind Kitabs, 1947.
Cadell, Elizabeth, *Sun in the Morning*, London: Hodder & Stoughton, 1951.
Chatterjee, Bankim Chandra. *Rajmohan's Wife*. 1864; rpt, Calcutta; R. Chatterjee. 1935.
Desai, Anita, *Clear Light of Day*. 1980; rpt, Harmondsworth: Penguin, 1980.
—— *Baumgartner's Bombay*. London: Heinemann, 1988.
Douglas, O. [Anna Buchan]. *Olivia in India*. London: Hodder & Stoughton, 1912.
Duncan, Sara Jeanette. *The Pool in the Desert*. 1903; rpt, Markham, Ontario: Penguin, 1984.
Farrell, J.G. *The Siege of Krishnapur* 1973; rpt, Harmondsworth: Penguin, 1979.
—— *The Hill Station*. London: Weidenfeld & Nicolson, 1981.
Forster, E.M. *A Passage to India*. 1924; rpt, Harmondsworth: Penguin, 1979.
—— *The Hill of Devi*. 1927; rpt, Harmondsworth: Penguin, 1965.
Godden, Rumer. *Black Narcissus*. 1939; rpt, Harmondsworth: Penguin, 1979.
—— *Kingfishers Catch Fire*. 1953; rpt, London: Reprint Society, 1955.
Golding, William. *Lord of the Flies*. London: Faber, 1954.
Hartley, L.P. *The Go-Between* 1953; rpt, London: Heinemann, 1963.
Jhabvala, Ruth Prawer. *A Stronger Climate*. 1968; rpt, London: Granada, 1983.
—— *A New Dominion* 1972; rpt, London: Granada, 1983.
—— *Heat and Dust*. 1975; rpt, London: Futura, 1983.
—— *Autobiography of a Princess, Also being the Adventures of an American Film Director in the Land of the Maharajas*, compiled by James Ivory; photographs by John Swope and others; screenplay by Ruth Prawer Jhabvala. London: Murray, 1975.
Kaye, M.M. *Shadow of the Moon*. 1959; rev. edn 1979; rpt, Harmondsworth: Penguin, 1980.
—— *The Far Pavilions*. 1978; rpt, Harmondsworth: Penguin, 1979.
Kipling, Rudyard. *Plain Tales from the Hills*. 1888; rpt, London: Macmillan, 1985.
—— *Life's Handicap*. 1891; rpt, London: Macmillan, 1982.

—— and Wolcott Balestier. *The Naulakha.* 1892; rpt, London: Macmillan, 1983.
—— *Kim.* 1901; rpt, London: Macmillan, 1985.
Malgonkar, Manohar. *Distant Drum.* Bombay: Asia Publishing House, 1960.
—— *The Princes.* London: Hamish Hamilton, 1963.
—— *A Bend in the Ganges.* London: Hamish Hamilton, 1964.
—— *The Devil's Wind.* New York: Viking, 1972.
Markandaya, Kamala. *The Coffer Dams.* New York: John Day, 1969.
—— *The Golden Honeycomb.* London: Chatto & Windus, 1977.
Masters, John. *Nightrunners of Bengal.* 1951; rpt, London: Sphere, 1977.
—— *The Deceivers.* 1952; rpt, London: Sphere, 1984.
—— *The Lotus and the Wind.* London: Michael Joseph, 1953.
—— *Bhowani Junction.* 1954; rpt, London: Sphere, 1983.
—— *Far, Far the Mountain Peak.* London: Michael Joseph, 1957.
—— *To the Coral Strand.* London: Michael Joseph, 1962.
Myers, L.H. *The Root and the Flower* [containing *The Near and the Far, Prince Jali, Rajah Amar*]. 1935; rpt, London: Secker & Warburg, 1984.
Nahal, Chaman. *Azadi.* New Delhi: Arnold-Heinemann India, 1975.
Naipaul, V.S. *An Area of Darkness.* 1964; rpt, Harmondsworth: Penguin, 1979.
—— *India: A Wounded Civilization.* 1977; rpt, Harmondsworth: Penguin, 1980.
Narayan, R.K. *Waiting for the Mahatma.* Michigan State University Press, 1955.
—— *The Vendor of Sweets.* 1967; rpt, Harmondsworth: Penguin, 1983.
—— *The Ramayana.* New York: Viking, 1972.
Rajan, Balachandra. *The Dark Dancer.* London: Heinemann, 1959.
Rao, Raja. *Kanthapura.* 1938; rpt, Bombay: Oxford University Press, 1947.
—— *The Serpent and the Rope.* London: Murray, 1960.
Rau, Santha Rama. *Remember the House.* London: Gollancz, 1956.
—— *A Passage to India* [a play from the novel by E.M. Forster]. London: Edward Arnold, 1960.
Rushdie, Salman. *Midnight's Children.* 1981; rpt, London: Picador, 1982.
—— *Shame.* 1983; rpt, London: Picador, 1984.
—— *The Satanic Verses.* London: Viking, 1988.
Sahgal, Nayantara. *Storm in Chandigarh.* New York: Norton, 1969.
—— *Rich Like Us.* London: Heinemann, 1985.
Scott, Paul. *The Jewel in the Crown.* 1966; rpt, London; Granada, 1980.
—— *The Day of the Scorpion.* 1968; rpt, London: Granada, 1979.
—— *The Towers of Silence.* 1971; rpt, London: Granada, 1979.
—— *A Division of the Spoils.* 1975; rpt, London: Granada, 1979.
—— *Staying On.* 1977; rpt, London: Granada, 1980.
Scott, Sir Walter. *Waverley.* 1814; rpt, Oxford: Oxford World Classics, 1986.
Shakespeare, William. *The Merchant of Venice.* Ed. W. Moelwyn Merchant. Harmondsworth: Penguin, 1967.
Sidhwa, Bapsi. *The Bride.* 1983; rpt, London: Futura, 1984.
Simeons, A.W.T. *The Mask of a Lion.* London: Gollancz, 1952.
Singh, Kushwant. *Train to Pakistan.* 1956; rpt, New Delhi: Ravi Dayal, 1988.
Smith, Stevie. *The Holiday.* 1949; rpt, London: Virago, 1979.
Sterne, Laurence. *The Life and Opinions of Tristram Shandy, Gentleman.* 1759–67; rpt, Oxford University Press, 1983.
Tennyson, Alfred Lord. 'The Defence of Lucknow'. In *The Works of Alfred*

Lord Tennyson. London: Macmillan, 1932.
Vijayan, O.V. *The Saga of Dharmapuri.* New Delhi: Penguin, 1988.
Walker, David. *Harry Black.* London: Collins, 1956.
Weston, Christine. *Indigo.* 1944; rpt, London: Reprint Society, 1946.
Wood, Heather. *Third-Class Ticket.* 1980; rpt, Harmondsworth: Penguin, 1988.

SECONDARY SOURCES

Agarwal, Ramlal. 'Forster, Jhabvala and Readers'. *Journal of Indian Writing in English,* 3, no. 2 (1976), 25–7.
Ali, Ahmed. 'Illusion and Reality: The Art and Philosophy of Raja Rao'. *Journal of Commonwealth Literature,* no. 5 (1968), pp. 16–28.
Ali, Tariq. 'Fiction as History, History as Fiction'. *Indo-British Review: A Journal of History,* 11, no. 2 (1985), 72–8.
Allen, Charles. *Plain Tales from the Raj.* 1975; rpt, London: Futura, 1985.
—— *Raj: A Scrapbook of British India 1877-1947.* London: Deutsch, 1977.
Altick, Richard D. *Victorian People and Ideas.* New York: Norton, 1973.
Asnani, Shyam M. 'The Theme of Partition in the Indo-Anglian Novel'. *Triveni,* April-June 1979, pp. 58–67.
Banerjee, Jaqueline. 'A Living Legacy: An Indian View of Paul Scott's India'. *London Magazine,* 20, nos. 1 and 2 (1980), 97–104.
Batra, Shakti. 'Two Partition Novels'. *Indian Literature,* 18, no. 3 (1975), 83–103.
Beaumont, Roger. *Sword of the Raj: The British Army in India, 1747-1947.* Indianapolis: Bobbs-Merrill, 1977.
Beloff, Max. 'The End of the Raj: Paul Scott's Novels as History'. *Encounter,* 36, no. 5 (1976), 65–70.
Berger, John. *Ways of Seeing.* London: BBC and Penguin, 1972.
Bergonzi, Bernard. 'Fiction of History'. In *The Situation of the Novel.* 2nd edn London: Macmillan, 1979, pp. 214–37.
Binns, Ronald. *J.G Farrell.* London: Methuen, 1986.
Bloch, Marc. *The Historian's Craft.* Trans. Peter Putnam. Manchester University Press, 1954.
Boyer, Allen. 'Love, Sex, and History in *The Raj Quartet'.* *Modern Language Quarterly,* 46, no.1 (1985), 64–80.
Bradbury, Malcolm. 'Two Passages to India: Forster as Victorian and Modern'. In *Aspects of E.M. Forster.* Ed. Oliver Stallybrass. London: Edward Arnold, 1969, pp. 123–42.
—— Ed. *E.M. Forster: A Passage to India.* London: Macmillan (Casebook Series), 1970.
Brady, Veronica. 'Straddling Two Cultures'. Rev. of *The Tiger's Daughter,* by Bharati Mukherjee. *CRNLE Reviews Journal,* nos. 1 and 2 (1988), 109–16.
Brantlinger, Patrick. *Rule of Darkness: British Literature and Imperialism, 1830-1914.* Ithaca and London: Cornell University Press, 1988.
Brookner, Anita. *Watteau.* Feltham: Hamlyn, 1967.
Buckley, Jerome Hamilton. *The Triumph of Time.* Cambridge, Mass.: Belknap Press of Harvard University Press, 1966.
Burjorjee, Dinshaw M. 'The Indian Mutiny in Anglo-Indian Fiction Written after the Second World War'. *Chandrabhaga,* no. 8 (1982), pp. 1-32, and no.

9 (1983), pp. 33–69.

Burke, Kenneth. 'Social and Cosmic Mystery: *A Passage to India'*. In *Language as Symbolic Action: Essays on Life, Literature, and Method*. University of California Press, 1966, pp. 223–39.

Butterfield, Herbert. *The Whig Interpretation of History*. 1931; rpt, London: G. Bell, 1968.

Chew, Shirley. 'Fictions of Princely States and Empire'. *Ariel*, 17, no. 3 (1986), 103–17.

Collier, Richard. *The Great Indian Mutiny*. New York: E.P. Dutton, 1964.

Coombs, David. *Sports and the Countryside in English Paintings, Watercolours and Prints*. Oxford: Phaidon, 1978.

Cowasjee, Saros. Introd. to *Private Life of an Indian Prince*, by Mulk Raj Anand. London: Bodley Head, 1953, pp. 11–22.

—— 'Mulk Raj Anand: Princes and Proletarians'. *Journal of Commonwealth Literature*. no. 5 (1968), pp. 52–64.

Cronin, Richard. 'The Indian English Novel: *Kim* and *Midnight's Children'*. *Modern Fiction Studies*, 33, no. 2 (1987), 201–13.

Dayananda, James Y. 'Manohar Malgonkar on His Novel *The Princes*: An Interview'. *Journal of Commonwealth Literature*, 9, no. 3 (1975), 21–8.

Dessaix, Robert. 'India-phile'. Rev. of *The Trotter-nama*, by I. Allan Sealy. *24 Hours*, June 1989, p. 110.

Driesen, Cynthia Vanden. 'R.K. Narayan's Neglected Novel: *Waiting for the Mahatma'*. *World Literature Written in English*, 26. no. 2 (1986), 362–9.

Eagleton, Terry. *Literary Theory: An Introduction*. Oxford: Blackwell, 1983.

Fleishman, Avrom. *The English Historical Novel; Walter Scott to Virginia Woolf*. Baltimore: Johns Hopkins University Press, 1971.

Forster, E.M. *Aspects of the Novel*. 1927; rpt, Harmondsworth: Penguin, 1979.

Gardner, Philip. Ed. *E.M. Forster, The Critical Heritage*. London: Routledge & Kegan Paul, 1973.

Gooneratne, Yasmine. 'Irony in Ruth Prawer Jhabvala's *Heat and Dust'*. *New Literature Review*, no. 4 (1978), pp. 41–50.

—— 'Ruth Prawer Jhabvala: Generating Heat and Light'. *Kunapipi*, 1, no. 1 (1979), 115–29.

—— 'Film into Fiction: The influence upon Ruth Prawer Jhabvala's fiction of her work for the cinema, 1960–76'. *World Literature Written in English*, 18, no. 2 (1979), 368–86.

—— 'Paul Scott's *Staying On*: Finale in a Minor Key'. *Journal of Indian Writing in English*, 9, no. 2 (1982), 1–12.

—— *Silence, Exile and Cunning: The Fiction of Ruth Prawer Jhabvala*. Hyderabad: Orient Longman, 1983.

Goonetilleke, D.C.R.A. 'Colonial Neuroses: Kipling and Forster'. *Ariel*, 5, no. 4 (1974), 56–68.

Greenberger, Allen J. *The British Image of India*. Oxford University Press, 1969.

Greenberger, Allen J. and Edith L. Piness. 'The Legacy of the Raj: J.G. Farrell's *The Siege of Krishnapur'*. *Indo-British Review – A Journal of History*, 11, no. 1 (1984), 112–17.

Harris, Michael. '"Transformation without End": Salman Rushdie's India'. *Meridian*, 5, no. 1 (1986), 15–22.

Harrex, S.C. *The Fire and the Offering: the English-language Novel of India, 1935-*

1970. 2 vols. Calcutta: Writers Workshop, 1977–78.

Hibbert, Christopher. *The Great Mutiny.* 1978; rpt, Harmondsworth: Penguin, 1980.

Howe, Susanne. *Novels of Empire.* 1949; rpt, New York: Kraus Reprint, 1971.

Howells, Coral Ann. 'Ruby Wiebe's *The Temptations of Big Bear* and Salman Rushdie's *Midnight's Children'. Literary Criterion,* 20, no. 1 (1985), 191–203.

Hutcheon, Linda. *A Poetics of Postmodernism: History, Theory, Fiction.* London: Routledge & Kegan Paul, 1988.

Islam, Shamsul. *Kipling's 'Law': A Study of his Philosophy of Life.* London: Macmillan, 1975.

Jhabvala, Ruth Prawer. 'Disinheritance'. *Blackwood's Edinburgh Magazine,* July 1979, pp. 4–14.

Judd, Denis. *The Victorian Empire: A Pictorial History, 1837–1901.* London: Weidenfeld & Nicolson, 1970.

Jussawalla, Feroza. 'Fact versus Fiction: Attenborough's *Gandhi* and Salman Rushdie's *Midnight's Children'. ACLALS Bulletin,* 7th Series, no. 4 (1986), 70–8.

Kermode, Frank. *The Sense of an Ending.* 1967; rpt, Oxford University Press, 1968.

—— *Essays on Fiction 1971-82.* London: Routledge & Kegan Paul, 1983.

Lascelles, Mary. *The Story-teller Retrieves the Past.* Oxford: Clarendon Press, 1980.

Lukács, Georg. *The Historical Novel.* Trans. Hannah and Stanley Mitchell. London: Merlin, 1962.

Lutyens, Mary. *Effie in Venice.* London: Murray, 1965.

Mabbett, Ian W. *A Short History of India.* 2nd edn. North Ryde: Methuen Australia, 1983.

Mason, Philip. *Kipling: The Glass, the Shadow and the Fire.* London: Jonathan Cape, 1975.

Masselos, Jim. *Indian Nationalism: An History.* New Delhi: Sterling, 1985.

Masters, John. *Bugles and a Tiger.* 1956; rpt, London: Reprint Society. 1957.

Mehta, P.P. 'Malgonkar's "The Devil's Wind" The first great Indo-Anglian historical novel'. *Triveni,* 48, no. 2 (1979), 72–9.

Mehta, Ved. *Walking the Indian Streets.* 1963; rev. edn. 1971; rpt, Harmondsworth: Penguin, 1975.

Mellors, John. 'Raj Mahal: Paul Scott's India Quartet'. *London Magazine,* 15, no. 2 (1975), 62–7.

Meyers, Jeffrey. *Disease and the Novel, 1880-1960.* New York: St. Martin's, 1985.

Moorehouse, Geoffrey. *India Britannica.* 1983; rpt, London: Paladin, 1986.

Mukherjee, Meenakshi. *The Twice Born Fiction; themes and techniques of the Indian novel in English.* New Delhi: Heinemann, 1971.

Nair, Rukmini Bhaya. 'The Voyeur's View in *Midnight's Children* and *Shame'. ACLALS Bulletin,* 7th series, no. 1 (1985), 57–75.

Narasimhaiah, C.D. 'Raja Rao's *Kanthapura*: An Analysis'. In *Fiction and the Reading Public in India.* Ed. C.D. Narasimhaiah. Mysore University Press, 1967.

Natwar-Singh, K. 'Only connect...: Forster and India'. In *Aspects of E.M. Forster.* Ed. Oliver Stallybrass. London: Arnold, 1969, pp. 37–50.

Page, Norman. *A Kipling Companion.* London: Macmillan, 1984.

Parry, Benita, *Delusions and Discoveries*. London: Allen Lane, 1972.
—— 'Paul Scott's Raj'. *South Asian Review*, 8, no. 4 (1975), 359–69.
Pradhan, N.S. 'The Problem of Focus in Jhabvala's *Heat and Dust*'. *Indian Literary Review*, 1, no. 1 (1978), pp. 15–20.
Raleigh, John Henry. 'The English Novel and the Three Kinds of Time.' *Sewanee Review*, 62, no. 3 (1954), 242–52.
Rance, Nicholas. *The Historical Novel and Popular Politics in Nineteenth-Century England*. London: Vision, 1975.
Rao, A.V. Krishna. 'Identity and Environment: Narayan's *The Guide* and Naipaul's *A House for Mr Biswas*'. In *Inventing Countries: Essays in Post-Colonial Literatures*. Ed. William McGaw. Wollongong: SPACLALS, 1987, pp. 165–77.
Rao, K. Bhaskara. *Rudyard Kipling's India*. Norman: University of Oklahoma Press, 1967.
Reeve, N.H. 'Reflections on "Fictionality"'. In *The Contemporary English Novel*, Stratford-upon-Avon Studies, 18. Eds. Malcolm Bradbury and David Palmer. London: Arnold, 1979, pp. 112–30.
Riemenschneider, Dieter. 'History and the Individual in Salman Rushdie's *Midnight's Children* and Anita Desai's *Clear Light of Day*'. *Kunapipi*, 7, no. 2 (1984), 53–66.
Ross, Alexander. 'Remnants of the Raj'. *Equinox*, May–June 1986, pp. 22–40.
Ross, Robert L. 'The Emerging Myth: Partition in the Indian and Pakistanian [sic] Novel'. *ACLALS Bulletin*, 7th Series, no. 4 (1986), 63–9.
Rubin, David. *After the Raj: British Novels of India Since 1947*. Hanover and London: University Press of New England, 1986.
Rushdie, Salman. '*Midnight's Children* and *Shame*'. *Kunapipi*, 7, no. 1 (1985), 1–19.
Said, Edward W. '*Kim*, The Pleasures of Imperialism'. *Raritan*, 7, no. 2 (1987), 27–64.
Sandison, Alan. *The Wheel of Empire: A Study of the Imperial Idea in Some Late Nineteenth and Early Twentieth Century Fiction*. London: Macmillan, 1967.
Sarachchandra, Ediriwira. 'Illusion and Reality: Raja Rao as Novelist'. In *Only Connect: Literacy Perspectives East and West*. Eds Guy Amirthanayagam and S.C. Harrex. Adelaide and Honolulu: Centre for Research in the New Literatures in English & East–West Center, 1981, pp. 107–17.
Scott, Paul. 'India: A Post-Forsterian View'. In *Essays by Divers Hands*, no. 36. Ed. Mary Stocks. Oxford University Press, 1976, pp. 113–32.
Sen, K.M. *Hinduism*. Harmondsworth: Penguin, 1981.
Shahane, Vasant. 'Jhabvala's *Heat and Dust*; A Cross-Cultural Encounter'. In *Aspects of Indian Writing in English* [Essays in honour of Professor K.R. Srinivasa Iyengar]. Ed. M.K. Naik. Madras: Macmillan, 1979, pp. 222–31.
Sharrad, Paul. *Raja Rao and Cultural Tradition*. New Delhi: Sterling, 1987.
Shaw, Harry E. *The Forms of Historical Fiction*. Ithaca: Cornell University Press, 1983.
Singh, Bhupal. *A Survey of Anglo-Indian Fiction*. 1934; rpt, London: Curzon, 1975.
Singh, Frances B. 'Progress and History in J.G. Farrell's *The Siege of Krishnapur*'. *Chandrabhaga*, no. 2 (1979), 23–39.
Singh, Shailendra Dhari. *Novels on the Indian Mutiny*. New Delhi: Arnold-

Heinemann India, 1973.

Spurling, John. 'As Does the Bishop'. In *The Hill Station*. London: Weidenfeld & Nicolson, 1981, pp. 141–60.

Stallybrass, Oliver. 'Forster's "Wobblings": The Manuscripts of *A Passage to India'*. In *Aspects of E.M. Forster*. Ed. Oliver Stallybrass. London: Arnold, 1969, pp. 143–54.

—— *The Manuscripts of A Passage to India*. The Abinger Edition of E.M. Forster, vol. 6a. London: Arnold, 1978.

—— Introd. to *A Passage to India*, by E.M. Forster. Harmondsworth: Penguin, 1979, pp. 7–28.

Stone, Wilfred. *The Cave and the Mountain, A Study of E.M. Forster*. Stanford University Press, 1966.

Swann, Joseph. '"East is East and West is West"? Salman Rushdie's *Midnight's Children* as an Indian Novel'. *World Literature Written in English*, 26, no. 2 (1986), 353–62.

Swinden, Patrick. *Paul Scott: Images of India*. London: Macmillan, 1980.

Tarinayya, M. 'Two novels: Kushwant Singh's *Train to Pakistan* and Bhabani Bhattacharya's *So Many Hungers!' Indian Literature*, 13, no. 1 (1970), 113–21.

Tedesco, Janis. '*Staying On:* The Final Connection'. *Western Humanities Review*, 39, no 3. (1985), 195–211.

Theroux, Paul. 'An Interrupted Journey'. *The Sunday Times*, 26 April 1981, p. 42.

Thompson, Elizabeth Boyd. 'E.M. Forster's *A Passage to India*: What Really Happened in the Caves'. *Modern Fiction Studies*, 34, no. 4 (1988), 596–604.

Tompkins, J.M.S. *The Art of Rudyard Kipling*. London: Methuen, 1959.

Verghese, C. Paul. *Problems of the Indian Creative Writer in English*. Bombay: Somaiya, 1971.

Walsh, William. *R.K. Narayan: A Critical Appreciation*. London: Heinemann, 1982.

Weinbaum, Francine S. 'Paul Scott's India: *The Raj Quartet'. Critique*, 20. no 1 (1978), 100–10.

White, Hayden. *Tropics of Discourse*. Baltimore: Johns Hopkins University Press, 1978.

Wilson, Angus. *The Strange Ride of Rudyard Kipling*. London: Book Club Associates. 1977.

Wilson, Edmund. 'The *Kim* that Nobody Reads'. In *The Wound and the Bow*. 1952; rpt, London: Methuen, 1961.

Wood, Christopher. *Victorian Panorama: Paintings of Victorian Life*. London: Faber, 1976.

Woodcock, George. 'A Distant and A Deadly Shore: Notes on the Literature of the Sahibs'. *Pacific Affairs*, 46 (1973), 94–110.

—— 'The Sometime Sahibs: Two Post-Independence British Novelists of India'. *Queen's Quarterly*, 86 (1979–80), 39–49.

Woodruff, Philip. *The Founders*. vol.1 of *The Men Who Ruled India*. London: Jonathan Cape, 1953.

—— *The Guardians*. vol. 2 of *The Men Who Ruled India*. London: Jonathan Cape, 1954.

Unsigned. 'The Indian Mutiny in Fiction'. *Blackwood's Edinburgh Magazine*, Feb. 1897. pp. 218–31.

Index

208